Murder Stories

ISSUES IN CRIME & JUSTICE

Series Editor
Gregg Barak, Eastern Michigan University

As we embark upon the twenty-first century, the meanings of crime continue to evolve and our approaches to justice are in flux. The contributions to this series focus attention on crime and justice as well as on crime control and prevention in the context of a dynamically changing legal order. Across the series, there are books that consider the full range of crime and criminality and that engage a diverse set of topics related to the formal and informal workings of the administration of criminal justice. In an age of globalization, crime and criminality are no longer confined, if they ever were, to the boundaries of single nation-states. As a consequence, while many books in the series will address crime and justice in the United States, the scope of these books will accommodate a global perspective, and they will consider such eminently global issues such as slavery, terrorism, or punishment. Books in the series are written to be used as supplements in standard undergraduate and graduate courses in criminology and criminal justice and related courses in sociology. Some of the standard courses in these areas include introduction to criminal justice, introduction to law enforcement, introduction to corrections, juvenile justice, crime and delinquency, criminal law, white collar, corporate, and organized crime.

Titles in Series:

Effigy: Images of Capital Defendants, by Allison Cotton
Perverts and Predators: The Making of Sexual Offending Laws, by Laura J. Zilney and Lisa Anne Zilney
The Prisoners' World: Portraits of Convicts Caught in the Incarceration Binge, by William Tregea and Marjorie Larmour
Racial Profiling: Research, Racism, Resistance, by Karen S. Glover
State Criminality: The Crime of All Crimes, by Dawn L. Rothe
Punishment for Sale: Private Prisons and Big Business, by Donna Selman and Paul Leighton
Forensic Science in Court: Challenges in the Twenty-first Century, by Donald E. Shelton
Threat Perceptions: The Policing of Dangers from Eugenics to the War on Terrorism, by Saran Ghatak
Gendered Justice: Intimate Partner Violence and the Criminal Justice System, by Venessa Garcia and Patrick McManimon
Murder Stories: Ideological Narratives in Capital Punishment, by Paul Kaplan

Murder Stories

Ideological Narratives in Capital Punishment

Paul Kaplan

LEXINGTON BOOKS
Lanham • Boulder • New York • Toronto • Plymouth, UK

Published by Lexington Books
A wholly owned subsidiary of The Rowman & Littlefield Publishing Group, Inc.
4501 Forbes Boulevard, Suite 200, Lanham, Maryland 20706
www.lexingtonbooks.com

Estover Road, Plymouth PL6 7PY, United Kingdom

"Forgetting the Future: Cause Lawyering and the Work of California Capital Trial Defenders," by Paul Kaplan (2010), was originally published in *Theoretical Criminology*, 14(2). Reprinted with permission of SAGE Publications Ltd.

British Library Cataloguing in Publication Information Available

Library of Congress Cataloging-in-Publication Data

Kaplan, Paul, 1968–
  Murder stories : ideological narratives in capital punishment / Paul Kaplan.
    pages cm.—(Issues in crime & justice)
  Includes bibliographical references and index.
  ISBN 978-0-7391-7170-7 (cloth: alk. paper)—ISBN 978-0-7391-7171-4
(electronic)
    1. Capital punishment—United States. 2. Trials—United States. 3. Murder—
United States. I. Title.
  KF9227.C2K37 2012
  364.660973—dc23   2011046173

∞™ The paper used in this publication meets the minimum requirements of American National Standard for Information Sciences—Permanence of Paper for Printed Library Materials, ANSI/NISO Z39.48-1992.

Printed in the United States of America

To Sylvia

Contents

List of Tables

Acknowledgments

My work on capital cases began in 1996 when I was convinced by my friend Sarah Weiner to volunteer at the Center for Capital Assistance in San Francisco, a nonprofit organization dedicated to providing mitigation expertise to lawyers defending persons facing death sentences or executions. In the years since, my professional life has—in one way or another—focused on America's institution of state killing. Along the way, I have worked as a mitigation investigator on cases and published articles about the death penalty. This book thus represents a kind of culmination for me, an encapsulation of my career to this point. As with all books of this kind, *Murder Stories* is the result of many collaborations, conversations, and arguments with smart and dedicated people. Of course, everything in this book, including any errors or flaws, should be attributed exclusively to me.

First and foremost, I thank Scharlette Holdman, who introduced me to the world of capital mitigation and provided a paragon example of intelligence and dedication. My time under Scharlette was short, but her tutelage stays with me today. Next, I thank Courtney Bell, Susan Garvey, and Charlie Pizarro, the team of investigators who took me in, trained me, and became some of my closest friends. To this day, I look to these beautifully fierce persons for inspiration, laughter, and hijinks. Thanks to Peter Blair for keeping me sharp for the last twenty years. Sylvia Valenzuela gets special recognition for putting up with me. Thank you, my darling darling, for being wonderful.

I thank Val Jenness, who stepped in and saved this project from falling through the cracks when it began in graduate school. I would never have written this book were it not for Val's guidance, vision, and dedication. I would like to thank Kitty Calavita for her always incisive commentary on this work, and also for her example as a scholar. Kitty is the ultimate scholarly role model. Thanks to Simon Cole, for his perceptive commentary, intellectual inspiration, and wonderfully dry humor. I also thank Richard Leo for his early stewardship of this project and mentorship in general. Richard always thought long and hard about my work, and provided probably the best constructive criticisms I have ever been lucky enough to receive.

Thanks to my collaborator Kerry Dunn for her intellectual integrity and remarkable dedication to social justice. I would also like to thank the following scholars from around the world for their various assistances and inspirations: Bill Bowers, Jesse Cheng, John Cleary, Susan Coutin, Howie Erlanger, Ben Fleury-Steiner, David Garland, David T. Johnson, Beth Loftus, Mona Lynch, Liisa Malkii, Bill Maurer, Karl Shoemaker, Bill Thompson, Austin Sarat, Elizabeth Vartkessian, and Frank Zimring. I am especially thankful to Daniel LaChance for reading the entire manuscript of this book. His comments were exceptionally thoughtful and helpful.

I am grateful to Kate Coyne for her help with introducing me around various courthouses. Thanks to Jesse Rodriguez for his help. Thanks to all the prosecutors, defense attorneys and others who agreed to be interviewed for this project. I enthusiastically thank all of my friends in the world of capital defense, both for inspiration and for being there to answer my legal questions.

My colleagues at San Diego State University have proven to be invaluable friends, collaborators and mentors; I thank them heartily: Mounah Abdel-Samad, Salvador Espinoza, Shawn Flanigan, Stuart Henry, Larry Herzog, Alan Mobley, Dana Nurge, and Paul Sutton.

A deeply felt debt of gratitude goes to family and friends who believed in me all along—even when I didn't—and who have inspired me in all kinds of ways over the years. I am deeply grateful to my immediate family: Jeff Kaplan, Barbara Kunkel (RIP), Ben Kaplan-Good, Sam Kaplan-Good, and Peri Lou Good. Thanks to the following friends for their unconditional love, support, and inspiration: Courtney Bell, Susie Bennett, Peter Blair, Dimitri Bogazianos, Michael Braun, Stone Clement, Ryan Fischer, Susan Garvey, Scott Kaminski, Glenda Kelmes, James Lingen, Christian Muro, Charlie Pizarro, Darcy Purvis, Kim Richman, Anastasia Tosouni, Michael Smyth, David Weiner, and Kyong Yi. Thanks to the basketball posse for forcing me go to my left once in a while: Mounah Abdel-Samad, Trent Biggs, Alessio Bloesch, Brian Goeltzenleuchter, Jeff Kaplan, and Dana Nurge.

I would like to acknowledge and pay respect to those persons who suffer the violence of murder, and their counterparts who suffer the violence of the law.

I thank the National Science Foundation (Grant # SES-0518071), and the School of Social Ecology at the University of California, Irvine for financial support of this project.

Thanks to Gregg Barak for taking an interest in this book, the anonymous reviewers of this manuscript for their comments, and also to the editorial staff at Lexington Books.

Finally, I am indebted to the American Bar Association/Wiley-Blackwell, Elsevier/Emerald, and Sage Publications for permission to reproduce and adapt from the following of my articles: "American Exceptionalism and Racialized Inequality in American Capital Punishment." *Law and Social Inquiry* (Vol. 31, Issue 1, 149–75); "Facts and Furies: The Antinomies of Facts and Law, and Retribution in the Work of Capital Prosecutors." *Studies in Law, Politics and Society. Special Issue: Is the Death Penalty Dying?* (Vol. 42, 135–59); "Forgetting the Future: Are Capital Trial Defenders Cause Lawyers?" *Theoretical Criminology* (Vol. 14, No. 2, 211–35).

Introduction

On a foggy December night in 1979, near a tiny central California town, a thirty-year-old man named Bernard Sampson killed his twelve-year-old stepdaughter, Sally.[1] Sally's body was found less than a day after she died. The local medical examiner determined that the cause of death was strangulation and the severing of the carotid artery. The crime scene was especially gruesome—after her death from the fatal wounds, Sally had been cut deeply from her pubic bone to her breast bone, exposing her internal organs. Because Bernard was the last person seen with Sally, police were immediately suspicious of him and he was soon arrested, shortly after which he confessed to the murder. In bringing capital murder charges, the prosecution alleged that Bernard also raped and sodomized Sally, a charge he has always denied, but that seemed plausible in light of rumors Bernard had been sexually abusing Sally for several years. Bernard was convicted by a jury of capital murder and sentenced to death. Several years later, an appellate court found that the trial judge erred when giving jury instructions, and Bernard was granted a re-trial of the "penalty phase"[2] of his trial, after which he was again sentenced to death. At the time of this writing, Bernard Sampson's appellate process continues as he waits in line for execution among over 650 men at San Quentin State Prison near San Francisco.[3]

Bernard Sampson was an outsider, even in his own community. His large, insular family moved to California's agricultural central valley when Bernard was eight years old in an attempt to escape grinding poverty in Arkansas; the casual observer might categorize the Sampsons as "Arkies." The extremely impoverished family compound turned out to be a den of horrors for the many Sampson children, including Bernard. Many of the young Sampson boys and girls, especially Bernard, were physically and sexually abused serially by parents, uncles, and a few other adults who came to drink moonshine concocted by Bernard's father and uncles. Everyone in the family worked in agriculture, and Bernard was exposed to pesticides and other toxins regularly from before his birth. Bernard's teachers classified him as mentally retarded, and his Full Scale IQ at the time of his first trial (1980) was 74, which mental health professionals classify as "borderline mentally retarded." Subsequent testing suggested that Bernard's brain is damaged in such a way as to impair his mental capabilities, including controlling impulses. In short, Bernard's social history was characterized by long-term extreme poverty, significant abuse and neglect, and his mental capabilities were severely diminished at the time of the crime (and remain so).

I came to know about Bernard's case, and to know Bernard personally, through my professional work as a "mitigation investigator" prior to entering academics.[4] Mitigation investigators work on behalf of men facing the death penalty, primarily investigating their social histories. This work was akin to anthropological field work, but driven by a prerogative to save the client's life rather than by a research question. Much of the labor consists of locating and interviewing family witnesses ("going into the field"), creating family genealogies ("delineating kin networks"), and identifying and collecting life history and legal documents ("gathering archival data"). This evidence was driven by and then drove the defense team's theory of the client's "story." Eventually, some of these materials would be organized and submitted to legal decision-makers (juries or appellate courts) as exhibits—as "facts" used to "prove" the truth of the defendant's mitigating social history story.

During these years, I spent a great many hours parked on dusty, empty roads waiting for someone's uncle or cousin to come home so I could gently interview them about their relative's (the defendant) inevitably sad and invariably troubled life. During these lonely hours, I often found myself thinking about the complicated meanings of the legal stories of men facing execution. I knew that Bernard Sampson was much more than a sick man who decided to kill his step-daughter. I knew that the story of Sally's death went beyond that deadly winter night. Those violent seconds were, it seemed to me, a small vignette within a much larger story having to do with complex and elusive social factors. It became obvious to me, for example, that Bernard Sampson was not capable of interacting in the social world in the way I or most persons I knew were. Nearly every piece of evidence I gathered in the field pointed to a severely impaired "man-child" who could barely function in society, despite the fact that he married and held down a handful of menial jobs.

But I was also aware that my understanding of his "mental health" was intimately connected to the question of Bernard's limited ability to control his actions. From the point of view of his defense team, Bernard's constitutional lack of self control—his so-called "diminished autonomy"[5]—*equated* to something called "mental illness." This somewhat tautological line of thought made me think about the relationship between conceptualizations of "mental health" and the norms around human agency that construct and are constructed by a variety of discourses in a capitalist liberal democracy like the United States. After all, at their roots, capitalist liberal democracies are systems in which all members of society are supposed to be (or are understood as) autonomous monads, contracting with one another. It seemed to me that our understandings of mental health and mental illness must surely be bound up with these basic fabrics of our society. I now recognize that this was a rather deterministic way of thinking about mental health discourse; nonetheless, the point is that it got me wondering, about broad questions regarding legal knowledge and the limitations of the legal milieu for contemplating the meanings of murder and execution.

What was the *cause* of Sally's death, I wondered? Was it Bernard Sampson's evil soul? Was it his mental illness? Was it sexual mores that made sex with a child a taboo? Was it ostracization from the local community? Was it the effects of the "double-edged sword" of individualistic American capitalism? Where did the story of Sally's death begin? Was the story temporally short—limited to a few moments of violence in a parked car in a raisin vineyard? Or was it temporally long—beginning generations before among Sally's and Bernard's relatives in Arkansas? I wanted to know these things, waiting around in my hot little rental car. Of course, on some level, I knew that all of the factors floating in my mind were in some way involved in Bernard's violent act. But what were the ideological implications of the different versions of the story?

One thing I did know was that I was not going to be able to answer these questions while working as a mitigation investigator. Philosophical ponderings about the relationship between capitalism and conceptualizations of individual autonomy, while perhaps acceptable during late-night beer sessions with other defense team members, simply had no place in the day-to-day labor of putting together a mitigation social history for a capital case. The imperative was to gather the "facts" that the lawyers and mental health professionals back at the office could plug in to a DSM-IV diagnosis.[6] But although I was deeply committed to saving the lives of my clients, I was sometimes frustrated by the intellectual limitations imposed by the legal and life-and-death imperatives inherent to capital cases. Not unlike police investigating a high-profile murder, capital defenders sometimes suffer something like tunnel vision. It sometimes bothered me when other defenders railed against the police bias, or small-town racism, or prosecutorial dirty tricks but were reluctant to talk about the larger ideological frameworks within which these specific problems were taking place.[7]Thinking about the larger ideological picture—analyzing the death penalty abstractly rather than pragmatically—eventually led me to graduate school.

As I moved from the rather concrete world of capital defense to the somewhat more abstract world of academics, my interest in the cause of murders such as those committed by Bernard Sampson became more complex. I realized that identifying a straightforward cause-and-effect relationship would be impossible, and began to become preoccupied with the *legally constructed narratives of causation*, rather than any particular empirical factor or factors that might explain murder or execution. Thus, my own focus of analysis shifted, as I took seminars, wrote papers, and endured exams, to the concept of stories of defendants rather than the particulars of any given story. I especially wanted to explore why the prosecution version of the defendant's story usually began and ended in the moments surrounding the crime, while the defender's version often began three generations ago in a sharecropper's cabin.

It is probably true that both academics and lawyers participate in constructing something of a false dichotomy between "ideas" and "practice." A deep understanding of the larger ideological picture ought to matter for attorneys seeking to mobilize latent cultural values in juries in favor of their clients. Likewise, the quotidian life of death penalty litigation ought to matter for theorists of the death penalty. Part of the goal of this book is to bridge the gap between these worlds.

What follows is in-depth investigation into narratives of murder and murderers. In the chapters below, I describe the content of the stories told in a set of California capital trials, their embedded ideological "cargo," and also the processes of their construction—all with an eye toward understanding their relationship to ideology.

What emerges is a story about the hegemonic power of particularly "American" ideologies and the rather limited potential to resist them. Murder stories told by prosecutors, not surprisingly, invoke and support dominant (and repressive) ideologies about what it means to be a victim and killer. Defense versions of these stories sometimes challenge the assumptions underlying prosecution narratives. However, defendant stories often rely on the same dominant and repressive ideologies called upon by prosecutors. In many of the "murder stories" analyzed in this book, defense arguments were constructed through the same "ideological grammar" as those of the prosecutor, even as they battled the prosecution's goals of conviction and death sentencing. As I show in the pages that follow, this situation elucidates the complex relationship between law and ideology—the stories told by potentially subversive legal actors can only approach subversion through alternative versions *of* dominant ideologies, *not* by directly challenging the dominant ideologies themselves.

PLAN OF THE BOOK

In chapter 1 I introduce to the reader the extensive literatures on a) capital punishment, b) the academic theory of "narrativity," and c) the sociolegal theory of hegemony and resistance to hegemony. In chapter 2, I take up the question of whether or how the U.S. death penalty is related to deep "American" cultural commitments having to do with individualism and other ideologies—sometimes referred to as the "American Creed." In chapter 3, I delineate an "anatomy" of capital trials, discussing in detail the legal structure of capital trials in general, and the specific empirical characteristics of the trials in this data set. In chapter 4, I analyze the hegemony of and occasional resistance to ideologies embedded in the narratives produced in thirty-seven California death penalty trials. In chapter 5, I focus on the work of capital defenders, describing their process of constructing narratives and investigating whether or how they might be engaging in "cause lawyering." In chapter 6, I turn to the work of capital prosecutors and investigate their process of constructing narratives, with a particular focus on what prosecutor discourses can tell us about U.S. capital punishment's "life or death." Throughout, my interest is in tracing the ways in which ideologies are constituted and challenged in legal discourses.

NOTES

1. All names in this book are pseudonyms.

2. Death penalty trials in California (and most states) consist of two distinct phases—the so-called "guilt phase" and the so-called "penalty phase." In the former, the jury determines whether the defendant is legally guilty of capital murder; in the latter (usually) the same jury decides whether the defendant should receive a sentence of death or Life Without the Possibility of Parole (LWOP).

3. There are also nineteen women facing execution in California. They are housed at Valley State Prison for Women near Chowchilla, a small town in the San Joaquin Valley.

4. "Mitigation" is a term of art within the capital defense bar that means "evidence intended to mitigate the defendant's crime" and is often comprised of records and testimony about trauma and abuse in the defendant's background. Mitigation investigators work closely with capital defense attorneys to find mitigation evidence.

5. "Diminished autonomy" is another term of art among capital defense attorneys that should not be confused with the legal defense of "diminished *capacity*," which specifically refers to a state of mind in which a defendant cannot fully comprehend the nature of the criminal act.Leading mitigation specialist Russell Stetler defines "diminished autonomy" this way: "[The goal is] to show the client as someone with "diminished autonomy"—and therefore worthy of protection from the ultimate sanction of capital punishment. We diminish the client's degree of responsibility, his or her capacity to exercise free will, by demonstrating how his or her decisions in life have been drastically curtailed by biological, social, and psychological influences which were not chosen" (Stetler, 1999).

6. The Diagnostic and Statistical Manual-IV is a phonebook-sized reference manual published by the American Psychiatric Association that lists diagnostic criteria for mental illnesses.

7. Perhaps understandably, many of my colleagues in the capital defense community think that this attitude is somewhat self-indulgent, naïve, foolish, and most importantly, dangerous to the welfare of their clients. When a person's life is at stake, questions about the political economy can wait. Nevertheless, situating the defendant and his or her crime within an encompassing web of social organization is usually a primary goal of capital defenders—but one driven by a specific set of legal imperatives rather than a pursuit of knowledge.

1

• • •

Capital Punishment Conflicts, Narrativity, Hegemony, and Resistance

CAPITAL PUNISHMENT CONFLICTS

Many analysts of the death penalty find the contemporary presence of capital punishment in the United States somewhat unexpected. Indeed, several empirical factors seem to militate against American retention of capital punishment, including 138 erroneous capital convictions since 1973 (Death Penalty Information Center, 2011), (former) Illinois Governor George Ryan's highly publicized 2003 blanket clemency for all 167 persons on Illinois's death row, the move in Europe to abolish capital punishment worldwide, and moderately declining public support at home in the United States.

Moreover, the use of capital punishment seems to some observers to be inherently antinomic to the modern liberal legal order purported to be exemplified by the United States:

> The fulfillment of Enlightenment that ought to have resulted in Kant's Maturity of reason, reason also ought to have been accomplished in such a way that criminal acts would come to be considered as irrational, and criminals would become known as beings who are subject to correction if possible and containment if not. Indeed, in a well-ordered, fully enlightened society, punishment is supposed to fade away and penalties would continue to exist only as forms of reassurance. To actually kill in the name of containment would be to abandon the reason that knows perfectly the fallibility of its all too human execution by persons not fully endowed with the capacity to reason—the insane, infirm, or imbecilic. (Dumm, 2000, p. 471)

Put less elegantly, it seems irrational or contradictory to execute within a modern, rational, and purportedly enlightened society.[1] Such a conceptualization of the death penalty is in alignment with Foucault's (1977) vision of punishment as delineated in *Discipline and Punish*, which imagines "criminal justice today as fundamentally rational and bureaucratic, and as a largely cold and routinized expression of growing administrative control" (Smith, 2003, p. 28). According to Smith (2003), Foucault's rationalist vision imagines a situation in which "primordial symbols and mythologies no longer play a significant part in punishment discourse. Punishment is now explicable as a rational and instrumental application of social control, not an expression of meanings" (Smith, 2003, p. 29). Indeed, as Dumm (2000) argues:

> Michel Foucault's thesis—most fully announced in *Discipline and Punish* (1977)—supposedly is that the rise of practices of visibility, order, and micromanagement of bodies culminated in the penal reforms that ended the spectacle of the scaffold and gave rise to disciplinary society, effectively foreclosing any meaningful purpose in killing criminals. The practice of state killing as a punishment for crimes ought to have withered away as a disciplinary society extends its reach and the ensemble of corrective measures becomes more extensive. (p. 471)

Considering this theoretical view of punishment and criminal justice, along with the empirical trends that seem to be working against capital punishment, its lingering presence becomes a striking paradox for many scholars.

Nevertheless, one wonders whether the death penalty is really so contradictory with the modern, liberal legal order. A tautological response would be to argue that its presence proves its logical place in American society. This perspective underlies the proretention argument that the death penalty "fits" in American society because it is apparently vaguely popular. A more convincing argument for the death penalty's fit comes from Smith (2003), who, invoking Durkheim's functionalist notions of punishment as expression of collective moral outrage, as well as empirical evidence of "affective" and "mythological" use of the guillotine in eighteenth century France,[2] argues that "there is no necessary antinomy between technological reason within the disciplinary complex and affective mythology" (p. 31). Smith's point is that a strict application of the Foucauldian notion of rationalized punishment overstates the relationship of rationalism to punishment, while bracketing out the empirically verifiable role of emotion and symbolism. I address the tension between "rationality" and "emotion" in the law in chapter 6.

More radically, Dunn (2000) suggests that the death penalty may actually represent the ultimate aim, or *telos*, of the Enlightenment because it operates to establish order upon disorder: "We still seek to bring back to order the disorder the polity suffers, a disorder initiated at the moment when a criminal confronts or evades the sovereign by violating the sovereign's laws. In a bloody paradox, we seek to re-order what has been disordered, by killing those who have introduced disorder into the fabric of polity" (p. 471).

Others have gone beyond theorizing by attempting to empirically explain why our government continues to impose death upon people like Bernard Sampson. Zimring (2003), for example, argues that the United States has deep, longstanding cultural values not in place in Western Europe, most importantly, *vigilantism* (especially in the American South). Garland (2005, 2010), on the other hand, has argued that such "American Exceptionalism" approaches are too deterministic, suggesting instead that American retention is *not* due to deep historical cultural traditions, but rather to relatively recent social and cultural changes occurring within "late modernity," especially the politics of crime control over the last thirty years (see p. 22), as well as the profoundly *local* nature of the American polity. Garland argues that it is a mistake to interpret the legal-institutional idiosyncrasies that have helped enable the retention of the death penalty as somehow reflective of a deep, essentialist American "creed" (in the case of Zimring, in the form of southern vigilantism) that demands capital punishment. I join this theoretical debate in chapter 2, arguing that the current voices on either side of the "American Exceptionalism" debate tend to bracket out or minimize the role of racialized inequality in American society when addressing the death penalty retention question.

Furthermore, capital punishment illuminates a number of conflicts in American criminal law, especially the competing values of retribution and due process (see Zimring, 2003), the paradox of distinguishing state violence from illegal violence (see Sarat, 2001), as well as other major legal tensions such as the competing values of rationality (nonarbitrariness) and individualization, and the contradictory doctrines of individual culpability and "diminished autonomy."

In Bernard Sampson's case, for example, the law required that Sampson be individually "contextualized" (in his penalty phase) while it (the law) maintained a respectable, consistent rationality. Unlike most criminal cases, capital cases are rather individualized—the punishment is as much connected to the *person* as to the *crime*. Indeed, the most important legal factor in capital cases—after guilt for homicide is determined—is the defendant's individual characteristics. And while it is not legally required for a verdict and penalty, the background of the victim (as well as the impact of his or her death on family members) is often prominently discussed in all stages of capital cases. This is one way that "death is different," and is an unexpected point of focus in American legal proceedings because it contradicts the value of *generalization* or *rationality* central to American formalism. This generalizing characteristic is often thought of as an essential tenet in modern liberal legal systems. As Milovanovic (1994) puts it (discussing Weber), rationality, means "following some criteria of decision which is applicable to all like cases." In other words, it stands for generality; it means dealing with all similarly situated cases in a similar way" (p. 41). This rationality is important to modern states because it makes for a highly predictable, stable legal framework, which is necessary for a smooth-running capitalist political economy. The introduction of extensive and detailed evidence about the characteristics of individuals is generally *not* something that fits with a rationalist legal system.[3]

Indeed, recent capital jurisprudence is one prominent instance in which the tension in the law between "individualization" and "reliability" has been played out. Recall that the essence of the Supreme Court's ruling in *Furman v. Georgia* (1972) was that death penalty statutes were too arbitrary.[4] The eventual response by legislatures in many American states was to rewrite their capital statutes to adhere to the principle of "guided discretion," which gave adjudicators detailed guidelines for deciding capital cases. The post-*Gregg v. Georgia* (1976) era was supposed to bring rationality or reliability back to the practice of capital punishment. However, with cases such as *Woodson v. North Carolina* (1976), *Lockett v. Ohio* (1978), and *Eddings v. Oklahoma* (1982), the court required that capital adjudicators consider defendants' individual characteristics when determining death sentences.[5] The result has been a rather contradictory and confusing body of jurisprudence that one analyst has described as "a Frankenstein's monster" (Zimring, 2003).

Of course, as Ewick and Silbey's (1995) work demonstrates, there is a basic and abiding conflict between individualization and generalization in the law. As an aspect of formalism, the principle of individual culpability in the law tends to preclude the use of generalizing or contextualizing stories in adjudication processes. A classic example cited by Ewick and Silbey (1995) is *McCleskey v. Kemp* (1987), wherein the Supreme Court rejected the mitigating effect of systemic racism because the social science evidence introduced on behalf of McCleskey (a black man convicted of murdering a white police officer) could not prove that McCleskey himself was individually discriminated against. Thus, the law, in this instance, valued particularity over generality. Nevertheless, in most criminal cases, extensive details about the background and characteristics of defendants and victims tend to be marginalized. Indeed, as Ewick and Silbey (1995) show, "legally organized narrativity helps produce the taken-for-granted and naturalized world by effacing the connections between the particular and the general" (p. 215). Generally speaking, the theory and practice of

American adjudication and punishment adheres to the egalitarian, Becarrian principle of "blind justice" where punishment is meant to "fit the crime" not the criminal.

However, as I have already suggested, this is significantly different in capital cases. Capital penalty phase proceedings are one of few locations in American law where stories connecting the particular and the general are explicitly allowed, and in fact required. As such, capital defendant narratives qualify as one of the few opportunities for the production of contextualizing stories in the law, which Ewick and Silbey (1995) refer to as "subversive" and identify as those that "make visible and explicit the connections between particular lives and social organization . . . Subversive stories are narratives that employ the connection between the particular and the general by locating persons and events within the encompassing web of social organization" (p. 222–23).[6] Locating the *defendant* and his crime within the "encompassing web of social organization" is precisely the goal of capital defenders—often developing a quasi-deterministic sense of "diminished autonomy"—while simultaneously downplaying the sociocontextual location of the *victim*. Conversely, capital prosecutors usually attempt to preclude or deny the defendant's context while foregrounding the social location of the victim.

Thus, the long story of the Sampson family's trek from Arkansas to California, the abuse and neglect of Bernard, the exposure to neurotoxins, and so forth, is something the law accepts reluctantly—a story required by the post-*Gregg* rulings, but at odds with the essential need for rationality. Connecting the "particular" of Bernard Sampson the killer to the "general" of his social history is undertaken by the law reluctantly, partially because it uncomfortably raises the possibility that individuals are not entirely autonomous (e.g., partially determined by their social history)—yet individual autonomy is one of the basic principles constituting American law. Moreover, this "connecting" has the potential to uncover tough questions about the *social* causes of crime, something the law is not well equipped to address.

Death penalty stories, like those about Bernard Sampson, are thus rather unusual and interesting artifacts in the American legal landscape. Despite the significance of the topic of capital punishment and the numerous theoretical questions raised by death penalty stories, little scholarly attention has been paid to the processes that produce legal representations of the executable (or non-executable) subject. While sociolegal scholars have analyzed capital defendant narratives, especially with regard to race (Fleury-Steiner, 2002; Fleury-Steiner and Argothy, 2004; Haney, 1995; Lynch and Haney, 2000; Sarat, 2001), relatively few have addressed the processes that produce them (Costanzo and Peterson, 1994; Cotton, 2008;

Lynch and Haney, 2000; Sarat, 2001). Almost twenty years ago, Amsterdam and Hertz (1992), called for just such an investigation:

> [A] level of questions has to do with the nature of the processes through which the lawyers themselves produce the sort of argumentation that we have detected in Jones: thickly textured tales in which the lawyer's explicit logical reasoning is backed by the implicit sending of additional messages, strikingly harmonious, mediated by the multiple devices of narration, allusion and linguistic coding. It is hardly plausible to suppose that all of these communicative strategies are employed deliberatively, or even deliberately. . . . So how [do lawyers] do it? Is the process involved akin to the workings of a computer program: once the lawyer chose the overall message that he wanted to send to the jury, all of the subroutines for sending that he had evolved throughout the course of his professional and personal life went "on line" and sent accordingly? Is there something here akin to the wisdom of the Zen masters who, after the most intensive preparation and discipline, are enabled to pass beyond a conscious concentration on technique and achieve the spontaneity of oneness with their art? We do not know the answers to these questions. We are thinking about them, and we hope this article may intrigue others to think about them also and to share their thoughts with us. . . . Such thinking is work for scholars who are interesting in understanding the complicated processes through which trials construct the reality which they are authorized by law to announce. (p. 21–22)

Following Amsterdam and Hertz, I systematically analyze how narrative representations of capital defendants are constructed, what they convey ideologically, and how they can contribute to knowledge about why the death penalty has persisted in certain parts of the United States.

NARRATIVITY

In order to address the theoretical issues raised above, I follow prior death penalty analysts by focusing on the narratives created in capital discourses. The theoretical and methodological starting point here lies in an understanding of what Bruner (1991) calls the "narrative construction of reality" (p. 1), meaning the human process of interpreting experience through the structural conventions of narrative. As narratologist Chatman (1981) puts it, "Narrative itself is a deep structure quite independent of its medium" (p. 117), and thus an important technology for the social construction of human reality. Thinking of narratives as "data" thus goes beyond a methodological approach and becomes an epistemological commitment. Invoking narratologists such as Roland Barthes and Hayden White, Ewick and Silbey (1995) point to narrative's constitutive function in human reality as evidence of narrative analysis' epistemological advantages:

> It is argued that narratives have the capacity to reveal truths about the social world that are flattened or silenced by an insistence on more traditional methods of social science and legal scholarship. According to this view, social identities and social action, indeed all aspects of the social world, are storied. Consequently, narrative is not just a form that is imposed upon social life . . . rather is it constitutive of that which it represents. To attempt to examine lives, experiences, consciousnesses, or action outside of the narratives that constitute them, it is argued, is to distort through abstraction and decontextualization, depriving events and persons of meaning. (p. 199)

As Franzosi argues, such a commitment "shifts sociologists" concerns away from variables to actors, away from regression-based statistical models to network, and away from a variable-based conception of causality to narrative sequences" (1998, p. 526–27). This approach is ideal for identifying "an understanding of social relations as embedded in linguistic practices" (p. 550). Looking for these embedded meanings in capital narratives yields knowledge about how "specific linguistic mechanisms underline social relations of gender or class" (p. 550), and also the relationship between the ideologies in the "American Creed"—the ideological matrix that Lipset (1996) describes as a nexus of values unique to and constitutive of the United States, namely "liberty, egalitarianism, individualism, populism, and laissez faire" (p. 19)[7]—and these social relations.

Importantly, however, the "truths" revealed in death penalty narratives are of a particular form of knowledge, a type of knowledge Bruner (1991) describes as verisimilitude:

> We organize our experience and our memory of human happenings mainly in the form of narrative—stories, excuses, myths, reasons for doing and not doing and so on. Narrative is a conventional form, transmitted culturally and constrained by each individual's level of mastery and by his conglomerate of prosthetic devices, colleagues, and mentors. Unlike the constructions generated by logical and scientific procedures that can be weeded out by falsification, narrative constructions can only achieve "verisimilitude." Narratives, then, are a version of reality whose acceptability if governed by convention and "narrative necessity" rather than by empirical verification and logical requiredness, although ironically we have no compunction about calling stories true or false. (p. 4–5)

Narratives are thus shaped by certain "necessities," including, as I argue in this book, necessities related to subtle, taken-for-granted ideologies

such as those constituting the American Creed. Put another way, the verisimilitude of narratives in capital cases is related not only to the prereq-
uisite forms of story, but also to themes around race, class, individualism
and other "American" ideological processes.

According to Riessman (1993), the essential feature of a narrative is
sequence. Narratives always respond "to the question and then what
happened?" (p. 17). Beyond this basic understanding of narrative form,
narratologists have developed various theories about the structural characteristics of narrative. Riessman (1993) discusses, for example, Labov's
classic delineation of narratives' formal properties:

> A "fully formed" [narrative] includes six common elements: an abstract
> (summary of the substance of the narratives), orientation (time, place situ-
> ation, participants), complicating action (sequence of events), evaluation
> (significance and meaning of the action, attitude of the narrator), resolution
> (what finally happened), and coda (returns the perspective to the present).
> (p. 18–19)

Other theorists have developed similar notions of narrative structure
(see Riessman, 1993, p. 19). Indeed, narratology is a diverse, sophisticated
field, with a long history and a wide array of scholars working through
complicated "problem of how to translate *knowing* into *telling*" (White,
1981, p. 1).

For a basic starting point, I rely on the model of narrative analysis proposed and exemplified by Amsterdam and Bruner (2000). Armed with an
impressive knowledge of narratology and law, these scholars offer what
they refer to as an "austere" definition of narrative:

> A narrative can purport to be either a fiction or a real account of events; it
> does not have to specify which. It needs a *cast of human-like characters,* beings
> capable of *willing their own actions, forming intentions, holding beliefs, having
> feelings.* It also needs a *plot* with a beginning, a middle, and an end, in which
> particular characters are involved in particular events. The unfolding of the
> plot requires (implicitly or explicitly):
>   (1) an initial *steady state* grounded in the legitimate ordinariness of things
>   (2) that gets disrupted by a *trouble* consisting of circumstances attributable
> to human agency or susceptible to change by human intervention,
>   (3) in turn evoking *efforts* at redress or transformation, which succeed or
> fail,
>   (4) so that the old steady state is *restored* or a new (*transformed*) steady state
> is created,
>   (5) and the story concludes by drawing the then-and-there of the tale that
> has been told into the here-and-now of the telling through some *coda*—say,
> for example, Aesop's characteristic *moral of the story* (113–14, italics in
> original).

Narratives following this structural framework are "deeply concerned with legitimacy: they are about threats to normatively valued states of affairs and what it takes to overcome those threats" (Amsterdam and Bruner, 2000, p. 121). The "steady state," "trouble," "restoration," and "moral message" of narratives are all about some type of moral question. And, most importantly, the kinds of moral questions handled by narratives are questions framed by *scripts*, which are the "hidden cargo" in narratives, and "embody the norms with whose violation narrative is preoccupied" (p. 121). It is precisely this "hidden cargo" that I tried to uncover in this project, particularly to the extent that scripts within capital defendant narratives can tell us something interesting about the relationship of law to ideologies of the American Creed.

Through my analysis of texts and interviews, I have identified a number of components that shape the construction of death penalty narratives. In the first place, obviously, the facts of the crime and the facts of the defendant's social history are the raw materials that constitute the narratives displayed in capital trials.[8] Secondly, legal requirements (statutes and case law) influence the contours of narratives. For example, cases such as *Lockett v. Ohio* (1978) opened up capital penalty phase proceedings to a wide range of mitigation evidence while cases such as *Payne v. Tennessee* (1991) allowed forms of victim impact into evidence. Third, various strategic factors influence the form of defendant narratives. For example, as discussed earlier, capital defenders often create a story of "diminished autonomy" in hopes of explaining (not excusing) the murder. However, in cases where the defendant clearly does not have compelling mitigation evidence, but may conceivably be innocent of the murder, defenders sometimes try to carefully emphasize the plausibility of innocence in hopes of appealing to whatever lingering doubt some jurors may have. Fourth, the requirements of narrative are important in shaping representations of defendants. That is, if it is true that human reality is "narratively constructed" (Bruner, 1991), the rules about what makes narratives ring true (their "verisimilitude") will influence the construction of defendant stories.

Perhaps most importantly—and in relation to their verisimilitude—ideological forces play an important role in shaping the form of defendant narratives. For example, as I discuss in detail in the chapters that follow, defendant narratives operate as mechanisms for sustaining or challenging ideologies such as the American Creed. Indeed, one of my central claims in this book is that the ideological tenets of the American Creed form a "master component" under which the other components of the process fall. That is to say, the American Creed underlies other factors such as legal prerogatives or trial strategies because ideologies tend to run through or suffuse legal processes in subtle ways (e.g., basic principles that inform Supreme Court decisions or prosecutor tactics are ideological components of the Creed, such as individualism).[9]

But whereas the Creed partially underlies capital punishment, capital punishment arguably also underlies the Creed. Put another way, to the extent that the American Creed "causes" capital punishment, it is simultaneously also true that capital punishment "causes" or *instantiates* the Creed. To borrow a notion from Austin Sarat, the death penalty is necessary for the staying power of the American Creed precisely because the Creed is, in a sense, weak: "Capital punishment may be necessary to demonstrate that sovereignty can reside in the people. In this view, if the sovereignty of the people is to be genuine, it has to mimic the power and prerogatives of the monarchical forms it displaced and about whose sovereignty there could be few doubts" (Sarat, 2001, p. 17). As Lipset (1996) has pointed out, the United States came into being through ideas, such as "popular sovereignty," *not* through historical or geographically based ethnic traditions. Part of Sarat's argument about the "necessity" of capital punishment is that the ideologies in the United States that underlie its sovereignty are somewhat weak, threatened by governmentality and globalization, and in need of edification or perpetual instantiation through symbolic displays like capital punishment.[10] This study aims to reveal just how it is that death penalty narratives instantiate and underlie the Creed.

HEGEMONY AND SUBVERSION

A wide range of sociolegal scholars have taken up narrative analysis, generally, to study a diverse array of legal issues such as constitutional law (Farber and Sherry, 1996), judicial retention elections (Olson and Batjer, 1999), family law (Richman, 2002) and plea bargaining (Maynard, 1990), to name only a few. Ewick and Silbey (1995) provide a blueprint for using narrative analysis toward an understanding of how narratives both sustain and challenge—perhaps sometimes simultaneously—"hegemonic tales" (p. 197), in which "the structure, the content, and the performance of stories as they are defined and regulated within social settings often articulate and reproduce existing ideologies and hegemonic relations of power and inequality" (p. 212).[11] This notion of "hegemonic tales" takes Comaroff and Comaroff's (1991) theory of hegemony—wherein "power and ideas are so embedded as to be almost invisible, so taken for granted as to go without saying, because, being axiomatic, they come without saying" (Ewick and Silbey, 1995, p. 212, FN: 10)—and applies it to the narrative construction of reality. Ewick and Silbey begin with the idea that human reality is constructed through narrative and add to it the idea that these narratives are (or become) suffused with hidden ideological content.

According to Ewick and Silbey, narrative can be analyzed in a variety of ways. First, narratives can be the *objects* of inquiry, where scholars "examine how stories are produced through social action and function in mediating action and constituting identities" (p. 201–2). In this approach, "narrative is used as a fundamental sociological concept, analogous to role or status, to denote processes by which people construct and communicate their understandings of the world" (p. 202). The idea here is to see how human beings socially construct reality through narratives, or more simply stated, "narrate life." Second, narratives can be a *means* of analyzing human social reality: "Rather than the *object* of study themselves, here narratives are the *means* of studying something else such as class consciousness, familial power, or jury decision-making" (p. 202), or, in the case at hand, hegemonic tales and subversive stories having to do with liberty, egalitarianism, individualism, populism, and laissez-faire in capital cases. In this version of narrative analysis, the researcher collects and analyzes narratives in order to obtain knowledge about some aspect of the social world. A third conceptualization of narrative analysis is what Ewick and Silbey (1995) refer to as "sociology *as* narrative" (p. 204), meaning that scholarly representations can themselves be narratives. In this book, I employ a combination of the first and second of these three versions of narrative analysis, namely the examination of the production of capital narratives, and also the use of them (capital narratives) as a means of understanding ideologies (the American Creed) in capital cases.[12]

In analyzing death penalty narratives, it is important to attend to what Ewick and Silbey (1995) refer to as "the social organization of narrative" (p. 205), which describes the "rules" about when, where, how, and why narratives may be displayed. As Ewick and Silbey point out, narratives emerge and are shaped by various contextual and institutional factors: "The content of narratives is also governed by social norms and conventions. Content rules, as they operate within different cultural and institutional settings, define *what* constitutes an appropriate or successful narrative" (p. 207, emphasis in original). In the law, these rules often come in the form of statutes and caselaw. Moreover, legal narratives are often quite strategic (see p. 207–8). Accordingly, some death penalty narratives represent what Spivak calls "strategic essentialism," which refers to a "*strategic* use of positivist essentialism in a scrupulously visible political interest" (1996, p. 205).

In completing their blueprint, Ewick and Silbey describe the characteristics of narratives that can be either "hegemonic" or "subversive." Hegemonic tales are often *heteroglossic*, meaning that their strength or staying power lies in the fact that they are "constituted through variety and contradiction" (p. 212).[13] This is an important methodological point because it suggests that hegemonic tales involving themes such as race or individualism may turn out to incorporate or subsume potentially subversive stories. As Fleury-Steiner (2002) has shown in his study of capital jurors, for example, potentially subversive stories about the harmful influence of growing up in poverty can be inverted into hegemonic tales of failed individual responsibility by "ghetto lost souls" (see p. 564).

Second, narratives can function "specifically as mechanisms of social control" (Ewick and Silbey, 1995, p. 213), meaning that stories can demarcate what is or is not acceptable, and what the consequences are of violating norms of acceptability (p. 213).[14] Third, "the hegemonic potential of narrative is further enhanced by narratives' ability to colonize consciousness" (p. 213), meaning that the (apparent) coherence, believability, and plot of narratives can function to mask or bracket alternative stories, and thus solidify or reproduce hegemonic tales embedded within. Finally, "narratives contribute to hegemony to the extent that they conceal the social organization of their production and plausibility" (p. 214), meaning that "as narratives depict understandings of particular persons and events, they reproduce, *without exposing*, the connections of the specific story and persons to the structure of relations and institutions that made the story plausible" (p. 214, emphasis added). This potential for hegemonic "masking" in narratives is one of the major discursive themes in capital cases, and is an important point of focus in my analysis.

Nevertheless, narratives can also be subversive, as Ewick and Silbey show by citing sociolegal scholarship focusing on counter-hegemonic stories that expose or unmask relations between the individual and his or her social world: "subversive stories recount particular experiences as *rooted* in and part of an encompassing cultural, material, and political world that extends beyond the local" (p. 219, emphasis in original). Moreover, beyond the general characteristic of connecting the particular to the general, Ewick and Silbey argue that several conditions are probably necessary for subversive narratives to emerge. First, the narrator must be socially marginalized because it is "the marginal whose lives and experiences are least likely to find expression in the culturally available plots and characters" (p. 220). Second, the narrator must have an awareness of the structural or institutional plausibilities of creating a subversive story: "knowing the rules and perceiving a concealed agenda enhance the possibilities of intervention and resistance" (p. 221). Finally, according to Ewick and Silbey, "A third condition for generating subversive stories may lie in the circumstances of their telling where particular institutions create both a common opportunity to narrate and a common content to the narrative, thus revealing the collective organization of personal life" (p. 221).[15]

Each of these characteristics is on display in the context of capital cases. Defendants are almost always marginalized, their defenders understand the institutional parameters the law provides for telling their story, and the capital penalty phase furnishes one of the few venues in American law where these types of stories are not only accepted but also *required.*

One recent study directly analyzing death penalty narratives, hegemony, and resistance is Fleury-Steiner's (2002) "Narratives of the Death Sentence: Toward a Theory of Legal Narrativity." Drawing directly from the "narrative as a means" approach described by Ewick and Silbey, Fleury-Steiner analyzed interviews of sixty-six capital jurors who were on panels that handed down death sentences to black men to show how jurors use the law as a means of drawing identity boundaries that are grounded in hegemonic conceptualizations of race (p. 550). Fleury-Steiner argues that these hegemonic tales play out in jurors' legal consciousness as they draw distinctions between themselves and capital defendants; that is, Fleury-Steiner shows how "law as hegemonic narrative is mobilized and resisted at the intersection of the identities of both the punisher and the punished" (p. 552). This study builds upon Fleury-Steiner's work by investigating the shaping factors, content, and processes involved with the narratives created in capital *trials* (rather than juror consciousness).

Another recent study of death penalty narratives is Sarat's (2001) *When the State Kills: Capital Punishment and the American Condition* (2001). It is important to explain that *When the State Kills* is a central text within a strand of sociolegal research having to do with the relationship between law and violence. This small but theoretically vibrant body of work is indebted to the work of the late Yale law professor Robert Cover, who wrote several essays in the 1980s on legal narratives and violence. These essays, especially "Violence and the Word," turned out to be inspirational to a handful of leading contemporary sociolegal scholars. Cover's central thesis can be encapsulated as arguing that our legal order, our "normative world" of allegedly rational, formal, modern liberalism, relies upon violence and can only be understood in terms of the violence that it causes (see Cover, 1992, p. 203). The important point Cover makes, for the purposes of understanding Sarat's work (and this book), is that the law often relies upon violence, and that this violence is generally rather invisible in legal processes.

However, the law's violence is more visible in capital cases. The question of law's reliance upon violence becomes strikingly clear in capital cases, when the state's violence (execution) and criminal violence (murder) must be simultaneously addressed in the discourse of a death penalty trial. And it is because of this situation that the legitimacy of the "normative order" becomes complicated. As Sarat notes, state killing can only appear legitimate if it appears different from murder (see Sarat, 2001, p. 19). In light of this situation, Sarat is interested in understanding how the state differentiates its violence from that of the capital defendant:

> The proximity of law to, and its dependence on, violence raises a persistent doubt about whether state violence is different from and preferable to the violence beyond its boundaries. To address that doubt is a continuing necessity, especially when the state seeks to use death as a punishment. The opportunity to talk about violence and to distinguish capital punishment from murder occurs in those rare moments—capital trials—when both are spoken about at once. As a result, such trials, whether celebrated or not, are crucial and unusually revealing moments in the life of the law. (2001, p. 89)

This focus on legal rhetoric about violence is the central theoretical feature of Sarat's project, especially with regard to narratives of the defendant.

The antinomy of the law's violence becomes especially clear when we look at discourses in capital trials. In his case study of one capital trial (the retrial of a Georgia defendant named William Brooks), Sarat argues that there are two basic types of death penalty narrative: the state's "evil" narrative of murder and the defendant's "context" narrative of mitigation (p. 88). The first type of narrative, delineated by prosecutors, tells the story of a coherent, culpable individual deciding to mercilessly destroy an innocent victim to satisfy his selfish desires. The second type of narrative, delineated by defenders, tells the story of a not-fully-coherent, not-entirely-culpable individual victimized by damaging social conditions who ended up making a tragic mistake.[16] The "evil" narrative is simplistic and demands harsh punishment; the "mitigation" narrative is complex and begs forgiveness. As should be clear, these types of narrative deal in themes of particularity and generalization and correspond quite closely with Ewick and Silbey's dichotomous typology of hegemonic and subversive narrative—in this instance, the "evil" narrative might perpetuate hegemonic ideologies of individualism and the "mitigation" narrative might have the potential to be somewhat subversive of them. Note, however, that this dichotomous typology is something of a heuristic tool or very crude general construct meant to be used as a reference or starting point. As the data analyzed in this project demonstrate, mitigation narratives themselves often employ hegemonic themes, categories, or ideas (and vice-versa).

Ultimately, Sarat's varied analysis of the death penalty process (and its "cultural life" in popular media) leads him to conclude, "State killing is a distraction or, worse a force that makes our society neither safer nor saner" (p. 247). For Sarat, the victim-focused American practice of execution "is part of a strategy of governance that makes us fearful and dependant on the illusion of state protection, that divides rather than unites, that promises simple solutions to complex problems" (p. 247). Further, this "strategy of governance" creates tension for the legal order because it illuminates the violence that underlies the law: "When law . . . goes too far in facilitating state killing, it undermines its own claims to legitimacy and thus casts doubt on all its violent acts" (p. 22). This second point is that while all forms of modern law are predicated on violence (e.g., in modern, non-executing states), only in executing states is the law's violence *unmasked*. Again, as should be clear, the unmasking described by Sarat corresponds with Ewick and Silbey's notion of subversive narrative. If Sarat is correct, then, capital cases are a rather rare legal location where subversive stories have the potential to thrive. However, this is complex. The capital penalty phase narratives in the data set I analyze in this study do not appear especially subversive, at least from the cool distance of several years. Rarely did the defense in these cases actually come close to articulating something explicitly subversive of any hegemonic or dominant ideology. In most of these trials, any subversive aspects of defense argumentation were rather covert and unacknowledged.[17] I will discuss this in much more theoretical and empirical detail in chapter 5.

Aside from Sarat and Fleury-Steiner's work, there is not a great deal of sociolegal research on narrativity and the death penalty, and relatively little addressing the construction of capital narratives. Costanzo and Peterson (1994) analyze attorney arguments in several capital trial transcripts to identify oppositional rhetorical strategies. Similar to Sarat, they develop a dichotomous typology—prosecutors tell flat, simplistic stories, and defenders attempt to contextualize. Other treatments of death penalty rhetorical strategies (Haney [1995]; Haney [2005]; Cotton [2008]) turn out to delineate a similar dichotomous typology. Haney (1995), for example, shows how the "logic of mitigation" (p. 1) must be understood as an effort to debunk myths about capital punishment that "function to blur the core realities of capital punishment—the social causes of crime, the normative inadequacies of capital trials, and the horror of state-sanctioned executions" (p. 2). This is an important theoretical insight—one that Sarat builds upon later (as discussed above)—and important delineation of one half ("context") of the currently understood dichotomous typology of capital case narratives. Mona Lynch (2003) delineates the other half of the typology (the "evil" narrative) in her analysis of pro-death penalty discourse on the internet. As with other analyses, Lynch finds:

> The central issue relative to capital punishment has been pared down to a classic good guy/bad guy story, where goodness, innocence, and value of crime victims represents the counterpoint to convicted murderers' evilness and blameworthiness. Once transformed to this simple contrast, all arguments about problems in administration, such as bias and caprice in

sentencing, lack of instrumental value as crime policy, high costs, and even the risk of executing innocents can be significantly diminished because the inherent value of the victim is so much higher than any person who ends up on death row. (p. 222)

Lynch thus contributes to the literature emanating from Sarat and Haney by showing how narrations of capital defendants often function to bracket out or mask difficult social questions about the role and function of capital punishment. Cotton's (2008) case study of a capital trial in Colorado illuminates a similar dichotomous presentation—the prosecution constructed a flat, racist, stereotypical, and bracketing story of murder while the defense attempted to situate the defendant within a web of destructive social forces. As with Fleury-Steiner and Sarat's work, all of these findings are clearly in alignment with Ewick and Silbey's theoretical notion of hegemonic tales and subversive stories (even if this notion is not explicitly referenced in them).

Using a more historical and literary approach, Philip Smith (1996, 2003) argues against Foucault to show how narratives of the guillotine (and its victims) in the late eighteenth century represented more than a rationalist understanding of disciplinary punishment, but also signified something like the opposite—a grotesque, profane torture machine and also a terrifying antiscience technology producing "unknowable forces" (undead type characters) (see p. 27). For Smith's purposes, differential understandings of the guillotine and its victims "functioned to interrogate visions of perfection and rationality, order and discipline with its coded affirmations of materiality, decay and profanity" (p. 45). Ultimately, Smith connects his historical analysis to contemporary executions by arguing:

> We might also speculate that the lethal technologies that have survived into the present era are not merely those which are the least cruel, but also those which are best able to mute Gothic and grotesque undertones. Looked at from this perspective, the bureaucratic and medical protocols surrounding the poison injection, the most popular form of contemporary execution, are not just an expression of the dead hand of instrumental reason. Rather, they are a technological strategy that can be read as a textual strategy—a cultural innovation that has proven modestly resistant to an unseemly heterology. (p. 48)

Smith thus asks us to look for the rhetorics embedded in the semiotics of punishment; the narrative of lethal injection is thus, for Smith, more than just rational, but also erases the semiotic power of grotesquery. This is perhaps not an overwhelmingly surprising argument, but asks us to look again to Durkheim to think about what punishment "says." In this sense, Smith's use of historical narratives is important because it brings into the fold questions about the *semiotics* of punishment theory—how are themes involving deterrence, incapacitation and retribution at work in death penalty narratives?[18] This is an important question for death penalty research because punishment rationales have long been one of the key themes within debates for or against the policy of capital punishment.

One thing that these prior studies have not addressed in great detail, however, are the *components* and *processes* that produce capital narratives— the factors that shape the contours of capital narratives have not yet been theorized. This study thus builds upon previous important analyses of death penalty narratives in several ways: by focusing on the construction of the narratives I develop a theory of why they look the way they do; I aim to add to the familiar themes of race, class and gender by investigating the role of the ideologies that constitute the "American Creed"; I bring in to the fold questions of punishment theory, which have not been addressed in detail previously (with the exception of Smith); I use different primary sources than many of these previous treatments; and, as I make clear below, I use a systematic and comprehensive data set from California.[19]

SPECIFIC QUESTIONS AND METHODS

In order to investigate these theoretical issues surrounding the American death penalty, I take up two primary questions:

- What is the content of narratives created in capital trials?
- What are the factors that shape the contours of these narratives?

In addressing these questions, this study also investigates the processes involved in constructing these narratives, and explores the broad theoretical issues of what ideological work these narratives might carry out (e.g., do they support or challenge "the American Creed"?), what they can teach us about the meaning, mechanics, and effect of capital punishment in the United States, and what we can we learn generally about the law from these narratives (e.g., are there other legal venues which evince similar issues and tensions as those revealed in capital narratives?).

Specifically, I employ two primary methods: archival analysis of narratives in capital trial transcripts, and interviews with the producers of these narratives. Analyzing trial transcripts is useful for a number of reasons. In the first place, transcripts provide a window into the quotidian life of the law. They are a record of the law's actual being, as constructed by its commonplace practitioners, and as such are representative of the vast bulk of what actually constitutes "the law." This is in sharp contrast to judicial opinions—the modal source of data about capital punishment in legal scholarship—which represent the end point of a long filtering and abstracting process. In the second place, few sociolegal death penalty scholars have analyzed transcripts. Much of the sociolegal research on capital punishment has focused on other data sources, such as juror interviews, mock jury studies, media texts, historical texts, live courtroom observation, and judicial opinions. One important exception is Amsterdam and Hertz's (1992) article that closely reads the closing arguments of the prosecutor and defense attorney in a New York murder (although not capital) case.[20] In certain respects, this research follows in the tradition of that article. In general, however, sociolegal scholars have not utilized trial transcript data. Part of the reason for this may be that, until recently, transcripts were not available in electronic form and were inconvenient and expensive to obtain. This situation has changed in recent times with the advent of electronic transcript storage, allowing for somewhat more convenient access. Thirdly, trial transcripts are public record—but are very rarely examined by the public. One of the theories of conducting public trials is to create a sense of democracy and accountability for the law to the public. But the public almost never actually participates in the public nature of the law. It is true that journalists and legal scholars (and sometimes the curious civilian) sometimes attend trials or track down trial transcripts for various purposes, including, sometimes, to make public the law's daily life (especially in high profile cases). But this is rarely the case in mundane capital cases.[21] Indeed, capital trials are taking place all the time, in hundreds of counties across the country, but relatively few people have any idea what is actually transpiring in these trials.

The interviews in this study supplement and contextualize my analysis of the texts, further illuminate the processes of their construction, and also allow me to analyze the different institutional locations in which narratives are created and displayed. The ultimate goal of this project is to offer a fine grained analysis of the meaning and construction of death penalty narratives with regard to what they illustrate about the law, legal strategy, narrative, and ideology.

TRANSCRIPTS

In chapters 3 through 6, I analyze death penalty narratives within the primary public legal location constituting the day-to-day reality of capital punishment, namely trial transcripts. Specifically, I analyze the total population of capital trials that resulted in a death sentence in three large and diverse California counties between 1996 and 2004 (N = 37). California is a good location for studying death penalty narratives for several reasons. In the first place, California has the largest death row in the United States, with considerably more condemned inmates (714) than the next most death sentencing state, Florida (394) (Death Penalty Information Center, 2011). Secondly, California is economically, politically, and culturally diverse, providing something of a microcosm of the United States. This translates into diversity among all participants in death penalty processes, including victims, defendants, and caseworkers.

Moreover, practitioners of capital litigation recognize the counties I studied as locations where death penalty trials are conducted relatively competently and with relatively state-of-the-art methods (Coyne, 2004). This "professionalism" is important for this study because it offers a modicum of control against the effect of attorney competence (or incompetence) on the form of narratives. Also, each of these counties has had a relative abundance of cases resulting in death sentences. Since *Gregg*, the counties I studied collectively produced about 20 percent of California's death row (California Department of Corrections and Rehabilitation, 2011).[22] Further, each of the counties sentences to death a racially diverse array of defendants, as the following table demonstrates:

Table 1.1.   Race Demographics of Death Sentenced Defendants by County, 1996–2004

	White	Black	Hispanic	Asian/Other	Total
County 1:	8 (44%)[1]	3 (16%)	3 (16%)	4 (22%)	18
County 2:	4 (33%)	4 (33%)	2 (16%)	2 (16%)	12
County 3:	2 (25%)	3 (38%)	3 (38%)		8

[1]Percentages are approximate.

Further, at least one condemned person from each of these counties has been executed in the modern era, which is quite rare in California. Finally, each county is large and economically and culturally diverse, representing the diverse political and cultural demographics of California.

Following Ewick and Silbey's (1995) blueprint for narrative analysis, I use capital narratives found in these materials as a *means* of understanding their construction and also their relationship to the American Creed. Doing so entailed closely reading the texts and extracting the narratives from the larger body of text represented by the trials. Fortunately for me, I was able to obtain electronic copies of these transcripts, which allowed me to code them using the software program Atlas.ti. Because each trial transcript came in the form of dozens of very large text files, redacting out the narratives was a complex and onerous task. Because much of the bulk of the public record of a long and complex criminal trial like a capital case consists of pretrial hearings, voir dire, status conferences and the like, locating and extracting the parts of the trial wherein victims and defendants were "narrated" proved to be a bit like finding a needle in a haystack. I focused primarily on the opening and closing statements by prosecutors and defense attorneys—in both the guilt and penalty phase. These statements (sometimes called "arguments"), especially the closing statements, usually summarized the evidence and were given in rough narrative form. After locating these statements, I copied the text of them into a new file, which then allowed me to code it using Atlas.ti. I developed my coding schema inductively, reading through transcripts and adding codes corresponding to the theoretical issues discussed in this chapter. Obviously, this process entailed re- and re-re-coding transcripts as the list of codes grew. This process entailed carefully reading the transcripts and identifying passages that reflected analytical themes that I had already identified prior to the analysis, and also identifying new and sometimes unexpected themes that emerged from the data.[23] The process thus resembled the method of grounded theory, to the extent that I formulated new codes and analytical themes as I analyzed the data. For example, before reading a single passage of the transcripts, I knew from my prior experience with capital trials that a number of themes, such as for example, "retribution" or "incapacitation" would very likely be present as aspects of the narratives. This method also subscribes to Conley and O'Barr's (1998) theory that understanding macro-discourses (about ideology) require an analysis of micro-discourses (e.g., trial narratives).

Following Amsterdam and Bruner (2000), part of my coding process involved identifying the important characters, describing and theoretically contextualizing the "steady state" preceding the events of the story, describing the "trouble" that disrupts the steady state, describing "redress efforts" by characters, identifying the restoration of the steady state or transformation to a new steady state, and finally describing and theoretically contextualizing the "moral of the story." A generic type of narrative in this data is one in which the defendant and victim are the primary characters, the steady state is the victim's innocence, the trouble is the defendant's violence against the victim, the redress efforts are the law's intervention against the defendant, the transformation is the defendant's conviction and death sentence, and the moral of the story is that retribution is necessary for moral order (or retribution is the moral "right" of victims' families). But other generic types were at play also, including the type wherein the defendant was the primary character, the steady state was his innocence as a child, the trouble was abuse of the defendant, redress efforts were sorely lacking in the defendant's social history, the transformation to a new steady state would be a merciful decision by the jury, and the moral of the story was that people are not inherently evil, but a product of their environment. Still other general types showed up, including narratives where the *jury* was the protagonist, framed as "the hero" faced with the daunting task of resisting the prosecution's temptations to be vengeful against the defendant.[24] Each of these generic types of narrative is suffused or predicated upon scripts, which are, in turn, related to ideologies. I discuss this in detail in chapters 3 through 6.

INTERVIEWS

In addition to the text analysis, I conducted in-depth interviews among capital caseworkers who produce capital narratives. The primary purpose of the interviews was to investigate caseworkers' knowledge or consciousness about the shaping factors, content, and processes involved in the production of text narratives—with the ultimate aim of augmenting the analysis of the transcripts. Specifically, I interviewed twenty-six trial and postconviction death penalty caseworkers working in my study counties. Unlike other research on death penalty narrative (e.g., Sarat 2001; Fleury-Steiner, 2002), these interviews were not limited to elite defense attorneys or jurors. Rather, I interviewed a medley of professionals who participate in the quotidian construction of defendant and victim stories, including defense attorneys, prosecutors, investigators, and a judge. I define these "capital caseworkers" as professional legal workers engaged in the day-to-day labor of processing death penalty cases. Caseworkers are thus the persons who collectively produce capital defendant narratives. They are judges, attorneys, investigators, law enforcement agents, and expert witnesses.[25]

Most previous analyses of professionals working on death penalty cases have been limited to attorneys (e.g., Costanzo, 1994; Sarat, 1998; Sarat, 2001). One of the problems with limiting analysis to attorneys is that it tends to over-simplify the process of constructing defendant narratives. Sarat (2001), for example, observed and interviewed the prominent capital defender Stephen Bright in an analysis of a capital case in Georgia.[26] In discussing the case, Sarat conceptualized the relationship between fact-gathering and narrative construction linearly—in Sarat's understanding, someone goes and "gathers" facts, and then lawyers piece them together to make a narrative:

> Humanizing the client requires that death penalty lawyers engage in fact-intensive investigations designed to show that the mitigation stages of death penalty trials were constitutionally deficient. But the facts, once collected, do not speak for themselves. They must be put into a story line, with its own characters and plot. (174)

This framing of the process places the fact-gathering behavior before the narrative constructing behavior, and slightly misunderstands the process of constructing defendant narratives. The truth is that in everyday practice, the inverse is sometimes true. Narratives are "drafted" and then facts are gathered to gird them. Even when the facts come first, they are not typically "gathered" without serious consideration of the narrative to soon be constructed. Indeed, some "facts" are not "gathered" when discovered because of their potential for damage to the case, either for the prosecution or defense. Moreover, the fact-gatherers carry their own cultural baggage that influences what gets gathered and what gets left behind.

Nevertheless, the caseworkers most responsible for defendant narratives are attorneys—responsible both in the sense that they are key players in their construction and are also in the sense that they are held accountable for the stories that become official legal representations of defendants once trials are finished. Thus, prosecutors must follow rules that limit inflammatory portrayals of defendants, and defenders must likewise be careful about strategies or decisions that may lead to charges of ineffective assistance. No matter how much work other caseworkers devote to narrative construction, it is the lawyers who have their name on the official papers, and thus professionally on the line. Thus, prosecutors and defense attorneys made up the bulk of my interviews in this project. These interviews were semistructured, although I had a rough interview protocol that I followed in all the interviews. I came to each interview with a set of open-ended questions with the goal of initiating a conversation rather than administering a questionnaire. Each interview lasted between one and three hours; I recorded several of the interviews, but decided not to record several others due to my impression that recording tended to inhibit the interviewees. I analyzed the interview transcripts similarly to the trial transcripts, coding for some predetermined themes and developing new ones as I went along. Confidentiality was maintained throughout the process.

A WORD ABOUT GENERALIZABILITY

Readers may wonder whether studying capital punishment in California deleteriously limits the scope of this research. This is a legitimate and reasonable consideration. So, from the outset, let me make clear that this study is about capital punishment in California. However, because this data consists of the full set—not a sample—of death-sentence resulting capital trials over an eight-year period (which includes the years with the most and second most death sentences in the modern era, namely 1999 and 1996) for three of the largest and most diverse counties in the state, it represents the zenith of California's modern death penalty.

The question of generalizability of findings and arguments to other locations is important to address. Aside from the well-known and thoroughly analyzed fact that capital punishment in America is mostly a profoundly *Southern* institution, especially in terms of actual executions (e.g., Garland, 2010; Zimring, 2003), there are a number of issues in the capital states that are related to location. Different local death penalty practices are undoubtedly influenced by a number of factors, including differential patterns of death sentencing versus executing (California sentences many but executes few; Texas sentences many and executes many; Delaware sentences few but executes most of them), different local statutes and jurisprudence (e.g., statutes in Alabama, Florida, and Delaware allow for judges to override jury recommendations on sentencing), but also including regional norms along several dimensions (differential courtroom workgroup norms, local cultural values, and so forth).

However, regional differences between locations do not entirely determine the ideological content of trial stories. While statutory and cultural differences certainly matter in the construction of trial narratives, I do not believe they prohibit, significantly inhibit, or radically encourage one or another ideological framework. Put another way: In Alabama prosecutor and/or defender stories might be *more* individualistic or populist than in California, but not so much more that trials in either state are so different as to be incomparable. There is no reason to believe that the California counties analyzed in this study are *relevantly*—in terms of the role of ideology—incomparable from the counties containing, say, Denver, Phoenix, Cleveland, or Atlanta (just for example).

This is especially true in terms of ideology. Whether a state's statute delineates (or doesn't delineate) which kinds of evidence can count as aggravators or mitigators, or whether that state's courtroom workgroups operate differently than in California would not preclude a prosecutor or defender from telling (or not telling) a story instantiating individualism, populism, or libertarianism. The late-twentieth-century jurisprudence on penalty phases—especially *Payne v. Tennessee* (1991) and *Lockett v. Ohio* (1978—assures this. American ideological commitments might be stronger or weaker here or there, but they may be ultimately deeper than and somewhat impervious to statutes or local norms.

Because this study is limited to California, only comparative research to other death penalty states can tell us if this is true. Based on my own recent analyses of judicial death sentences "overriding" jury recommendations for life in Alabama, Florida, and Delaware, there is at least some support for the claim that murder stories all over the United States are infused with ideologies of the American Creed. In their memos, judges in those states construct narratives of murder that seem to operate in ideologically similar ways to the trial stories I examine in this manuscript.[27] Moreover, recent studies of capital trials in other locations that focus on different themes than my own but also rely on trial transcripts suggest that creed ideologies are in display in places other than California (e.g., Cotton, 2008; Sarat 2001).

With these theoretical and methodological considerations in mind, I now turn to a detailed look at the role of the American Creed as a master frame in American capital punishment.

NOTES

1. See also Kaufman-Osborn (2002) for a detailed discussion of the complex relationship between the death penalty and contemporary states practicing "liberal law."

2. Which is precisely the technological example Foucault drew upon in *Discipline and Punish*.

3. Although it is relatively rare in the criminal law, this situation is not totally unique to capital cases. As Coutin (2000) shows, political asylum and immigration cases often focus on the individual. Like capital defendants, asylum applicants are required to fit a general category but simultaneously individualize their cases.

4. *Furman v. Georgia* (1972) was the landmark case that temporarily rendered the death penalty unconstitutional.

5. As I discuss in subsequent chapters, however, defendants are usually described in somewhat predictable narratives. Indeed, as I argue later, these predictable narratives are intimately connected to the ideologies of the American Creed.

6. "Subversive" may be too strong a word to describe the potential effect of these contextualizing stories because they do not, in-and-of-themselves, subvert or overthrow the hegemonic power relations that they illuminate. A different terminology, such as "potentially destabilizing" might be more befitting, but considering Ewick and Silbey's consistent use of the term, I will use it here for simplicity's sake.

7. Definitions of these ideologies are probably somewhat indeterminate and in flux. In the name of brevity, I leave a detailed exploration of the meanings of these ideologies for another time.

8. This truism is complex because the law creates a complicated filtering process between the empirical reality of "facts," and the representations *of* those facts in court.

9. It is important to note that, of course, Lipset's notion of the American Creed is itself rife with tensions, which complicate its status as what I call a "master component"; it's easy to see how, for example, "egalitarianism" and "laissez-faire" could manifest themselves in contradictory ways. Thanks to Daniel LaChance for pointing this out.

10. For a concise summary of this theoretical proposition, see p. 16–22 in Sarat's (2005) *Mercy on Trial*.

11. Ewick and Silbey also discuss the ways narrative can be used in *The Common Place of Law* (1998).

12. While it is true that my book will form a narrative of its own, I purposely downplay this version of narrative analysis in the hopes that bracketing my own narrativity will allow me to better focus on my empirical data.

13. The notion of "heteroglossia" comes from the Russian theorist Bakhtin. Smith (2003) very briefly describes heteroglossia as a situation in which "discourses . . . become layered and mutate in complex and unanticipated ways as formal models encounter folk models in a migration from center to periphery" (p. 43). Ewick and Silbey also discuss the multiplicity of legal meanings in *The Common Place of Law* (1998, see p. 17).

14. Although Ewick and Silbey do not mention it, this is a rather Durkheimian way of thinking of narratives. As I discuss below, Philip Smith (1996, 2003) has used a Durkheimian frame to analyze capital narratives.

15. For a similar formulation of the requirements for subversive stories, see Ewick and Silbey (1998).

16. Again, see Stetler (1999) on "diminished autonomy" for an elaboration on this type of narrative.

17. As I alluded to in a footnote in the prologue of this book, this should not be surprising. Openly "calling out" the hegemonic ideologies that are involved in producing deadly violence is thought to be tantamount to a suicide mission by practicing defense attorneys—if such a thing even ever occurs to them. Indeed, one of the reasons for writing this book is simply to note this fact and try to explain why it is so.

18. Smith makes somewhat similar point in his 1996 article, "Executing Executions: Aesthetics, Identity, and the Problematic Narratives of Capital Punishment Ritual."

19. As I discuss in the next chapter, David Garland has recently written comprehensively about capital punishment in America. However, Garland's (2010) *Peculiar Institution* is a broad overview and argument about American retention of the death penalty rather than a fine-grained study of the empirical and quotidian life of the institution of state killing.

20. Costanzo and Peterson's (1994) article analyzes transcripts from capital penalty phases, but does so from a social psychological perspective, somewhat different than the sociolegal framework I am working in. Cotton (2008) also analyzes a capital trial.

21. For example, during my research on this book, I sat in attendance for an afternoon of testimony in a capital trial after having interviewed a capital prosecutor that morning. This testimony was during what appeared to be an important part of the guilt phase where the prosecutor was questioning law enforcement officers who had captured the defendant. The courtroom was nearly empty, with only a small handful of the victim's and defendant's family present, as well as one or two others who may or may not have been from the media.

22. Los Angeles County accounts for the largest percentage of condemned inmates with about 30 percent (see California Department of Corrections and Rehabilitation, 2011).

23. I focused almost exclusively on the opening statements and closing arguments in both the guilt and penalty phases, although I also sometimes read parts of the pretrial materials and evidence.

24. Amsterdam and Hertz theorized this generic type of legal narrative in "An Analysis of Closing Arguments to a Jury." *New York Law School Law Review* 55 (1992).

25. Other court personnel, such as bailiffs and court reporters, might also be considered capital caseworkers, because they participate in the mundane bureaucracy of capital trials. However, these roles are peripheral to the production of defendant narratives, and are thus left aside in this study. I also do not investigate the role of jurors precisely because they are the ones who legally *interpret* narratives, not create them. Moreover, juror narratives have been studied extensively by the Capital Jury Project. In this book, I aim to address similar questions as the Capital Jury Project, but by studying the legal authors of defendant narratives rather than the legal interpreters of them.

26. This case was a retrial of a defendant whose original conviction and death sentence were overturned.

27. The discourses in the memos are different than those produced by lawyers in trials, largely because they are not created for the purpose of convincing the decider to vote one way or another on the question of death. They are declarative. Moreover, the rules governing these memos are different than those for trial arguments. Nevertheless, these memos require (at least formally) the sentencing judge to state his or her reasons for overriding the jury's recommendation of life. As such, they include "murder stories" describing homicides that are not unlike the narratives created by prosecutors in California capital trials.

2

•••

The American Creed and
American Capital Punishment

As I discussed earlier, the death penalty remains hale and hearty in the United States, both as state policy and as a widely discussed topic in academics, law, politics and culture despite several factors that would seem to militate against its presence as a penal policy, notably erroneous capital convictions at home and a worldwide movement to abolish the death penalty. Recently, a scholarly debate has emerged in the United States over whether or not the somewhat puzzling retention of capital punishment can be explained by "American Exceptionalism," meaning deep, longstanding cultural differences between the United States and Western Europe that equate to very different understandings of the death penalty. These features are sometimes collectively referred to as the "American Creed." I join this conversation now in order to interrogate the ways in which the "American Creed" may operate as master frame for death penalty narratives.

Two recent books explicitly make the exceptionalism claim: Franklin E. Zimring's (2003) *The Contradictions of American Capital Punishment* and James Q. Whitman's (2003) *Harsh Justice: Criminal Punishment and the Widening Divide between America and Europe*. Using approaches as innovative as they are different, Zimring and Whitman each illuminate an apparently unique disjuncture in the United States between public discourse about the death penalty and the day-to-day practice of execution. According to Zimring and Whitman, this disjuncture allows decision makers (be they voters, legislators, or Supreme Court Justices) to support capital punishment without participating in the morbid processes of execution. Moreover, they each independently make the novel argument that a

27

longstanding and particularly American distrust of state power counterintuitively allows for extremely harsh punishments such as the death penalty. The collective upshot of their arguments is that capital punishment is understood in Europe as an unacceptable expression of state power (and travesty against human rights), while in the United States it is imagined as a public service conducted on behalf of victims. For Zimring, the essential feature of U.S. culture that leads to this difference is a longstanding and deep commitment to "vigilantism" in the South; for Whitman, the explanation is a uniquely prominent role of "degradation" in especially egalitarian U.S. punishment.

In response, David Garland (2005) has argued that "American Exceptionalism" is too deterministic, suggesting that U.S. retention is *not* due to deep historical cultural traditions, but rather to relatively recent social and cultural changes occurring within "late modernity," especially the politics of crime control over the last thirty years (see p. 22), coupled with the United State's longstanding commitment to local democracy (Garland, 2010, p. 309–310). Garland believes that it is a mistake to interpret the legal and institutional idiosyncrasies that have helped enable the retention of the death penalty as somehow reflective of a deep, essentialist American "creed" that demands capital punishment. Rather, Garland argues that the answer to the question of America's retention can be found primarily in its "radical local version of democracy," which, with support from U.S. Supreme Court jurisprudence, has placed the question of using (or not using) the death penalty into the hands of local, politically motivated actors such as prosecutors and judges (Garland, 2010, p. 310).

The "exceptionalism" debate is complex, involving complex arguments on all sides. Indeed, one important aspect of the exceptionalism discussion has to do with what exactly is meant by "exceptionalism" in the first place. In this chapter, I outline the exceptionalism conversation, using the recent books by Zimring and Whitman, as well as Garland's response essay and recent book as centerpieces. Along the way, I also briefly discuss the work of Poveda (2000) and Lipset (1996) and attempt to bring to the exceptionalism debate the issue of racialized inequality in the U.S. legal landscape. It may be that the United States is exceptional, but that its uniqueness has as much to do with its complex history of racialized inequality as with other longstanding sociocultural forces, which are the primary focus of the materials reviewed here. My goal is thus to identify the cultural features that these prominent death penalty scholars think are intimately related to the U.S. use of capital punishment so that I can then analyze them (the features) in my own empirical data. I explicate this "exceptionalism" debate in order to have a nuanced understanding of the "American Creed," and to see how the creed may be operating within contemporary capital trials.

FRANKLIN ZIMRING ON
PRIVATIZATION AND VIGILANTE VALUES

The central question Zimring poses is this: "Why did the United States reintroduce the death penalty after 1976 when the trend in most other developed democracies was to abolish the penalty as a matter of domestic policy and to press for the prohibition of capital punishment in all civilized nations?" (p. 13). His answer is twofold. First, the practice of death penalty prosecution in the United States has become "privatized," or reconceptualized "as a service that the government provides to the relatives of crime victims rather than as a manifestation of the power of the state" (p. 14). And, second, longstanding cultural traditions based on what Zimring calls "vigilante values" outweigh traditions of "due process values" in the South, leading to support for death penalties and executions in that region (p. 14).

As a prelude to his two primary arguments, Zimring sketches "the peculiar present of American capital punishment" (p. 3) by dispelling two false impressions the casual observer might have when contemplating the death penalty in the United States: that death sentences are distributed evenly throughout the United States, and that people given death sentences are regularly executed. In contrast, Zimring notes that twelve U.S. states do not have capital statutes at all, and shows that the rate of actual execution varies widely in those states that do sentence people to death. For example, California, which has the largest condemned population in the United States (630 men and 6 women on death row), has executed only 14 people since reinstatement (California Department of Corrections, 2006), at the time of this writing. And most important for Zimring's arguments, U.S. executions take place almost exclusively in the South. For example, in the year 2000, "two-thirds of all American executions were conducted in just three of the thirty-eight American states that authorize executions: Texas, Oklahoma, and Virginia" (Zimring, 2003, p. 7). This stark variation is essential to Zimring's argument because, he believes, "privatization" and "vigilante values" are primarily southern phenomena.

The Privatization Thesis

Zimring begins from the position that the contemporary era of U.S. capital punishment is altogether different from the death penalty before *Furman v. Georgia* (1972). The key feature of this new era, according to Zimring, is the centrality of the victim in death penalty discourse and practice (p. 52). How did the victim become so important in capital cases? Zimring lays much of the blame on post-*Gregg v. Georgia* (1976) Supreme Court rulings that established guidelines for the penalty phase, an issue that had not been addressed before *Furman*. For example, Zimring notes the ruling in *Lockett v. Ohio* (1978), which "provided the defendant in a capital penalty trial with the right to present evidence and arguments on virtually any aspect of his life that was of potential importance in the choice between life and death" (p. 52). One consequence of post-*Gregg* decisions such as *Lockett*—which were aimed at making capital cases fairer for defendants, in accordance with *Gregg* and its concomitants—was a successful move by prosecutors to advocate for the inclusion of information "on the nature and extent of the harm suffered by the particular victims of the murder as well as by their relations" (p. 53). With a subsequent series of rulings allowing such "victim impact" testimony, penalty phase proceedings have developed into hotly contested discursive locations, where each side has considerable freedom to bring in contextual factors not typically allowed as evidence in criminal trials. Zimring's view of penalty phase proceedings is that they have turned into "status competitions" between the offender and the victim's family (p. 55)—a "zero-sum game" between two *private* parties rather than a dispute between the defendant and the *state*. Under these circumstances, jurors might feel that handing down less than a capital sentence is a "vote against the victim."

Zimring thus draws an insightful connection between the fairness impulse in post-*Furman* capital jurisprudence and contemporary "zero sum" capital trials. Under this interpretation, the phenomenon of "privatization" emerged because prosecutors developed a line of argument essentially saying, "If the defendant can make a particularized appeal, so can the family of the victim."

With the notion of "privatization" in mind, Zimring introduces a very interesting contribution to the capital punishment literature—a careful analysis of the use of the word "closure" in death penalty discourse. Death penalty advocates often cite "closure" for the families of murder victims as an important benefit or purpose of capital punishment. For example, former attorney general John Ashcroft set up a private broadcast of Timothy McVeigh's execution for the victims of the Oklahoma bombing because he believed it would help them "close this chapter in their lives" (Lauerman, 2001). Considering the prominent and relatively recent use of this terminology, Zimring wonders: What does "closure" *mean*? His answer is that its use in death penalty discourse is vague, ultimately seeming to mean little more than "something good that execution brings to those mourning the murder of loved one" (p. 59). Is "closure" supposed to mean the end of the disturbing and seemingly endless litigation inherent to death penalty trials and appeals? It might mean that, says Zimring; but if so, it suggests that the family's suffering could have been avoided if the death penalty had not been sought in the first place (p. 59). Does "closure" mean a psychological satisfaction produced somehow by the death of the defendant? But what might such a benefit be, if not raw vengeance? In pondering these questions, Zimring raises the question of whether or not we might expect to see differences in adjustment to the loss of a loved one between states that do or do not carry the death penalty.

In addition to pointing out the vagueness of the meaning of "closure" as it applies to the death penalty, Zimring makes an effort to demonstrate that the concept seems to have surpassed utilitarian arguments (deterrence and incapacitation) in favor of the death penalty in the public's imagination. Zimring's empirical evidence is that "closure" in political discourse and the media has increased over several years, and one poll showed that people supported the idea that the death penalty is fair because it "gives closure to families" (see p. 60–61). The point is, "closure" has made Americans think that executing defendants is essentially a psychotherapeutic "right" for victim's families (see p. 61–62).

All in all, Zimring makes three important points about the phenomenon of "closure" in the privatization of capital punishment in the United States: (1) in contrast to naked vengeance, "closure" seems like a positive rationale for execution that the public can easily support (p. 62); (2) when execution is carried out on behalf of the interests of victims' families rather than the interests of the state, the issue of excessive state power is bracketed out of the discourse (p. 62); and (3) executing on behalf of victims' families makes it seem as though the policy of execution is actually a policy of community control (p. 62).[1]

The Vigilante Thesis

Zimring's other primary argument is that cultural locations with "traditional vigilante values" also support execution. To a casual observer, the significant regional difference in execution rates in the United States might seem like a mundane point, but Zimring focuses on its relationship to federalism, which allows for extremely wide regional variation in criminal justice policy generally (p. 68). In addition to the data on contemporary executions, Zimring illustrates regional differences by analyzing historical data about lynching, public opinion, vigilante behaviors,[2] and execution. These statistics, he argues, demonstrate the correlation between vigilante values and executions. The key finding is that there is a tighter correlation between older geographic patterns of *lynching* and contemporary patterns of execution than between older patterns of *execution* and contemporary execution: "When the regional patterns of both executions and lynchings of a century ago is compared with the geography of recent executions, it is *the lynching pattern* rather than the earlier distribution of legal executions that best approximates the extremes found in the 695 executions recorded from 1977 to 2000" (emphasis added; p. 93).[3]

For Zimring, the theoretical significance of these findings is twofold: vigilante values equate to an understanding of punishment as "local"; and this "local" vision of punishment militates against the fear of state power typically engendered by harsh state punishment.[4] Considering the importance of this proposition to Zimring's argument, he is worth quoting at length:

> I do not think that the major influence of the vigilante precedents on contemporary capital punishment comes from any inherited enthusiasm for killing as a form of social control. Instead, the tradition of regarding the punishment of criminals as a local concern acts to remove one major argument against the death penalty where the punishing agency is regarded as a government that may itself be a potential adversary to citizen interests. If this is the case, viewing punishment as a community rather than state response should leave a citizen less worried and conflicted about executions even though his or her general view of governmental power may be distrustful. (p. 98)[5]

The vigilante thesis is thus obviously closely related to the privatization thesis, insofar as both suggest that capital punishment in the United States is imagined as a private, local matter somewhat removed from any sort of oppressive display of state power.

If Zimring's arguments are on the mark, it is likely that vigilante values— like privatization— allow for the emergence or reintroduction of vengeance as a primary ideology for capital punishment. Nevertheless, "vigilante values" contradict another important traditional American value, namely a commitment to due process rights in criminal proceedings (see p. 119). Indeed, this is the primary contradiction to which the title of Zimring's book refers. In mapping the regional variation of capital punishment, Zimring invokes the image of a scale with "vigilante values" on one side and "due-process values" on the other. In locations where the vigilante side is slightly heavier than the due process side, we will see executions; the heavier that vigilante side, the more executions.

Moreover, while vigilante and/or due process values may be (at least abstractly) important to many Americans, the facts of murder and execution touch relatively few Americans. The upshot of this situation is that, unlike our European peers, who generally lack the vigilante tradition and are slightly less committed to due process, we in the United States are faced with a deep and powerful cultural conflict when contemplating a topic that does not impact very many of us. To put this in instrumental terms, Zimring believes that the power of vigilante values must diminish significantly in order for the United States to abolish the death penalty (p. 138). One way for this to occur is to reframe executions not as a service for the families of victims, but as a terrifying exhibition of state power: "When states disguise the use of extreme governmental power as instead a neutral public service, that misrepresentation is a worthy enemy for all who would wish to render the United States an execution-free zone" (p. 138). This reframing, of course, would be in alignment with the orthodox view in Europe that capital punishment is, at its roots, a human rights violation.

With regard to the question of American exceptionalism, it is clear that Zimring believes that U.S. retention is due to a uniquely U.S. (and especially Southern) culture of vigilantism (manifest in processes of "privatization"), which is based upon a deep and longstanding fear of the state that is less prevalent in Europe. Nevertheless, Zimring's study is not explicitly comparative—he does not empirically demonstrate a relative *lack* of vigilantism in Europe. In this sense, Zimring seems to take American exceptionalism for granted and focuses on "those *exceptional* elements in American history and governmental structure that account for why the United States is pursuing a different policy [than Europe] at the beginning of the twenty-first century" (p. 65, italics added). Zimring's project is thus not an offer of proof of American exceptionalism, per se, but rather an argument that accepts the premise of American exceptionalism and seeks to explain it.

JAMES Q. WHITMAN ON
STATUS, MERCY, AND HARSHNESS

Like Zimring, James Q. Whitman wants to explain the difference between the United States and its modern peers when it comes to harsh punishment.[6] Put as simply as possible, Whitman's counterintuitive argument is that the United States evinces much harsher punishment than its European peers because deep American cultural characteristics of egalitarianism and distrust of state power inhibit the merciful and respectful treatment of defendants (p. 6). In place of mercy and respect, American defendants are more degraded than their European counterparts because degradation has been exposed and rejected in Europe but masked in the United States. According to Whitman, these differences can be attributed to Europe's strong hierarchical culture and America's deep egalitarianism (p. 7). Furthermore, the mixture of democratic electoral politics and formal equality in the law makes for an oddly perfect recipe for harshness:

> Harshness and democratization go hand in hand, and for a simple reason: voters never have individual offenders before their eyes; they are never in a position to *feel* the Montesquieuian impulse toward mercy. Ordinary voters

are never capable of the routinized, sober, and merciful approach to punishment that is the stuff of the daily work of punishment professionals. . . . Behind the harshness of the sentencing guidelines thus lies a painful American irony—painful, at least, to liberals who think of themselves as subscribing to Enlightenment values. When formal equality in sentencing is married to the electoral quality of mass politics, the consequences are explosive. It is simply too easy for politicians to mobilize support by advocating harsh punishment for abstractly conceived "criminals." (p. 55–56)

Put another way, voters who influence criminal justice policy (e.g., in supporting policies such as capital punishment or determinate sentencing) are detached from offenders but also influenced by political discourse, unlike punishment bureaucrats, who are somewhat insulated from politics and who work closely with offenders.[7]

In contrast, (some) modern European nations' weaker historical traditions of egalitarianism and state distrust contribute to the contemporary respectful and merciful treatment of defendants. The essential reason for this difference, according to Whitman, is that the Europeans have long had a two-tiered system of punishment: a respectful and merciful tier for the small number of elites punished by the state, and a less respectful and merciful tier for commoners (p. 11). Eventually, according to Whitman, *all* punishment in Europe "leveled up" to the characteristics of the elite tier, while in the United States, the (egalitarian) absence of an elite tier led to uniform harsh treatment for all: "Where nineteenth-century continental Europeans slowly began to *generalize* high-status treatment, nineteenth-century Americans moved strongly to *abolish* high-status treatment. From a very early date, Americans showed instead, at least sporadically, a typical tendency to generalize norms of *low*-status treatment—to level down" (emphasis in original, p. 11).

From the outset, it is important to note that Whitman does not take careful account of Federalism and state variation in death sentencing and execution. If Whitman's explanation is valid, it would follow that his proposed cultural values that equate to "harshness"—egalitarianism and distrust of the state—would be especially influential in the region actively practicing executions, namely the U.S. South. This seems implausible, at least with regard to egalitarianism, because Southern culture has generally been more hierarchical than Northern culture. This is a conceptual problem to the extent that Whitman wishes to explain U.S. retention of capital punishment, in particular, but it is less problematic for the general question of U.S. harshness, because Northern states can be quite harsh without using the death penalty. However, because capital punishment represents the zenith of "harshness," the overloading of executions in the South casts an uneasy shadow over Whitman's basic argument.

At first blush, Whitman's argument that egalitarianism could be related to harsh treatment seems ironic. It is taken for granted in the United States that "blind justice" is a good thing that should lead to fair and reasonable treatment for all defendants. Many Americans rejoice when they see wealthy white-collar criminals taken from courtrooms in handcuffs because it symbolizes the profoundly American values of "rule of law" and "equality." In 2005, for example, the celebrity businesswoman Martha Stewart had recently served a prison sentence for perjury. One of the jurors declared that her case "sends a message to bigwigs in corporations that they have to abide by the law. No one is above the law" (Toobin, 2004, p. 71). Whitman's point, however, is not that egalitarianism leads to unfair treatment of defendants, but that the powerful U.S. version of egalitarianism has led to consistently harsh punishment for everyone, including the wealthy and powerful.[8] Put another way, Whitman suggests that mercy is incompatible with the egalitarianism of a rational formal legal system:

> A merciful justice looks down on the offender, and asks: what is it that might entitle this offender to milder punishment than others who have committed the same offense? In this sense mercy involves individualization of justice—a willingness to distinguish between more deserving and less deserving persons. The contrary of mercy, as understood in this sense, is formal equality: a system that operates by the principle of formal equality is a system that aims to treat all persons alike, extending no special mercy to anyone. (p. 12)

This understanding of U.S. harshness makes for an interesting contrast with Zimring's privatization thesis because it suggests that a legal impulse toward individualism should equate with *mildness*, whereas in Zimring's conceptualization, traces of individualism inevitably embedded in a "private" capital adjudication (in the detailed invocation of victim's and defendant's characteristics in penalty phase proceedings) turn out to enable or cultivate *harshness* in the form of death penalties and executions.

Perhaps even more counterintuitive than an equation between egalitarianism and harshness is Whitman's notion that the historical American deep distrust of the state equates to harsh punishment by the state. Again, it is usually assumed in the United States that procedural protections in criminal prosecutions should inoculate against excessive state punishment. However, as Whitman implies in the quote above, the due process protections built into the U.S. formal legal system (which embody or represent the American cultural value of "distrust of state") do more than just create equity for defendants, they also prevent the state from delivering discretionary, merciful, punishment. Whitman suggests that U.S. state agents are relatively weak in terms of their autonomy in disseminating punishment, which inhibits their ability to be merciful. By contrast, both Germany and France have relatively *strong* state apparatuses, vis-à-vis punishment practices, which allow them to be merciful:

> Germany and France have state apparatuses that are both relatively *power-ful* and relatively *autonomous.* They are powerful in the sense that they are relatively free to intervene in civil society without losing political legitimacy. They are autonomous in the sense that they are steered by bureaucracies that are relatively immune to the vagaries of public opinion. The relative power and autonomy of these continental states, I am going to argue, has done a great deal to keep the values of mercy alive in continental society and to promote other forms of mildness in criminal punishment as well. (p. 13–14, emphasis in original)

This is most strikingly true in the case of capital punishment, as exemplified by the fact that public opinion favors capital punishment in both the United States and Europe, but that powerful, autonomous bureaucrats in Europe have been able to lead the way to abolition while American mass politics has so far prevented abolition (see p. 200).

Here, again, we can note how Whitman and Zimring oddly complement each other. Both scholars think that uniquely American distrust of the state (rather inadvertently) allows for capital punishment—but for different reasons. Zimring thinks that distrust of the state is at work in the cultivation of vigilante values (which correlate with executions), whereas Whitman believes that distrust of the state cultivates formalism and precludes mercy (which is necessary for mild punishment). But while the conclusions match, the supporting arguments are contradictory: Zimring's theory of distrust involves the vigilantist *circumvention* of formalist impulses (wherein formalism seems to equate to "the state" for Zimring) whereas Whitman's theory on distrust is that distrust *equates* to formalism. Thus, although both scholars believe that a uniquely American distrust of the state allows for capital punishment, they do not agree on the *meaning* of that distrust.

Status and Punishment on the Continent and in the United States

Having stated his theory of difference between the United States and continental Europe in general terms, Whitman sets out to delineate the details of his theory in great historical and comparative detail. Thus, a full chapter is dedicated to defining the meaning and importance of "degradation" and "harshness." Degradation refers to the "treatment of others that make them feel *inferior, lessened, lowered*" (p. 20, italics in original), but its status-lowering character is obscured by traditional modern explanations for punishment policy, such as deterrence or incapacitation (p. 23). Contemporary punishment policy discourse tends to bracket out the status-lowering function of degradation, which is inherent to harsh punishment.[9] Thus, whereas Zimring argues that discourses of privatization allow for vengeance, Whitman suggests that discourses of deterrence and incapacitation mask degradation.

A large portion of Whitman's book is devoted to explicating the historical development of nondegrading, relatively mild punishment in continental Europe. I will not reconstruct this meticulous history, but will note a few key points. First, Whitman argues that the underlying factor in U.S. egalitarian law derives from the Enlightenment notion of *rejecting* an individualized, hierarchical "respect for persons" in favor of "act-egalitarianism," as exemplified by Beccaria's arguments for focusing on the crime rather than the criminal. This anti-individualizing theme has become foundational in U.S. punishment practices (especially since the mid-1970s, as manifest by policies such as determinate sentencing), but is much less prevalent in European punishment practices. Second, the standard Foucauldian interpretation of European change from violent corporal punishment to incarceration leaves out the important theme of *status* (p. 98). That is, as far as Whitman is concerned, "the disappearance of such [violent] punishments [is] a history, not so much of a declining toleration for *inflicting pain*, as of a declining tolerance for *degradation*" (emphasis in original, p. 98). The point here is that punishment functioned not just to display sovereign power, but also to demonstrate the "hierarchical ordering of society" (p. 104).

These points are part of Whitman's overarching argument that society in continental Europe has historically been much more hierarchical than in the United States, and that this is reflected quite clearly in the laws of European punishment. Notions of "infamy," "honor," and "grace" were far more important in Europe than the United States, and these factors played an important role in the development of mild punishment. Whitman devotes a great deal of attention to carefully developing this point, but two important examples, the histories of beheading and "fortress imprisonment," are particularly salient to studying capital punishment. With regard to beheading, Whitman shows that the *methods* of execution in Europe were historically connected to the status of the offender. This was especially true in France, prior to 1792. Low status offenders were usually hanged, and also sometimes mutilated. High status offenders were beheaded because this was perceived to be less painful and also more dignified (for a variety of reasons, see p. 111–13). But in 1792, beheading with the guillotine was codified as the general form of execution, signifying, for Whitman, an early movement toward "leveling up" all punishment to the "mildness" that had previously been reserved for the elites (p. 113).

Whitman's discussion of "fortress confinement" makes a similar point. For a very long time, and up through the mid-twentieth century in continental Europe, certain elite prisoners of the state (especially political prisoners) were incarcerated in "fortresses." The inhabitants of these institutions, such as *Sainte-Pélagie* in Paris, were treated with respect and allowed to wear their own clothes, receive food, books, and materials from the outside, were not subjected to forced labor, and could receive regular visitors in comfortable surroundings (p. 122). Whitman cites continental elites, such as Voltaire, who were subjected to fortress confinement. In both France and Germany, "leveling-up" processes eventually led to respectful treatment for *all* prisoners. In France, the change was related to a slow but consistent theme of reimagining *all* prisoners as "politicals" (enemies of the state), rather than inherently evil "criminals" (see p. 129). The German transformation is somewhat more difficult to pin down, but the key factor seems to be a moralistic/behaviorist theme in German punishment policy. During the Weimar era, for example, prisoners evincing "good character" were rewarded with the privileges of "fortress confinement" (p. 139). This model survived during the Nazi period (for "regular" prisoners) and by the 1970s all prisoners were treated relatively respectfully (p. 142).

As for U.S. history regarding punishment and status, the key point for Whitman is that the American revolution was precisely a revolution *against* hierarchy: "As Gordon Wood stirringly describes the radicalism of the American Revolution," it was a radicalism that especially targeted the patterns of hierarchical deference that had always shaped all complex human societies—not, to be sure, a Marxian *economic* radicalism, but a radicalism of *status*" (p. 170). Concomitant with the radical egalitarianism of the revolution came a *decline* in high status punishment, which had been in evidence in the colonial period. Indeed, according to Whitman, this decline corresponded to the well-known U.S. innovation of the penitentiary. This is another of Whitman's ironic arguments: the seemingly "mild" punishment of incarceration actually turns out to equate, in the long run, to harshness. The reason for this, according to Whitman, is that nineteenth-century incarceration in the United States closely resembled another notorious American policy, slavery:

> The story of American punishment as it developed with the rise of the prison movement became, fatefully, a story of the generalization of *low*-status treatment. Corporal punishment became the norm in American prisons. So did forced labor. Indeed, it is the most striking fact of early-nineteenth-century punishment in America that the status of prisoners came, by the time of the Thirteenth Amendment, to be explicitly assimilated to that of slaves. (p. 173)

Indeed, as Whitman points out, the degrading parallel between prisoners and slaves is codified in the Thirteenth Amendment: "Despite some loosening of the early-nineteenth-century practices of degradation, the Thirteenth Amendment expressly permitted prisoners to be reduced to the status of slaves: "Neither slavery nor involuntary servitude, *except as punishment for a crime whereof the party shall have been duly convicted*, shall exist within the United States" (emphasis in original, p. 177).

Taken together, Whitman's points about egalitarianism, democratic mass politics and state power suggest that hierarchical culture, along with relatively powerful, autonomous state punishment apparatuses in continental Europe, have enabled mild punishment (including abolition of capital punishment), while democratic, radically egalitarian culture and relatively weak state punishment apparatuses in the United States have enabled harsh punishment (including capital punishment). According to Whitman, this counterintuitive situation is especially true because continentals' memory of harshness under the *ancién regime* cultivates a "leveling up" sort of egalitarianism in punishment, while our memory of slavery has the opposite effect:

> But the fact is that the history of slave-society just does not have the same resonance in American society that the history of ancién regime Europe does in France and Germany. For Europeans, it is an imperative consequence of the abolition of the ancién regime that dignity must be extended to all. We do not draw the same conclusion from our own abolition of slavery. . . . For, on the deepest level, what must drive continental European sensibilities is the natural identification that most Europeans are able to feel with their low-status ancestors. *We were all*, most of them say, *once at the bottom*. It is precisely the nature of American slaveholding that we Americans were not all once at the bottom; most Americans do not by any means identify with African slaves. (p. 198)

By the strict measure of majority (that is, "most" or more than fifty percent), it is no doubt correct that most Americans do not identify with slaves, but it is certainly possible that very many Americans *do* identify with slaves.[10] But even if this is true, Whitman's point is well taken: unlike Europeans, many Americans may imagine offenders as practically subhuman, which, in turn, makes harsh, degrading punishment seem more appropriate.

Whitman's study is a comparative history, and more explicitly "exceptionalist" than Zimring's book. His project is to delineate what he believes to be very different histories of punishment in the United States and on the Continent. At the risk of being reductionist, it is probably safe to say that both scholars believe that they have identified a deep, longstanding and unique American cultural value that essentially "causes" harsh punishment (and capital punishment): distrust of the state. For Zimring this distrust is manifest in vigilantism; for Whitman it is manifest in radical egalitarianism.

American Exceptionalism and the American Creed

But is the exceptionalist frame too deterministic? From the outset it is important to note that, to the extent that U.S. leaders understand or interpret capital punishment very differently than European leaders, the United States certainly seems "exceptional." Few would dispute that the U.S. government's position is that the death penalty is a domestic criminal justice issue, while the European Union's position is that it is a travesty against human rights, which are universal and transcend state borders. This latter view—what Zimring calls the "human rights orthodoxy"—is in line with what Fine and Chernilo (2004) have called "the new cosmopolitanism," which describes an emerging global order based on human rights and democracy (rather than surveillance). In the cosmopolitanist imaginary of globalization, international law would take precedence over state law when it comes to basic human rights issues, such as capital punishment.[11] Covering similar themes, Lisa Hajjar (2004) advocates a new "universal jurisdiction," which would allow foreign officials accused of human rights violations to be prosecuted domestically rather than in (ineffectual) international courts. Hajjar describes universal jurisdiction as both "chaotic" (because it would subvert the current paradigm of state supremacy) and "utopian" (because it would elevate human rights concerns over state concerns). The point relevant to this book is that there is a prominent movement afoot, mostly in Europe, to make human rights a high priority in international relations, and opposition to capital punishment is a major feature of this "new cosmopolitanism." To the extent that the United States does not abide by the "human rights orthodoxy" of cosmopolitanist discourse about the death penalty, it is certainly "exceptional."

This raises the question of what precisely is meant by "exceptionalism." Garland (2005) suggests that the exceptionalist take on American retention of capital punishment is rooted in a strand of thought epitomized by Lipset (1996), who argued that a nexus of values in the United States, namely "liberty, egalitarianism, individualism, populism, and laissez faire" (p. 19), distinguishes it from its European peers.[12] Lipset refers to this collection of values as the "American Creed," and notes that it stems from the fact that "America" is defined by ideology, not ethnicity. That is, unlike most European states—in which most citizens define themselves by common history and birthright—"America" is, at its roots, an ideological construction, or even itself an ideology (p. 18).[13] To the extent that Whitman draws attention to some of the themes identified by Lipset as part of the American Creed, especially egalitarianism, he can be understood as an innovator working within this tradition. Considering that Zimring does not explicitly allude to the values nexus discussed by Lipset, his position looks somewhat different than Whitman's. Indeed, as Garland (2005) notes, the "vigilante thesis" appears to be a rather novel argument, somewhat removed from the political texture of what we might call "Lipsetian" exceptionalism. Still, the idea of "the vigilante tradition" is basically an argument about fear of the state, which at least reflects (if not explicitly) the essential features Lipset attributes to American culture, especially notions of liberty, populism, and laissez-faire.

Preceding Zimring, Whitman and Garland, Poveda (2000),[14] drawing on Lipset, attributes U.S. retention of capital punishment to a late-twentieth-century renaissance in conservative and exclusionary social policies that revivified longstanding values that cultivate poverty and exclusion, ultimately creating a sort of "executable class": "The several themes (the "dark side" of the American Dream, traditions of social exclusion, and social Darwinism) combine to form a distinctive American cultural logic—American exceptionalism—that continues to justify the execution of criminal offenders at a time when other Western democracies have abandoned the practice" (p. 7–8). Poveda thus takes the core idea in Lipset—that American society's values of egalitarianism and individualism produce a "double-edged sword" that leaves a class of "losers"—and applies it to capital punishment, essentially arguing that the "loser class" is understood in the mainstream as so hopelessly and chronically marginal that they deserve whatever punishment comes their way, including and especially execution. Poveda thus looks like a quasi-Mertonian, or "strain theorist" in the sense that he believes the Creed functions to exclude a class of Americans who end up becoming deviant (violent) and ultimately alienated and executable.[15]

This line of argument is somewhat similar to Whitman's, to the extent that both believe that something like an American Creed severely "disincorporates" a large class of people, casting them as nearly subhuman, except that Poveda focuses on egalitarianism in the society at large whereas Whitman focuses on egalitarianism specifically in punishment. It is important to also note—as Whitman probably would—that Poveda's argument seems to apply to *all* harsh punishment in the United States (as does Whitman's), not just the death penalty. Indeed, if America's "double-edged sword" allows for capital punishment, it probably also allows for determinate sentencing policies such as California's notorious Three Strikes law. In this sense, Poveda makes a similar bottom line point as Whitman: American exceptionalism—of the type identified by

Lipset—accounts for harshness in the United States. The difference is that Poveda limits his discussion to capital punishment.

The type of especially "American" individualism discussed by these analysts is rooted in the notion of "possessive individualism," a theoretical concept delineated by McPhereson (1962). In defining "possessive individualism," MacPherson draws on English scholars from the Enlightenment, especially John Locke. Thus, in "possessive individualism:"

> The individual was seen neither as a moral whole, nor as part of a larger social whole, but as an owner of himself. The relation of ownership, having become for more and more men the critically important relation determining their actual freedom and actual prospect of realizing their full potentialities, was read back into the nature of the individual. The individual, it was thought, is free inasmuch as he is proprietor of his person and capacities. The human essence is freedom from dependence on the wills of others, and freedom is a function of possession. Society becomes a lot of free equal individuals related to each other as proprietors of their own capacities and of what they have acquired by their exercise. Society consists of relations of exchange between proprietors. Political society becomes a calculated device for the protection of this property and for the maintenance of an orderly relation of exchange. (p. 3)

This is perhaps a somewhat deterministic conceptualization of Enlightenment-era liberal political ideology, but it captures the essence of the "naturalization" of individualized ownership that is central to the American Creed. This is not to imply that possessive individualism is the sole or most dominant ideology of politics or law in contemporary liberal states such as the United States. It goes without saying that socialist or welfarist impulses and policies thrive even in America's hypercapitalist society, deregulated. It is to say, however, that the ideology of possessive individualism is certainly *prominent* in American society, perhaps especially in our rational, formal legal system.

DAVID GARLAND ON AMERICA'S RADICAL LOCALISM

David Garland (2005, 2010), however, is not so sure that American exceptionalism—whether it be explicit (á la Whitman and Poveda) or implicit (á la Zimring)—is a good candidate for explaining U.S. retention in the first place. This is because Garland believes that, whatever the merits of American exceptionalism as a *general* political theory might be, it simply does not apply to capital punishment. The mistake, says Garland, is looking to the eighteenth or nineteenth century to explain a very recent American uniqueness. It is probable, Garland argues, that the United States is simply lagging behind in abolishing capital punishment. After all, if the *Furman* decision had never been reversed, the U.S. version of abolition would have taken place during the same approximate time as France's. From Garland's point of view, this is an awfully close call on which to base a theory involving longstanding cultural characteristics. Indeed, rather than looking to the past for clues to American retention, Garland suggests closely examining the recent vicissitudes of the American penal and judicial landscape. Such an investigation would focus on:

> how specific forms of action (such as the campaign of anti-death penalty federal litigation) interacted with specific features of the American polity (Constitutional law, the separation of powers between legislatures and courts; the local nature of criminal law jurisdiction; the elected nature of criminal justice officials; the political character of criminal justice decision making) and specific cultural circumstances (the "crime complex" of the 1970s, the backlash against the Court's liberal activism, the conservative reaction against civil rights gains and the "moral decay" of the 1960s) to produce the reform and retention of the death penalty. (Garland, 2005, p. 23)

As we can see, Garland's basic argument against exceptionalism is that U.S. resumption of the death penalty occurred as a result of a confluence of factors, many of which are, he argues, unrelated to longstanding "American" cultural traits.

Garland followed his own suggestion and produced a comprehensive analysis of the U.S. death penalty with *Peculiar Institution: America's Death Penalty in an Age of Abolition* (2010). Following scholars such as Zimring (2003), *Peculiar Institution* constitutes a kind of sweeping, totalizing argument about capital punishment in America. In a nutshell, Garland's answer to the question of American retention is that:

> The short answer does not point to Puritanism, or punitiveness, or violent vigilantism. . . . It points instead to one of America's chief values and virtues—a radically local version of democracy—which is the primary cause of capital punishment's persistence into the twenty-first century. . . . American capital punishment persists, despite its conflict with contemporary liberal and humanitarian norms, because of the structure of the American polity. That structure makes it difficult to abolish the death penalty in the face of majority public opinion and deprives governing elites of the opportunity for top-down, countermajoritarian reform of the kind that has led to abolition elsewhere. (That same structure helps shape the political attitudes of these elites, which is why America's leaders are so much less abolitionist than their equivalents elsewhere.) America's pluralist state, its popular local democracies, and the Supreme Court's constitutional decisions have empowered local majorities that support the death penalty, while simultaneously restraining, refining, and restricting its implementation. (p. 309–10)

Garland arrives at this conclusion after a meticulous review of the history, jurisprudential mechanics, and politics of the American death penalty, including a rigorous focus on its short abolition and subsequent reinstatement in the 1970s. Perhaps most interesting and original of Garland's arguments in this book is his discussion of contemporary "uses" of capital punishment that are implicated in its retention (see chapter 11). The essence of this argument is that the current purpose of the death penalty is discursive—talking about murder and execution provide symbolic benefits for people from many different groups (although few benefits for victims' families or, for that matter, murderers).

In this respect, most analysts of capital punishment in the United States would probably agree—the death penalty's *effect* is largely symbolic. Few serious analysts of capital punishment are likely to believe that the contemporary death penalty has much utilitarian value.[16] Its purpose is to send messages, often about the messenger's political identity. Advocates are either cynical (they support or employ the death penalty to appear "tough on crime") or "true believers" (they wish to provide a retributive sense of "closure" to victims family and, perhaps, society). The conservative backlash against several progressive Supreme Court decisions of the 1960s and early 1970s (such as *Roe v. Wade*, 1973), but also exemplified by *Furman*) gave the death penalty new symbolic meaning, ultimately leading to its resumption. Likewise, once reinstated and allegedly more fair, it obtained a veneer of legitimacy and established itself as a staple of conservative law and order discourse.[17] Garland's view is that this symbolic transformation is so new and so connected to other recent sociocultural shifts that it could not possibly be caused by deep, longstanding cultural values.

The discursive "uses" of capital punishment, according to Garland (2010), include the obvious political profits reaped by advocates of capital punishment, but also less obvious benefits to defense attorneys (intensity, excitement and "even a hint of glamour," p. 291), as well as a strange kind of psychological benefit for all of us discussing murder and execution:

> The murder story is a disruptive, anxiety-producing narrative, prompting fear as well as fascination in the onlookers. To impose a sentence of death on the murderer is a psychically satisfying resolution. We get to talk about, and to imagine, the killer's death in a way that produces pleasure rather than anxiety, a sense of moral order rather than amoral chaos. His is a deserved death, a controlled killing, a legally approved sacrifice that may, in any case, never happen. The death sentence brings death within the reach of power. It tames death and puts it to work. (p. 306)

Whether this last type of benefit exists or not is anyone's guess— Garland's book is not an empirical test of this argument, nor does he cite any evidence of the pleasure we are supposed to be enjoying by discussing execution. Moreover, as Justice John Paul Stevens (2010) argued in his review of *Peculiar Institution*, symbolic or discursive "uses" of capital punishment are not *legitimate* in the same sense that utilitarian ones might be: "Deterring crime is a valid reason to punish. Neither political strategy nor deference to the mass media, however, provides an adequate justification for [execution]" (p. 2).

More to the point of this book, one wonders whether "the structure of the American polity" is itself related to ideologies such as individualism. Is localism a reflection of deep reverence for the rights of the individual? Pondering the relationship between the structure of the American polity and creed ideologies, of course, presents a chicken-and-egg problem, a problem I don't intend to resolve in this book. Suffice to say, for now, that features of the American polity such as localism, hyper-democracy, and politicized criminal justice decision making are probably especially American because of their compatibility with ideologies such as individualism, egalitarianism, and populism.

Whether or not the American Creed *causes* the use of capital punishment, it is certainly involved in the construction of the criminal law—and vice versa. The basic principles of criminal law in a common law system rely on the same ideological conceptualizations of selfhood and agency as those in possessive individualism. *Mens rea* is an entirely individualistic idea. But the constitutive relationship between the individualistic aspects of the American Creed and the law operates in both directions—the law is perhaps the most important institution in a liberal democracy and as such teaches us about selfhood and agency, just as possessive individualism teaches the law about these same concepts.

Where I differ from previous "exceptionalist" analysts of the death penalty is that I am *not* trying to prove whether or not the "American Creed" specifically underlies the death penalty. Instead I show in subsequent chapters the ways in which the death penalty's stories of murder, victims, criminals, and execution *instantiate* the American Creed and also sometimes *subverts it.* I take the basic features of the Creed somewhat for granted in this study. For now, I do not question whether the United States is exemplified by or constructed through liberty, egalitarianism, individualism, populism, laissez-faire, or moreover that vigilantism is integrated into these cultural discourses, or—perhaps most important— that the Creed (even as vaguely as I have described it here) is implicated in the oppression and subordination of classes of persons in the United States (regardless of whether it is precisely the "cause" of U.S. retention of the death penalty). However, although I take the Creed's presence for granted, I do not perpetuate its hegemony. Instead, one of the primary goals of this study is to explicitly point out the presence of the Creed and how it operates within the law.

HOW DO RACISM AND INEQUALITY FIGURE IN THE EXCEPTIONALISM AND RETENTION DEBATE?

One important feature of American culture left out in the "exceptionalism" debate so far is race. In his introduction, Whitman states that he is willing to "leave to one side" race, violence, and religion in order to draw attention to his counter-intuitive themes, egalitarianism and state power (p. 6). But it seems likely that America's legacy of slavery, its longstanding racism in various forms, deep, abiding and diverse cultural commitments to religion, and its relatively high level of violence—all in comparison with Europe—might be more important factors in harsh U.S. punishment than Whitman allows by "leaving them to one side." Despite his acknowledgment that nineteenth-century prisoners in the United States resembled slaves, there is very little discussion of *who* is now being degraded—a lot of poor people of color. Likewise, although Zimring's argument is based on an analysis of the practice of lynching, he does not say much about who was getting lynched, and who is now getting executed.[18] It is likely that wealthy and middle class white Americans would not tolerate the degrading violence of harsh punishment and execution if the degraded and executed looked more like them.

Racialized inequality as a feature of American society, especially in the justice system, surely matters more to the question of retention than Whitman or Zimring give credit for in their studies. Forty-two percent of persons executed in the modern (post-*Furman*) era were nonwhite (Death Penalty Information Center [DPIC], 2011) and 56 percent of persons currently on death row are nonwhite 2011). An abundance of empirical evidence has shown that the race of a murder victim is likely to influence the chance that a defendant will be charged with capital murder or receive the death penalty—when victims are white, the likelihood of capital charging or sentencing goes up (U.S. GAO, 1990).[19]

At the very least, Whitman's argument about egalitarianism neglects the fact that egalitarianism is an ideology, not an empirical description of punishment in the United States. That is to say, if Whitman's thesis requires that the justice system in the United States *actually* be egalitarian (rather than only purport to be so), it quickly becomes clear that this thesis dissolves in the face of studies demonstrating stark inequality in American justice. For instance, Cole (1999) shows how the grand sounding and supposedly egalitarian due process protections laid out in cases such as *Miranda v. Arizona* (1966) turn out—in the everyday real life of the justice system—to apply primarily to middle class or wealthy white Americans rather than poor people of color.[20] Cole shows how the law on the books differs radically from the law in action at every level of the justice system: from police practices, to trials, to punishment policy, to the rules of appellate courts. Just for instance, Cole describes how the egalitarian spirit of *Gideon v. Wainwright* (1963) (which guarantees defense counsel for any felony defendant) is not on display in the normal practice of public indigent defense, where public defenders are usually at a severe disadvantage against prosecutors, and also has been undermined repeatedly and thoroughly in subsequent cases, such as *Strickland v. Washington* (1984), which requires appellants to meet a nearly impossible two-pronged standard of incompetence and prejudice when making claims of ineffective assistance of counsel (see Cole, 1999, p. 76–81). In effect, this situation actually protects the rights of those able to afford quality representation while only ostensibly protecting those who cannot. Cole ultimately shows how the egalitarian rhetoric of criminal jurisprudence tends to mask a two-tiered system of justice, one for poor people of color and one for middle-class and wealthy whites:

> The rhetoric of the criminal justice system sends the message that our society carefully protects everyone's constitutional rights, but in practice the rules assure that law enforcement prerogatives will generally prevail over the rights of minorities and the poor. By affording criminal suspects substantial constitutional protections in theory, the Supreme Court validates the results of the criminal justice system as fair. That formal fairness obscures the systemic concerns that ought to be raised by the fact that the prison population is overwhelmingly poor and disproportionately black. (p. 8–9)

Moreover, this two-tiered system is necessary for the maintenance of the recent program of crime control in the United States because wealthy whites would never tolerate the *proportionate* punishment that would result if the system were truly egalitarian and harsh: "Absent race and class disparities, the privileged among us could not enjoy as much constitutional protection of our liberties as we do; and without those disparities, we could not afford the policy of mass incarceration that we have pursued over the past two decades" (p. 5).[21]

This point of view contradicts Whitman's suggestion that the United States has (or has ever had) a single-tiered, degrading justice system for everyone because it shows how wealthy and middle class whites are effectively exempt from degrading prison terms and death sentences. The occasional examples of (white) white collar criminals such as Martha Stewart or Bernard Madoff notwithstanding, most wealthy white people in the United States never experience the harsh, degrading justice described by Whitman—indeed these rare cases would seem rather to perpetuate the hegemony of race inequality by burnishing the law's on the books veneer of legitimacy with high profile but rare examples of "egalitarian" punishment. Racialized inequality in the justice system might simply be such an obvious and well-trodden topic that Whitman and Zimring feel no need to repeat it. Still, questions linger about the relationship between Zimring's and Whitman's independent variables—vigilantism and egalitarianism—and structural racism in the United States.

Could it be that vigilantism is something like an intervening variable between racism and executions? One wonders if some other social facts about the South, such as rates of membership in white supremacy groups, correlate as well with executions as do vigilante values.[22] Recall that Zimring's best measure of vigilantism is lynching. But why would vigilantism—rather than antiblack racism—be the primary construct embodied in or measured by lynching? One response would be that it is not the racism inherent in lynching that is important for the question of current retention of capital punishment, but instead the "localized" nature of lynching that equates to a contemporary understanding of capital punishment, a "community response to crime" rather than an example of oppressive state violence. This may make sense on its own terms, but it begs the question of why Southerners desired (and now understand capital punishment as something like) extragovernmental punishment in the first place. One might speculate that this desire has something to do with dissatisfaction—perhaps quite implicit, covert, or unconscious—over the lack of state suppression of black people. Zimring might agree with this point, yet he does not discuss it in his book; he occasionally notes the racist nature of lynching (for example, p. 90), and when mentioning the Civil War does not characterize it as a war about slavery but as "the revolt of a society against its national government" (p. 110). Further, Zimring argues that "the race codes and racism of the late nineteenth and twentieth century have been for the most part rejected by citizens in the South" (p. 110), but offers no empirical evidence on the point.

Zimring seeks to disentangle racism from vigilantism in the South, by arguing that the explicit "racist terrorism" of the Ku Klux Klan (KKK) has been rejected, while the "legacy of rebellion" epitomized by the Confederate flag has not (p. 110). But this assertion assumes quite a bit about the symbolic meaning of the Confederate flag (i.e., that it is primarily a symbol of rebellion against the government not a symbol of antiblack racism), and also about white supremacy (i.e., that it has been disavowed because the KKK is much less popular and powerful than it once was). As Zimring himself would likely agree,[23] disentangling vigilantism and racism is surely a difficult conceptual and empirical problem, but one that should be taken up if his theory is to be validated. The South may be "exceptionally" vigilante, but it seems likely that its vigilantism is rooted in or connected to its unique history of racism.

A less straightforward line of criticism may be made against singling out egalitarianism as an independent variable causing harsh punishment. As critical race theorists have argued, the individualized juridical subject in American law is bound up with concepts of race. U.S. processes of constructing the juridical subject can be seen as part of a broad Western historical process of creating "civilized" subjectivities. As Fitzpatrick has argued in *The Mythology of Modern Law* (1992), law in the West must be understood as a component of modernity's "myth" of "progress," constituted through a negation of "the savage":

> The mythology of European identity is founded in an opposition to certain myth-ridden "others." These are constructed not as the exemplary affirmations of a classic mythology but in terms of a negative teleology: "so far as I know, we are the only people who think themselves risen from savages: everyone else believes they descended from Gods (Sahlins, 1976, p. 52–53). Occidental being is impelled in a progression away from aberrant origins. It is formed in the comprehensive denial of the "other." (ix–x)

The law has thus been used in the West generally—not just in the United States—as a socially constructed means of defining "white identity" through that which it is not—the "savage." The law thus creates order by allowing "us" to define ourselves as that which "we" are not, as not the Other.[24] In the United States, these processes of "selfizing" and "otherizing" emerged partially through legal racialization after the Civil War. As Gates (1997) has pointed out, the institution of slavery—and more importantly, its deinstitutionalization—engendered legalized understandings of different race categories that allowed for the discipline and control of "blacks" that have since become naturalized (see Gates, 1997, p. viii):

> During this period [pre-constitutional America], the doctrine of possessive individualism—the belief that the individual exists independent of her social relationships, i.e., exists in and for herself, fully in command of her own personal characteristics and ends—had not yet fully emerged. For that to occur, social acceptance of a new, alternate mode of appropriation would prove necessary, a development that only became possible with the conceptual severance, and the discrete annexation of human labor power in place of the appropriation of entire human beings. This move, which conferred markedly greater autonomy upon the broad mass of nonenslaved laborers, facilitated the legal expression of individuality, which in its turn gave rise to the legal expression of the concept of "race." (Gates, 1997, p. vii)

Thus, if the American Creed is based, in part, on possessive individualism, and possessive individualism is based, in part, on racism, the American Creed was born, in part, out of racism. If this syllogism has any validity, the American Creed takes on a different character, becoming suffused with the issues raised by America's particular history of defining white identity as *not* the "black savage."[25]

But even if racism is not especially implicated in vigilantism, and even if the social construction of race categories makes "race" conceptually difficult, few would dispute that the criminal justice system in general and capital punishment in particular have long oppressed poor people of color (even if the precise meaning of "color" is complex). Without endeavoring to explain the undoubtedly complex reasons why, it seems likely that the current disproportion in punishment is associated with the inequity of the past, when racism was much more blatant. Black people have always been feared and oppressed in the United States—from slavery to the convict leasing system to Jim Crow to the current racialized carceral society.[26] Perhaps the best explanation for why we retain the death penalty is the simplest reason: because the people being executed do not look like—and never have looked like—the people doing the executing.[27] The fact that this difference is well known does not mean that the point should not be made again—especially given the Supreme Court's reluctance to accept repeated empirical demonstrations of a race effect on capital case outcomes (see Dieter, 1998). The lacunae in Whitman's and Zimring's (and the other American exceptionalists) work is not that they fail to offer important theories of harsh punishment, but that they write as though U.S. harshness and capital punishment can be discussed without explicitly addressing racism and inequality. By doing so, Zimring and Whitman run the risk of taking race out of the equation, and thus mirroring the Supreme Court's jurisprudential "resolution" of racial bias in capital punishment.

Recall that the Supreme Court's decision in *Furman* that death penalty statutes were too arbitrary was partially connected to a concern that capital case outcomes reflected a bias against black defendants. Of course, this concern over racial bias only went far enough to raise questions about the implementation of capital punishment, not to a deep and general critique of racism in the administration of justice. Hence, as legislators retooled capital statutes to include provisions for "guided discretion," bias against minorities was supposed to be eliminated. But here again is an example of a gap between the law on the books and the law in action—post-*Gregg*, so far as I have been able to determine, there has been little reduction in arbitrariness or bias in capital case outcomes.[28] The intended effects of guided discretion have not been found. Thus, while the issue of systemic race bias has been officially "resolved" in death penalty law, it still lurks below the surface. The bottom line is that the nature of death penalty jurisprudence in the United States guides death eligibility and jury decision-making only so far—something about the capital trial process seems to still allow for covert racism. To ignore this in any exceptionalist treatment of U.S. capital punishment risks minimizing racism's role *in* the American Creed and U.S. retention of the death penalty.[29]

DOES IT MATTER IF THE
UNITED STATES IS EXCEPTIONAL?

Most analysts would probably agree that there are two plausible routes for formal abolition of capital punishment in the United States: (1) legislative change in each death penalty state, and (2) a new Supreme Court ruling finding capital punishment unconstitutional. At the time of this writing, the momentum of state-by-state abolition appears to be growing, with abolitions in New Jersey, New York, New Mexico, and Illinois in between 2007 and 2011, and the likelihood of a 2012 ballot measure in California to abolish capital punishment. However, it seems unlikely that this will happen in *all* states, even over the course of decades. Rather, in light of recent Supreme Court rulings that chip away at capital punishment (such as *Atkins v. Virginia* [2002] and *Roper v. Simmons* [2005]), it seems more likely that if capital punishment is abolished, it will be by the Supreme Court (although this also appears to be rather unlikely any time soon, given the Court's makeup).

Considering this state of affairs, what difference does it make whether U.S. retention is rooted in longstanding "exceptional" cultural characteristics—whether they involve vigilantism, egalitarianism, racism, or a combination of these factors—or is instead the result of a jumble of events taking place within the recent judicial/penal landscape, or is simply due to America's radically localized polity. This is a rather complex sociolegal question. Garland would probably argue that the very fact that the whole question would disappear if the composition of the Supreme Court changed slightly disproves the exceptionalism argument. Zimring, Whitman or Poveda might respond by arguing that the only way the Supreme Court would ever make such a ruling would be if "exceptional" American cultural characteristics (such as vigilantism or egalitarianism, or racism) were eclipsed by some other "American" value (Zimring would say "due process"). As Garland suggests, retention is probably due to the interaction between somewhat unique American characteristics (federalism) and the vicissitudes of the penal/judicial scene (such as the rise of the victims' rights movement). Consequently, abolition is likely to arrive only with a different interaction. As Stuart Banner has noted (2005), abolitions in the past and abroad have taken place during times when courts were limiting the practice of capital punishment (like the present) and the public was concerned about the prospect of wrongful execution (like the present).

However, if racism is as entwined within vigilantism and egalitarianism as I have suggested, and if the Supreme Court is the most plausible government agent of abolition, then the legal reasoning about race and inequality will probably have to change in the high court. Unless a few cases appear that demonstrate explicit, intentional and prejudicial racism against the particular defendant, which seems unlikely, the court will have to change the reasoning displayed in *McCleskey v. Kemp* (1987) (in which the court ruled that statistical evidence showing a systemic race effect on death penalty outcomes did not prove that the defendant himself was individually discriminated against). Such a change may not take place within the next few years, but considering that capital appellate defenders continue to bring appeals based on explicit racism, such as *Dobbs v. Zant* (1989) (Dobbs's trial took place in the 1980s; jurors, the judge, the prosecutor, and the defense attorney all were shown by appellate defenders to harbor racist beliefs and use derogatory terms such as "nigger" [see Cole, 1999, p. 135]), just enough Supreme Court justices might eventually be swayed to abandon the *McCleskey* doctrine and face up to the failure of guided discretion. Racism is probably deeply implicated in U.S. harsh punishment and execution, but it may also be the linchpin for abolition. The racism that underlies the disproportional punishment and execution in this country is overtly or officially vilified by most Americans, and certainly the political elites. If its role in capital punishment can be convincingly uncovered, perhaps it will finally prompt the Supreme Court to outlaw executions.[30]

CONCLUSION

As I have tried to show in this chapter, Zimring and Whitman each make an interesting case that several unique and longstanding characteristics of the American legal and cultural landscape allow for the persistence of capital punishment (and harshness in general). However, each argument is susceptible to criticism, such as Garland's, that the exceptionalist approach to retention can be undermined, is too deterministic, fails to account for recent changes in the judicial/penal landscape, and de-emphasizes the radically local democracy of the United States. Furthermore, even if the United States is exceptional, both Zimring's and Whitman's analyses seem to suffer from their lack of attention to "exceptional" racism and inequality in U.S. law, society, and capital punishment.

Still, these authors invite us to rethink the characteristics and purposes of modern punishment in the United States. On the one hand, Zimring shows how vengeance—through processes of "privatization"—has crept to the fore of American punishment rationales, at least with regard to capital punishment. On the other hand, Whitman shows how deep hierarchical cultural traditions in Europe eventually lead to the rejection of degrading punishment. What can students of the sociology of punishment—those not necessarily especially interested in capital punishment—learn from these studies? As Garland (2001) argues in *The Culture of Control: Crime and Social*

Order in Contemporary Society, the institutional arrangements and practices of punishment that had characterized American punishment for much of the twentieth century changed in the 1970s from "penal welfarism" (p. 3) to a "culture of control." Put a bit more simply, punishment ideologies changed from utilitarian/correctional to punitive. The key point is that "late modernity—the distinctive pattern of social, economic and cultural relations that emerged in America . . . in the last third of the twentieth century—brings with it a cluster of risks, insecurities, and control problems that have played a crucial role in shaping our changing response to crime" (p. viii). Zimring and Whitman suggest that, within "late modernity," obscured punishment ideologies of vengeance and degradation may be supplanting utilitarian ideologies such as deterrence, incapacitation or even retribution (even if retribution is most often invoked by contemporary death penalty advocates). Put another way, if we agree with Garland (1990, 2001) that U.S. punishment has been facing something of an "identity crisis" since the 1970s, then these books can help us see some ways in which this crisis is playing out in capital punishment.

In joining the discussion on capital punishment and the American Creed, I do not intend to resolve the exceptionalism debate. Instead I focus on how the Creed and the criminal law, in the form of capital trials, are involved in processes of constructing and challenging each other. I take up this question explicitly in the following chapter. In some respects, this approach follows the contemporary work of Garland, who has called for abandoning the endless normative discourse about capital punishment and instead studying it as an institution or a social fact to be explained. That is, like Garland, I do not approach the study of the death penalty with a normative axe to grind, although I am personally opposed to the death penalty. Instead of the normative approach, which Garland argues *inhibits* understanding of the death penalty institution, I look to the mutually constitutive (and deconstitutive) interplay between the criminal law and the Creed in hopes of learning something about each feature of American society. Finally, as I have tried to briefly explicate here, the American Creed is *inherently* racist. My subsequent examination of the Creed's relationship to the death penalty is undertaken with this knowledge in hand.

NOTES

1. One wonders if Zimring has gone far enough in his discussion of "closure." What "closure" *signifies* in death penalty discourse is unclear and sometimes contingent or suffused with a sort of veiled ideological hue. But despite the indeterminate meaning of "closure," Zimring does not use insights to be found in fields

such as semiotics, law and literature, or cultural studies, all of which contend with questions of linguistic indeterminacy. One can imagine drawing on the work of, for example, Gerwitz (1996) to investigate how "closure" is used in the narrative construction of reality in capital trials; that is, how "closure" is used rhetorically to narrate certain types of ideologically charged stories or characters. As Zimring points out, the emergence of "closure" as a justification for the death penalty provides a number of rhetorical functions for death penalty advocates. However, Zimring does not draw any connections between these rhetorical functions and the ideological position of those advocating the death penalty. *Who*, we wonder, is employing the use of "closure" and *why*?

2. Zimring's measures of behavioral indicators are the presence of "non-discretionary" concealed weapon laws and rates of self-defense killings, but he acknowledges that the validity of these measures is rather weak (p. 108).

3. Zimring compares two time periods: 1889–1918 and 1977–2000. During the first era, the South accounted for 88 percent of lynchings, while the Northeast accounted for 0.3 percent. During this same era, the south accounted for 56 percent of executions, while the Northeast accounted for 23 percent of executions. During the contemporary era, the South accounts for 81 percent of executions while the northeast accounts for 0.05 percent executions (see Zimring, p. 94).

4. In light of evidence showing that rates of interpersonal violence are higher in the *rural* South, scholars such as Nisbett and Cohen (1996) have argued that a "culture of honor" or "culture of violence" exists in the rural South. Zimring briefly mentions this "culture of violence" and suggests that the south should instead be seen as a "culture of punishment," which, according to Zimring, cannot be separated from the "vigilante tradition" (see p. 116–17).

5. A statistical study by Messner et al. (2006) suggests that the nexus between vigilantism and distrust of the state is racialized and more complex than Zimring proposes here.

6. Whitman does not limit his attention to *capital* punishment. Rather, he focuses on philosophies and practices of punishment in general, with special attention to the historical sociology of incarceration and execution. Nevertheless, in my reading, Whitman's explanation for American "harsh" punishment includes, and may be exemplified by, capital punishment.

7. This argument reflects Zimring's point about the gap between the day-to-day practice of execution and U.S. Supreme Court justices whose decisions shape the contours of death penalty law (see p. 10).

8. As I discuss below, this argument ignores the striking class and race disparities in U.S. punishment.

9. Whitman briefly mentions John Braithwaite's (1989) theory of re-integrative shaming, and suggests that it is unrealistic (see p. 24).

10. For example, if we were to take half of the roughly 13 percent of Americans who are descendants of African slaves, and combine them with whatever proportion of nonblack Americans who are under the control of the justice system, we obtain a significant number of Americans who may very well identify with African slaves, perhaps as many people as 10 or 12 percent of the population. Wacquant (2000) has explained how American society has continued the marginalization and control of African Americans through new forms of slavery's "peculiar

institution," specifically in the forms of Jim Crow laws, the mid-twentieth-century "metropolitan ghetto," and most recently, prison.

11. Indeed, there is a rift within the Supreme Court about the role of international opinion on legal issues, as evinced by the controversy over the court's citation of international treaties condemning capital punishment in the *Ropers v. Simmons* (2005) case, which outlawed executing juvenile offenders. For a brief overview, see Yen (2005).

12. Lipset follows in the footsteps of de Tocqueville, who is usually understood to be the first or at least one of the earliest prominent figures to posit "American exceptionalism." Note also that the concept of American Exceptionalism is not limited to the sort of political theory typified by Lipset. Madsen (1998), for example, looks to cultural artifacts such as novels and films to identify themes or characteristics thought to be especially "American," such as "the idea of discovering perfection through a return to primitive simplicity" (p. 123) by exploring frontier lands.

13. This is probably an overly simplistic rendering of "America" because it neglects much of the historical construction of "America" that has to do with *race.* See, for example, Gerstle's (2001) argument that two contradictory conceptualizations of American nationalism—one based on *ethnic purity* the other on *civic philosophy*—have profoundly shaped the history of the United States.

14. Steiker (2002) also preceded Zimring, Whitman, and Garland with a law review article entitled "Capital Punishment and American Exceptionalism," in which she discusses ten interconnected "theories" of what uniquely American sociocultural traits might explain retention of the death penalty. Candidates include "homicide rate," "public opinion," and "federalism," to name a few.

15. Lipset refers to Merton frequently in *American Exceptionalism*, relying almost entirely on the Mertonian notion of a means/ends disjuncture to explain high U.S. crime rates.

16. Some economists continue to cling to the notion that the death penalty has a deterrent effect (see for example, Rubin, 2006).

17. For more on these points, see Garland (2005) and Steiker (2002). This line of thought reflects the work of Austin Sarat (2001), who inverts the question of capital punishment's "cause" and seeks to explain its effect. To put it in overly simple terms, Sarat suggests that the presence of the death penalty bolsters or enables the very characteristics that exceptionalists believe enable the death penalty.

18. It may be that Zimring assumes that the topic "lynching" inherently equates to "racism," and did not feel the need to explicitly discuss race in his analysis of lynching. Nevertheless, Zimring's point of focus in discussing lynching is its vigilantist character *not* its racist character.

19. This GAO report is based on an "evaluation synthesis" (a nonstatistical form of meta-analysis) of empirical studies of race and capital punishment. While their report found a clear and strong "race of victim influence," it found only equivocal support for an independent effect of race of defendant (see p. 272). The GAO report validates the work of Baldus and his colleagues, who pioneered the study of race effects in capital outcomes.

20. It is likely that poor whites are also treated harshly. However, the empirical research on a "class effect" is not as substantial as that on a "race effect." There

is extensive empirical research showing the independent effect of race from other factors that might explain differential justice system outcomes for blacks. For an overview of the recent empirical research showing this "race effect," see chapter 4 of Brown et al. (2003).

21. These race and class disparities are well-documented in the empirical literature on punishment. See, for example, Wester et al. (2002), who break down incarceration rates by age, race, and educational background (a plausible measure of class, although the authors do not discuss it as such) while discussing the effect of mass incarceration on employment rates. These data dramatically demonstrate the racialized inequality in punishment described by Cole:

> Prison incarceration rates are about eight times higher for blacks than for whites, and high school dropouts are more than twice as likely to be in prison than high school graduates. Consequently, much of the growth in imprisonment in the three decades after 1970 was concentrated among young minority men with little education. By the late 1990s, about two-thirds of all state prison inmates were black or Hispanic, and about half of all minority inmates had less than twelve years of schooling. (p. 165)

See also Mauer (1999) for an overview (with supporting empirical evidence) of profound race and class disparities in punishment. See also Tonry (1996) where he notes that the racial consequences of harsh policies were entirely foreseeable by the architects of those policies.

22. It turns out that support for the death penalty in a given locale is associated with higher percentages of African Americans in the local population and racial prejudice. See Barkan and Cohn (1994), and Soss et al. (2003).

23. For example, Zimring notes:

> It is likely that the long tradition of viewing punishment as a community rather than state institution and the coercive white supremacist context in which punishments took place were defining elements of the Southern propensity to punish rather than a separate process from it. The larger willingness to punish was a function of the particular targets and the particular context of punishment, so that what I have been calling vigilante values are not only a cause of willingness to execute but may also be a contributing cause also of the broader enthusiasm for harsh treatment of offenders in the South. (p. 117)

24. An implication of Fitzpatrick's argument is that the "occidental being" has no essential constitution; the being is constructed through a discourse of comparison, suggesting that it is nonessential, relative, indeterminate, and abstract. This insight helps to show how race categories are themselves nonessential, relative, indeterminate, and abstract.

25. As Michael Meranze argued at the 2005 Annual Meeting of the Law and Society Association, this situation might also apply to other former European colonies. Meranze argues that it might make more sense to compare the United States to other nations that emerged out of European colonialism (rather than the European countries themselves), such as the British Caribbean or India (which use the death penalty), because the sovereign legacy of colonialism is a more useful category of comparison than "modernity." An important part of Meranze's argument is that these states share not only capital punishment with the United

States, but also "a wounded sovereignty," high levels of violence, and racially conflicted histories—all of which may be implicated in the persistence of using the death penalty.

26. Again, see Wacquant (2000) on how African Americans have been simultaneously exploited and excluded in various ways throughout American history.

27. This truism can be empirically illustrated by the racial demographics of prosecutors in death penalty states, 97.5 percent of whom are white (Dieter, 1998). An interesting empirical question is whether those executed in Europe looked as different from the executioner as they do in the United States. In order to draw such a comparison, it would be necessary to investigate the demographic history of capital punishment in Europe, perhaps limiting the analysis to the post-Enlightenment era. This approach would invert the question of retention to the question of abolition. If the executed in France, Great Britain, and Germany often or sometimes resembled middle-class or wealthy citizens belonging to the dominant homogenous ethnic group, perhaps abolition came easier. Such a line of reasoning would partially resemble Whitman's explanation for American harshness, to the extent that it would agree that Europeans understood punishment as "something for everyone," not just reserved for "subhumans."

28. The (1990) GAO report (discussed above) showing a race effect on capital case outcomes provides some empirical support for this point, as does Paternoster's 1991 review (see chapters 4–5). For a discussion of more recent empirical research on this point, conducted subsequent to the GAO report, see Baldus and Woodworth (1998).

29. Garland (2010), who is explicitly *not* an exceptionalist, devotes significant attention to the role of race in *Peculiar Institution*.

30. It is also plausible that proof of a recent wrongful execution could push the court—even one comprised of conservatives—to declare the death penalty inherently unconstitutional.

3

•••

Death Especially Deregulated
Anatomy of California Capital Trials

One purpose of this book is to bear witness to one small but important moment in the life of the law, namely the mundane reality of state killing. In that spirit, this chapter aims to be a record of a record—a compendium of facts about contemporary death penalty trials. The goal of this chapter is to elucidate empirical characteristics of the death penalty in actual practice. My hope is that this undertaking will *complicate* the meanings of these particular trials, and capital trials generally, so that they can be understood and remembered as something more than "just" instances of evil, selfish persons killing innocent, virtuous victims.[1]

Robert Burns (1999) advocates analyzing trials:

> Theoretically, the trial in general, the jury trial in particular, is a central institution in our legal order. An appreciation of its distinctive languages and performances cannot but enrich, and often quite radically changes, standard understandings of "what law is." An adequate philosophy of law must take account of those languages and practices. The trial makes law in the overwhelming majority of tried cases; law is what emerges from those languages and practices as a matter of constitutional right. (p. 7)

This chapter takes up Burns's call to analyze *trials* as a method of understanding "what law is."

Specifically, because this chapter addresses *California* capital trials, it shows how the death penalty process operates when it is especially "deregulated" (even more deregulated than in other death-sentencing states). As prominent death penalty scholars have shown for over twenty-five years, the jurisprudence regulating capital trials has been a contradictory mess ever since *Gregg v. Georgia* (1976) (see, for example, Weisberg, 1984, and Zimring, 2003). But the doctrinal schizophrenia around trying to discipline state killing is especially vivid in California because the rules governing the capital penalty phase in California are radically indeterminate. As the research of Craig Haney and his colleagues has shown, California penalty phase jury instructions are among the most unstructured in death penalty states, and often lead to significant juror confusion (Haney, Sontag, and Costanzo, 1994). Specifically, the California rules about penalty phase jury instructions do not require the court to "identify for the jury which factors may be aggravating and which may be mitigating" (CAL-CRIM, 2008, No. 763), providing very little guidance for jurors (which, as I discuss below, can lead to jurors "converting" mitigation to aggravation). Analyzing the empirical characteristics of these California trials thus provides an opportunity to see what the practice of capital punishment looks like when it is especially deregulated.

One key finding in this study is that the racial and socioeconomic demographics of capital defendants correspond to previous death penalty research on the demographics of capital defendants. African Americans are disproportionately represented in this data set when compared to their numbers in the respective counties, and nearly all of the defendants were poor.

This is important because it suggests that, despite the theoretical promise of "guided discretion" to eliminate bias in the death penalty process,[2] capital sentences continue to fall on the marginalized, the persons bracketed out of the American Dream by way of American society's ideologies of exclusion. This chapter is a literal illumination of this "executable class." As such, it demonstrates that guided discretion seems to be something of a false promise; an instance of "repressive formalism," where substantive justice is precluded by formal equality.[3] That is to say, despite the *formal* promise of equality offered by *Gregg v. Georgia* (1976) and the other cases meant to "rationalize" capital punishment (Garland, 2010), these data demonstrate again that the death penalty machine remains quite repressive. Indeed, it represses the same people it did prior to *Furman v. Georgia* (1972).

In the pages that follow, I first describe the basic characteristics of California capital trials in general, and then discuss the empirical characteristics of these particular cases. Specifically, I discuss the race and gender of defendants and victims, the socioeconomic status of defendants, the degree of "heinousness" of these murders, and the "special circumstances" charged. I also analyze the factors in aggravation and mitigation argued by prosecutors and defenders in these cases and discuss some of the issues raised by California's penalty phase jury instructions. Finally, I delineate a typology of stereotypical "characters" created by prosecutors and defenders when describing victims and defendants in capital trials. What emerges is a picture of dystopia—poor, often mentally ill and intoxicated people getting into lethal trouble. To paraphrase Austin Sarat (2001), the death penalty continues to be "a simple solution to complex problems," enduring in the twenty-first century to operate as an ineffective and blunt tool to contend with society's deep sicknesses of poverty and exclusion.

ANATOMY OF A CAPITAL TRIAL

Predicated on the principle of guided discretion laid out in *Gregg v. Georgia* (1976) and its companion cases[4] (and elaborated upon in subsequent cases, such as *Lockett v. Ohio* [1978][5]) death penalty trials in California consist of two distinct phases—the so-called "guilt phase" and the so-called "penalty phase." Generically, each phase is treated by capital litigators as a trial unto itself, although each phase normally has the same jury.[6]

Despite their generic status as individual trials, there are differences between the guilt and penalty phase in a capital trial, most notably the lack of a prosecution rebuttal during closing arguments in the penalty phase—unlike in the guilt phase (and most criminal trials), the prosecutor does not "get the last word" in a penalty trial. Generally, the process in the guilt phase of a capital trial unfolds in the following order:

1. Pretrial hearings
2. Jury selection (voir dire)
3. Prosecution's opening statement
4. Defense's opening statement
5. Prosecution's evidence
6. Defense's evidence
7. Prosecution's closing argument
8. Defense's closing argument
9. Prosecution's rebuttal

The guilt phase proceedings in these data nearly all mirrored this model, although, of course, the content of these proceedings varied widely.

Penalty trials are different primarily for two reasons: (1) the jury has already been selected by the attorneys and court (unless it is a penalty retrial), so a second round of voir dire is unnecessary, and (2) there is no "burden of proof" in a penalty phase, so the prosecutor is not entitled to a rebuttal—in the penalty phase, the defense "gets the last word." Thus, the generic procedural order of a penalty phase is as follows:

1. Prephase hearings
2. Prosecution's opening statement
3. Defense's opening statement
4. Prosecution's evidence
5. Defense's evidence
6. Prosecution's closing argument
7. Defense's closing argument

These are standard templates, and a few of the trials in this data set diverged from these outlines. For example, in two cases, the defendant pleaded guilty to capital murder, eliminating the need for a guilt phase. In one case, the defense put on no witnesses and made no argument in the penalty phase, deferring to the defendant's desire to simply address the jury himself. In a handful of other cases, the defendant's attorneys waived their guilt phase opening statements, or the order of closing arguments in the penalty phase was reversed. But these were exceptions; most of the trials followed these basic procedural forms.

EMPIRICAL CHARACTERISTICS OF
THIRTY-SEVEN CALIFORNIA CAPITAL TRIALS

Seventeen defendants have trials in County 1, twelve in County 2, and eight in County 3. Thirteen defendants are[7] white, eleven are black, seven are Hispanic, and six have been classified by the California Department of Corrections as "other." One of these "other" defendants is an Egyptian national, two are Vietnamese Americans, one is Samoan American, one is Chinese, and one I was unable to identify. Two of the Hispanic defendants are Mexican nationals.[8] The race demographics of these defendants do not correspond to race demographics in California—the U.S. Census for 2000 reported the California population as approximately 57 percent

Table 3.1.   Death Sentence Capital Trials by
County, 1996–2004

County	Death Sentence Capital Trials
County 1	17
County 2	12
County 3	8

Table 3.2. Race and Gender of Victim and Defendant[1]

Case	Race, Gender and Age Group of Victim	Race and Gender of Defendant
1	White Male Adult	White Male
2	White Female Adult	White Male
3	Black Female Adult	Black Male
	Black Male Adult	
4	White Female Adult	Black Male
5	White Male Adult	White Male
	White Female Adult	
	White Male Adult	
6	White Female Adult	Black Male
	Black Female Adult	
7	Asian Female Child	Black Male
	Hispanic Male Adult	
8	Asian Female	White Male
9	White Female Adult	White Male
10	White Female Adult	White Male
11	White Male Adult	White Male
12	Hispanic Male Child	Asian/Other Male
13	Hispanic Female Child	Hispanic Male
14	Hispanic Female Child	Hispanic Female
15	Black Female Child	Black Man
16	Asian Male Adult	White Male
17	White Female Child	Hispanic Male
18	White Male Adult	Asian/Other Male
19	White Female Adult	Hispanic Male
20	White Female Adult	Hispanic Male
21	White Female Adult	White Male
22	Multiple victims of both genders and multiple races[2]	Asian Male
23	Asian Male Adult	Asian/Other Male
	Asian Male Adult	
24	Hispanic Female Adult	Black Male
25	White Female Adult	Black Male
	White Female Adult	
	White Female Adult	
	White Female Adult	
	White Female Adult	
26	White Male Adult	White Male
	Other Male Adult	
	Asian Male Adult	
	Asian Female Adult	
27	White Male Adult	White Male
28	White Male Adult	Hispanic Male
	Asian/Other Female Adult	
	White Female Adult	

(*continued*)

Table 3.2.   (*continued*)

Case	Race, Gender, and Age Group of Victim	Race and Gender of Defendant
29	Asian/Other Male Adult	Asian/Other
30	American Indian Female Adult	Asian/Other Male
	American Indian Male Adult	
	Unknown Male Adult[3]	
31	White Female Adult	Black Male
32	Unknown Male Adult	Black Male
33	Unknown Female Adult	Black Male
34	White Male Child	Hispanic Male
35	White Male Child	White Male
36	White Female Adult	Black Male
37	White Female Child	White Male

[1]The source of the race and gender of defendant is the California Department of Corrections and Rehabilitation Condemned Inmate List (available on the CDCR web page). Sources for race, gender, and age of victims comes from trial transcripts, California Department of Justice reports, or personal communications with caseworkers.

[2]It is impossible to quantify the victims in this case because law enforcement discovered the remains of between twelve and twenty-five victims, many of which were difficult to identify by race.

[3]As of this writing, I have not been able to determine the race of three of the victims in this data set.

white, 6 percent black, 38 percent Hispanic, and 13 percent Asian (U.S. Census Bureau, 2006).[9] Although the small number of cases in this data set makes it impossible to draw any conclusive inferences, these data confirm what has become a truism about death row populations in the United States; people of color (especially black people) are disproportionately represented among the condemned.

This disparity held up when these demographics were compared to the race demographics in the individual counties. Table 3.5 shows a comparison between the U.S. Census data on race demographics in each county and race, by county, for condemned defendants from these counties.

Again, given the relatively small number of condemned persons from these counties and the percentage error inherent to the Census data, any inferences drawn from this comparison must be considered speculative. Nevertheless, this data set represents the total number of death sentence

Table 3.3.   Totals of Victim and Defendant by Gender[1]

Victims		Defendants	
Female:	31	Female:	1
Male:	22	Male:	36

[1]Tables 3.2 and 3.4 do not include the three victims for which I have not been able to determine race; they also do not include the multiple victims in the aforementioned case with between twelve and twenty-five victims.

Table 3.4. Totals of Victim and Defendant by Race

Victims		Defendants	
White:	29	White:	13
Black:	4	Black:	11
Hispanic:	5	Hispanic:	7
Asian/Other:	12	Asian/Other:	6

cases for each county for the years 1996 to 2004, meaning that this data set is not a sample but a total population being analyzed. Given this situation, it is notable, for example, that approximately 16 percent of the total death row population from County 1 (for cases tried in the years 1996 to 2004) is black whereas only approximately 2 percent of the population in County 1 was black in 2000.[10]

This suggests that the "race effect" on death sentences continues, twenty-five years after it was famously demonstrated by David Baldus (see Baldus et al., 1990, and Pierce and Radelet, 2005). We know, and these data support, that in homicides that ultimately become capital cases, the race of the persons involved matters at some point after the discovery of a dead body and before a jury sentences a person to death (and perhaps also after sentencing). Knowing *why* there is a race effect is, of course, a complex question, one that I addressed in part in chapter 2 of this book.

In any case, along with the race disparity truism, these data also support the standard view that most condemned persons in the United States are poor. All but one of the defendants in these data were officially indigent, meaning that they could not afford their own attorneys and had attorneys provided to them by the state. One defendant was financially able to start his trial with a private attorney, but eventually ran out of funds and switched to public defenders. Most of the defendants were represented by their respective county's public defender's office. A few were represented by private attorneys appointed by the court.

Table 3.5. Race Percentages of Condemned and Population by County[1]

	County 1		County 2		County 3	
	Cond.	Pop.	Cond.	Pop.	Cond.	Pop.
White	44%	65%	33%	49%	25%	67%
Black	16%	2%	33%	15%	38%	6%
Hispanic	16%	31%	16%	19%	38%	27%
Other	22%	13%	16%	20%	0%	9%

[1]Note that the Census percentages add up to more than 100 percent. This is apparently due to self-reporting errors. All of these figures come from the U.S. Census website (U.S. Census Bureau, 2006).

However, official indigence does not necessarily equate to poverty. Some of the defendants in these data were referred to by prosecutors and defenders as "middle class" or in two cases "upper middle class" or even "rich." In light of the overwhelming costs of litigating a capital trial, it would be misleading to rely on official indigence as a measure of the socioeconomic status of defendants. Very few persons in the United States could afford to finance their own capital trial. Therefore, by carefully reading the transcripts, especially the penalty phase proceedings (in which the background of the defendant was usually discussed in some detail), I was able to estimate the socioeconomic statuses of these defendants. In making this estimation, I relied on narrative descriptions of defendants made by both prosecutors and defenders, paying special attention to education, occupation, and income, and developed a four-level coding scheme: wealthy, middle class, working poor, homeless, and unable to determine. Thus, for example, I coded the defendant who had attended UCLA, owned his own business and drove a late model Mercedez-Benz as "middle class." I coded the defendant who panhandled and slept in a shed as "homeless." I coded a defendant described as a methamphetamine addict who was occasionally employed as a carpet installer as "poor." The Samoan gang member living with his brother in a crowded garage in the back of his mother's house was likewise classified as "poor."

Nearly all of the defendants in this data set fell into the "poor" category. This situation fits both with the common knowledge among capital litigators that most people charged with capital crimes and/or receiving death sentences come from the margins of society, and also other scholarly profiles of those charged with capital crimes and/or condemned prisoners (Bright, 1994; Haney, 2005; Holdman, 2007; Sanger, 2003; Steiker, 2005).

This also conforms to the logic of Poveda's (2000), "double-edged sword" theory of American retention of capital punishment, in which he argued that ideologies in the United States operate to create an executable class of persons understood as nearly subhuman in the mainstream. The race demographics, coupled with the socioeconomic demographics, suggest an interaction effect between race and inequality operating in American capital punishment. The bottom line is that the defendants in this data set were mostly poor and are disproportionately people of color—a group that looks very different than the judges, prosecutors, defense lawyers, and probably the jurors that processed their cases.[11]

Table 3.6. Capital Defendants by Socioeconomic Status

Status:				
Wealthy	Middle Class	Poor	Homeless	Unable to Determine
1	4	28	1	3

THE HORROR OF MURDER

Although it is difficult to identify an objective sense of the "facts" of a murder from reading the arguments of legal adversaries, it is possible to estimate a sense of "heinousness" for these cases by noting the quantities and ages of victims, and also extracting from the arguments enough information to intuit a crude rating of "heinousness" for each case. Of course, heinousness, like pornography, is a vague and relative term; difficult to define, let alone operationalize and measure (it is, however, also one of the statutorily defined special circumstances, although it was never alleged in these trials). In light of this situation, I made no attempt to assign "heinousness" codes to these cases. However, as I read the transcripts, it became clear to me that, although the crimes driving these trials tended generally to be terrifying and gruesome, there were outliers on either end of my interpretive sense of heinousness that seem worth noting.

In the first place, the cases with multiple victims stand out—especially the three defendants who were convicted of killing multiple strangers in separate events.

On the heinous end of the scale is the case in which the defendant raped and killed five women over the span of a few months in 1978 and 1979. In each event, the defendant broke into the apartments of women home alone and struck them in the head with an unknown blunt object, perhaps a hammer or mallet. He then raped or attempted to rape them after they were dead or unconscious. The defendant also raped and assaulted another woman in 1980, who was over nine months pregnant at the time of the assault. This victim survived the attack, but her fetus did not survive as a result of the trauma. After the assault, the 1980 victim's husband was wrongly convicted of murdering his unborn child and assaulting his wife. This man was sentenced to fifteen years to life and was in prison from 1980 to 1996 when DNA technology excluded him from this assault on his

Table 3.7. Numbers of Victims

Cases with more than five victims	1
Cases with five victims	1
Cases with four victims	1
Cases with three victims	3
Cases with two victims	4
Cases with one victim	27

Table 3.8. Child and Adult Victims

Cases with child victims	10
Cases with adult victims	27

wife, and he was thereafter exonerated.[12] Subsequently, law enforcement officers searched for matches on DNA found at one of the crime scenes to offenders in law enforcement databases and found a match with the defendant, who was serving a prison sentence for an unrelated sexual assault. Investigators visited the defendant and obtained statements in which he admitted the intent to assault and rape these victims, but claimed he never intended to kill any of them.

The defense did not dispute the basic facts argued by the prosecutor— that the defendant burgled the victims' homes, violently assaulted them, and then either raped or attempted to rape them. Instead, the points of dispute had to do with his mental state, essentially a combination of an intoxication and mental health defense, which together negated the intent to kill. In the guilt and penalty arguments, most of the testimony and argument had to do with emphasizing or deemphasizing the defendant's intent to kill and level of intoxication. For example, the defense repeatedly asserted that he did not believe that the blows to the victims' heads would kill them, which the prosecutor ridiculed by suggesting that blows to a human being's cranium with a hammer are almost certain to be deadly.

This particular defendant's story manifested a kind of "perfect storm" of deeply resonant, racialized, narrative features. The defendant, who is black, repeatedly lurked outside the apartments of young white women, watched them through a window to make sure they were alone, snuck in, bashed them in the skull with a heavy object, raped or attempted to rape them, and snuck out. Moreover, he had never been caught for any of these particular crimes. Making things worse for the defendant's hopes of acquittal or life without parole (LWOP) sentence was the fact that the husband of one of the victims had served sixteen years in prison for crimes committed by the defendant. Given all these facts, the defendant's addiction to alcohol and severe mental illness may have seemed to jurors, at first blush, to be somewhat beside the point or irrelevant—at least in terms of the question of incapacitation.[13]

On the other end of the heinousness spectrum, consider the case in which the defendant did not himself murder the victims. In this case, the prosecution's theory of the murder was that the defendant was the mastermind behind a botched computer store robbery during which an unexpected bystander was shot once (fatally) by a co-offender, and also "ordered a hit" from county jail against a second victim, a person who had information about the computer store robbery. According to the prosecutor, the hit was carried out by the defendant's girlfriend, after she tricked the victim into thinking she was going on a job interview. Compared to other cases in this data set, the evidence against the defendant appeared weak, including prejudicial identification evidence (a lineup presentation to a witness in which the defendant was the only African

American). Most notably, in neither killing was the defendant the "trigger man," yet he was the only one facing a capital charge.

This case does not appear especially "heinous" because, whatever involvement the defendant had in criminal activity (e.g., conspiring to rob a computer store or asking someone else to kill a witness), he himself did not actually injure anybody. Of course, this is a not *legal* defense to capital murder—felony murder, the legal doctrine that assigns culpability to anyone involved in a felony during which some person dies, is a capital crime in California.[14] But one could argue that, by whatever measure, a defendant who did not literally kill the victim is less "heinous" than a defendant who did. Moreover, both killings—the botched robbery and the "hit" on the witness—were relatively "clean," involving one fatal gunshot wound rather than prolonged torture or rape.

Most of the cases I analyzed fell somewhere in between these two, although more than half the cases involved a single adult victim. By definition, however, the details of homicide are terrifying and gruesome, the stuff of nightmares. With the exception of six cases that were botched robberies with a single victim, these trials were littered with the details of violence, sexualized depravity, suffering, and death that continue to haunt me as I write about them.

SPECIAL CIRCUMSTANCES

As in most death sentencing states, California requires a "special circumstance" to be attached to first-degree murder for prosecutors to bring a death punishable charge. Table 3.9 lists California's statutory special circumstances and the number of each charged in this collection of cases.

In more than half of these cases, the special circumstance charged by the prosecutor was murder committed in the act of another felony, delineated in the following list (California Penal Code 190.2.17):

(17) The murder was committed while the defendant was engaged in, or was an accomplice in, the commission of, attempted commission of, or the immediate flight after committing, or attempting to commit, the following felonies:

a. Robbery
b. Kidnapping
c. Rape
d. Sodomy
e. The performance of a lewd or lascivious act upon the person of a child under the age of fourteen years
f. Oral copulation
g. Burglary in the first or second degree

Table 3.9.   Special Circumstances Charged

California Special Circumstances	Number of Cases in this Data Set
Murder Committed During another Felony	20
Multiple Victims	9
Lying in Wait	4
Torture	4
Financial Gain	2
Murder of Law Enforcement Officer	1
Murder of a Witness to a Crime	1
Hate Crime	1
Drive-by Shooting	1
Prior Murder	0
Bombing	0
Previous Arrest	0
Mail Attack	0
Murder of Federal Law Enforcement Officer	0
Murder of Prosecutor	0
Murder of Firefighter	0
Murder of Judge	0
Murder of Elected Official	0
Heinousness	0
Poisoning	0
Murder of Juror	0
Defendant a Gang Member	0
Train wrecking	0

     h.   Arson
     i.   Train wrecking
     j.   Mayhem
     k.   Rape by instrument
     l.   Carjacking
     m. To prove the special circumstances of kidnapping in subparagraph (b), or arson in subparagraph (h), if there is specific intent to kill, it is only required that there be proof of the elements of those felonies. If so established, those two special circumstances are proven even if the felony of kidnapping or arson is committed primarily or solely for the purpose of facilitating the murder.

In this data set, the particular felonies charged against defendants included robbery, kidnapping, rape, molestation (lewd and lascivious acts against a minor), burglary, and oral copulation. Perhaps not surprisingly, no defendant in these data was accused of train wrecking. The second most charged special circumstance was "multiple murders," with seven defendants, followed by "lying in wait" and "torture."[15, 16]

AGGRAVATING AND MITIGATING FACTORS

California death penalty statutes delineate an array of "factors in aggravation and mitigation" that jurors are instructed to "weigh" when deciding between death and LWOP. Aggravation and mitigation factors are different than special circumstances. It is not necessary for jurors to "find" any of the factors to be relevant to render a decision. Moreover, there is no standard of proof. Instead, jurors are supposed to "assign a weight" to whichever of the factors they think might be important in deciding between death and LWOP. As Haney (1997) has pointed out, this is a psychologically complex process, especially in California, where the instructions on evaluating aggravation and mitigation are especially open-ended (see Haney et al., 1994).

Here is how a capital prosecutor explained "weighing the factors" to jurors during a penalty phase:

> This is a portion of an instruction that you'll be given, and we may have discussed this some months back, but the weighing of aggravating and mitigating circumstances, that's the good and the bad put really simply, the weighing of aggravated and mitigating circumstances does not mean a mere mechanical counting of factors on each side of an imaginary scale or an arbitrary assignment of weights to any of them. You are free to assign whatever moral or sympathetic value you deem appropriate to each and all of the various factors that you are permitted to consider. In relevant evidence which penalty is justified and appropriate—I guess that's a little awkward. Basically you consider what's relevant. You look at the case, what's relevant. Is it aggravating, is it mitigating, and some of these factors can only be viewed as mitigating. If anything at all. And then you decide what weights to give them and then you balance it as jurors. This instruction that I just read tells you it's not a mere mechanical counting, it's more qualitative than that. (Trial 2, 6440)

What this means subjectively to any particular individual is anyone's guess. Especially in California, the vagueness of jury instructions on penalty decisions creates an opportunity for a degree of indeterminacy that is diametrically opposite of the legal formality yearned for in the notion of "guided discretion"—jurors are allowed to consider literally whatever they want when rendering their decision. Yet the weighing of factors is one of the key features of the concept of "guided discretion" delineated in *Gregg*, theorized as a solution for the arbitrariness of pre-*Furman v. Georgia* (1972) capital trials. As Zimring (2003) has pointed out, "guided discretion" has *not* solved the arbitrariness problem, leaving a situation where indeterminacy is still alive and well in capital trial outcomes, despite the promises of guided discretion. Moreover, as Bowers et al. (1998) have demonstrated, it is likely that a disconcerting proportion of capital

Table 3.10. Factors in Aggravation and Mitigation Argued

Case No.	Aggravating Factors			Mitigating Factors							
	A	B	C	D	E	F	G	H	I	J	K
1	x	X	x								x
2	x							x	pros[1]		x
3	x	X	x					x			x
4	x	X	x								x
5	x	def[2]	def						x		x
6	x	X	x								x
7	x	X	x	X				x			x
8	x	X	x	X				x			x
9	x	X	x					x			x
10	x	X		X				x			x
11	x	X	x	X				x			x
12	x	X		X				x			x
13	x + def[3]	def	def				x		x		X
14	x + def	def	def	x			x	x	x	x	X
15	x	X	x	x				x			X
16	x	x	x					x			X
17	x	x	x					x			X
18	x	x	x								X
19	x	x						x			X
20	x	x						x			X
21	x	x	x					x			X
22	x	x	x				x	x			X
23	x + def	x							x		X
24	x	def	def	x				x			X
25	x	def	def	x					x		X
26	x	x	x	x			x	x			X
27	x	x	x								X
28	x	x									X
29	x	x									X
30	x	def	def						x		X
31	x	x						x			X
32	x	x		x				x			X
33	x	x	x						x		X
34	x	x						x	x		X
35	x	x						x			X
36	x	x						x			X
37	x	def	def						x		X

[1]Pros means that the prosecution argued that the defendant's age was an aggravating factor (not mitigating), which is an example of what Haney, Sontag, and Costanzo (1994) call "converted mitigation."

[2]Def means that the defense argued for the absence of this aggravating factor.

[3]X + Def means that the prosecution argued for and the defense for the absence of this aggravating factor.

Table 3.11. Definitions of Factors in Aggravation and Mitigation[1]

Factor	Definition
Aggravation	
A	The circumstances of the crime of which the defendant was convicted in the present proceeding and the existence of any special circumstances found to be true
B	The presence or absence of criminal activity by the defendant which involved the use or attempted use of force or violence or the express or implied threat to use force or violence (uncharged prior violent acts)
C	The presence or absence of any prior felony conviction
Mitigation	
D	Whether or not the offense was committed while the defendant was under the influence of extreme mental or emotional disturbance
E	Whether or not the victim was a participant in the defendant's homicidal conduct or consented to the homicidal act
F	Whether or not the offense was committed under circumstances which the defendant reasonably believed to be a moral justification or extenuation for his conduct
G	Whether or not the defendant acted under extreme duress or under the substantial domination of another person
H	Whether or not at the time of the offense the capacity of the defendant to appreciate the criminality of his conduct or to conform his conduct to the requirements of law was impaired as a result of mental disease or defect, or the effects of intoxication
I	The age of the defendant at the time of the crime
J	Whether or not the defendant was an accomplice to the offense and his participation in the commission of the offense was relatively minor
K	Any other circumstance which extenuates the gravity of the crime even though it is not a legal excuse for the crime (the "catchall" factor)

[1]California Penal Code 190.3

jurors in any given trial make their penalty decision *before* the penalty phase (see Bowers et al., 1998, p. 1489).

Table 3.10 lists California's penalty phase "factors" along with the number argued by prosecutors and defenders in this data set. Table 3.11 defines the factors.

Quantifying aggravation and mitigation factors in trial transcripts is difficult precisely because of the vagueness of jury instructions in California and the extraordinary freedom of argument afforded attorneys in the penalty phase of capital trials. For example, Factor I has to do with the defendant's age—defenders have the option of arguing that the defendant's youth (or old age) mitigate the murder to the extent that LWOP is more appropriate than death. But, constructing this argument is up to the discretion of the attorneys, meaning that the objective age of the defendant does not determine whether this argument is made to the jury. This creates the possibility in which lawyers representing a twenty-three-year-old might make the Factor I argument, but attorneys in another case representing a twenty-one-year-old might *not* make it.[17] Similarly, defenders in some cases may choose to argue the *absence* of factors A, B, or C, or they may not, depending on any number of variables (strategy, intuition about the jury, incompetence, etc.) that are impossible to know in this analysis.

Moreover, the "commitment to" or "power" (e.g., length, depth and strenuousness) of the argument about any factor is hard to know by analyzing transcripts. It is possible that one attorney's brief discussion of, say, Factor C (prior felonies) is more strenuous than another's—but this cannot be determined solely by reading the black and white print of a trial transcript. And, simply listing which factors were mentioned by attorneys could be misleading because some factors encapsulate several different type of "reason" for mitigation. For example, Factor H—whether or not at the time of the offense the defendant's capacity to appreciate the criminality of his conduct or follow the law was impaired as a result of mental disease/defect or the effects of intoxication—obviously includes at least two discrete concepts (mental defect and intoxication), each of which includes numerous sub concepts, running the gambit from schizophrenia to methamphetamine psychosis. Simply listing these factors thus obviously does not come close to capturing the texture of the rhetoric in these trials.

Nevertheless, it is useful to include this list, at least because it shows which factors were *not* invoked (or rarely were). For example, in none of these cases were Factors E (whether the victim was a participant in the defendant's homicidal conduct or consented to the homicidal conduct), F (whether or not the offense was committed under circumstances which the defendant reasonably believed to be a moral justification or extenuation for his conduct), nor J (whether or not the defendant was an accomplice to the offense and his participation in the commission of the offense was relatively minor) ever invoked by defenders. This is important because the absence of relevant factors puts defenders in the difficult position of having to explain why certain factors don't apply to their defendant, and creates a scenario (repeated in most of these case) where the prosecutor makes a "checklist" of factors (sometimes using visual displays) and crosses out the factors that do not apply to the defendant, implying that the defendant deserves death because "only" one or two of the factors apply to him.

Of course, CALCRIM (Judicial Council of California Criminal Jury Instructions) model jury instructions instruct the judge to say to the jurors: "Do not consider the absence of a mitigating factor as an aggravating factor" (CALCRIM No. 763). Nevertheless, prosecutors repeatedly employed the "checklist" approach in these data, suggesting that, as Haney et al.'s (1994) research indicates, this jury instruction may not mean very much to jurors (at least in the minds of prosecutors).

Moreover, as Haney et al. (1994) have shown, "Some [California jurors] took information that was introduced as mitigation and actually transformed it into aggravation (what we have called 'converted mitigation')" (p. 164). "Converted mitigation" describes the situation in which a juror might interpret a defense argument about, for example, the defendant's lack of a prior criminal record as evidence that the defendant had not experienced oppression and thus is deserving of harsh punishment. The current CALCRIM instruction that seems to have the potential to address the possibility of "converted mitigation" is so indeterminate and tautological that it seems almost devoid of any meaning at all: "You may not consider as an aggravating factor anything other than the factors contained in this list that you conclude are aggravating in this case. You must not take into account any other facts or circumstances as a basis for imposing the death penalty" (CALCRIM, 2008, No. 763). Moreover, the CALCRIM commentary section on No. 763 points out that current caselaw does not require the court to "identify for the jury which factors may be aggravating and which may be mitigating" (CALCRIM, 2008, No. 763), leaving entirely open the possibility of converted mitigation.

California's confusing form of "guided discretion" illuminates a tension in the formalist impulse to discipline the complex process of deciding the fate of another human being. Creating a list of seemingly discrete "factors" gives penalty phase proceedings a sheen of formalist discipline, but in practice equates to indeterminate processes. It is obvious that Factors A (the characteristics of the murder) and K (the "catchall" factor that instructs jurors to consider literally anything they want, including the vague concepts of mercy and sympathy) apply to all defendants. To count them as discrete factors in mitigation seems redundant, and points to something odd about the law's formalistic attempt to discipline the cognitive chaos of deciding another human being's fate. However, despite their apparent redundancy, the bulk of evidence in California penalty phases comes in through Factors A and K. Factor A allows the prosecutor to present victim impact evidence; Factor K allows for extensive social history evidence. It is mostly here that the "status competition" (Zimring, 2003, p. 55) between victim and defendant is played out.

In many of these cases, either Factor B (prior acts of violence) or C (prior felony convictions) or both applied to the defendant. Specifically, seventeen of the thirty-seven defendants (46 percent) had prior felony convictions, and, according to prosecutors, twenty-nine of the thirty-seven defendants (78 percent) had prior acts of violence that were never adjudicated. Of course, the Factor C felonies are easy to prove and are rather concrete forms of aggravation. Factor B violent acts are somewhat less clear because they have never been proved prior to the penalty phase. This means that prosecutors essentially try the defendant for these alleged prior acts during the penalty phase, bringing in witnesses and other evidence in a similar manner as in any criminal trial. The difference is that there is no burden of proof, meaning that Factor B evidence is sometimes more inflammatory than relevant to a death penalty decision. For example, prosecutors sometimes introduced evidence that defendants had gotten into what seem like routine scuffles while in county jail but characterized the jail conflicts as vicious assaults on other inmates.

Factor B and C evidence characterize defendants as dangerous and resistant to incapacitation, creating the impression—sometimes explicitly argued by prosecutors—that death is the only possible way to restrain defendants. In the opinion of one public defender, a defendant with a record of previous "bad acts" spanning months or years is the hardest thing to overcome in a penalty phase (Defender #2). In describing one of his most challenging cases—which is in this data set—this defender remembered the grueling experience of watching the prosecutor introduce into evidence a large cache of weapons found in the defendant's car (including an automatic rifle and hand grenades) during the penalty phase and then leaving the pile on a table in court for the duration of the day (Defender #2). The defender remembers noticing several jurors wince in fear as they repeatedly glanced at the pile of weapons (Defender #2). This particular defendant also had several prior felonies and "bad acts," including a bank robbery in which the defendant shot and injured a police officer. He had also nearly escaped from prison once before. In this defender's words, the cumulative effect of all the Factor B and C evidence created the impression that this defendant was "the most dangerous man in America" (Defender #2).

Aside from Factor K (the "catchall" factor), defenders most frequently invoked Factor H (impairment from mental problems or intoxication).[18] As mentioned above, this factor includes quite a wide range of possible mitigators, several of which turned up in these cases. For example, one defendant had been diagnosed as a schizophrenic prior to the murder. His defender characterized his mental illness as a brain sickness that could not be controlled by the defendant's willpower:

> The evidence is going to show that his actions are not the result of a sound mind. Beyond the fact that anyone who commits assaultive-type crimes obviously is not completely normal, the evidence is going to show that he has a physical illness that is not controllable by free will. That was not created by any of his own actions, an illness he was born with and an illness that he

can no more overcome without the help of medication and medical attention than somebody can will their way out of Parkinson's disease or epilepsy or diabetes or any other physical ailment that somebody is born with. (Trial 12, 2069)

Similarly, in a different case, the defendant had a very low IQ, which the defender argued made him "abnormal," and by implication, less culpable that "normal" people: "[He has] an IQ of 66. Now, what does that mean? What does that translate? To what does that translate? Out of a hundred people tested, he's the lowest one. He fits into the lowest, the first percentile of those tested. He's abnormal. That's right. He's impaired" (Trial 17, 5148).

This defender later extends his argument about low IQ to suggest that it is immoral to execute "abnormal" persons:

Ladies and gentlemen, you're dealing with a person who's developmentally between a third and a sixth grader. That's what [the defendant] is. He doesn't like me to say that about him, but that's what he is. Do you kill third and sixth graders? I hope not because I would then want to revoke my part aside. I would refuse to live in this society to do that, kill people that are at a third to six grade level. (Trial 17, 5149)

Defenders with drug or alcohol evidence attempted to characterize their drug-addled defendants as having a similar kind of "diminished autonomy." For example, this defender argues that his client's methamphetamine and alcohol intoxication makes him less culpable than "normal" killers:

But you can take into account the effect of those substances, those chemicals, on his brain. And you can distinguish him between the people I have in that little triangle, in that chart—the ones who do it cold sober, the ones who don't have beer and methamphetamine in them, the ones who do it cold sober; to make these kinds of decisions—for whatever reason—because they enjoy killing or whatever it might be—you can distinguish [the defendant] in his chemically driven mind at the time of these crimes. (Trial 2, 6590)

Aside from diminished autonomy, one of the most common factor-based arguments made by defenders was the concept of "lingering doubt," which does not correspond to its own enumerated factor but is allowable through Factor K. The lingering doubt argument presents one of the most striking antinomies in capital trials. Obviously, a conviction for capital murder indicates that the jury collectively believes—beyond a *reasonable* doubt—that the defendant is guilty of first-degree murder with a special circumstance. To then argue, in the penalty phase, that perhaps the defendant is *not* guilty seems entirely counter-intuitive. However, as

Bowers et al. (1998) have shown, jurors' lingering doubts can be powerful determinants of LWOP decisions, despite the illogic of defender arguments about lingering doubt at the penalty phase (see p. 1534).

In one of these trials, the defense relied entirely on lingering doubt, putting on no witnesses and simply asserting innocence in penalty phase arguments. In this case, the defendant was convicted of fatally shooting and robbing a man of $20,000 in cash he had just withdrawn for the purposes of having money on hand at his family's grocery and check-cashing business. The theory was that the defendant, who had been previously convicted of robbery, had inside information and knew that the victim was going to have a large amount of cash on the day and time of the murder. This case had languished for years because there was very little evidence at the crime scene. Eventually, one of the defendant's old crime partners (a woman with whom he had been romantically involved) told authorities that the defendant committed the murder. Aside from this "snitch" evidence, the primary prosecution witnesses turned out to be two eyewitnesses who believed they saw the defendant near the crime scene around the time of the crime. Neither the murder weapon nor the allegedly stolen cash were ever found. The defendant himself testified to an alibi in the guilt phase, and later complained to the judge that he got convicted because of his record. After the guilty verdict, the defense simply re-asserted innocence in the penalty phase. The tone of the argumentation bordered on defiant:

> Good afternoon, ladies and gentlemen of the jury. The mitigating factor in this case is lingering doubt because this man did not commit this murder. He's innocent of the slaying of [the victims]. And I am going to ask each and every on of you to look at the evidence, not his prior record. But to look at the evidence in this case, to make your determination is there a lingering doubt in your mind. Have the courage, have the courage, the intellectual honesty to look at the evidence. (Trial 1, 2063)

The first line of this closing argument—"the mitigating factor in this case is lingering doubt because this man did not commit this murder"—is striking because the defender in this instance directly contradicted the jury while simultaneously asking them to spare his client's life.

(STEREO)TYPES OF VICTIMS AND DEFENDANTS

I finally list here a tentative typology of (stereo)types of victims and defendants delineated in this data set. This typology cannot capture the nuances of the narratives in these trials, but it does give a sense of the stock characters relied upon by prosecutors and defenders when spinning their narratives in a deregulated context. I created this typology after carefully reading the narratives in the guilt and penalty arguments and identifying patterns in how victims and defendants were described. Prosecutor and defender descriptions of the victims and defendants—as well as their social worlds—were the criteria for deciding which cases fell into which categories. Prosecutors tended to narrate victims and defendants using simplistic, essentializing, and stereotypical language and themes, whereas defenders tended to employ a "throw-in-everything-but-the-kitchen-sink" approach in their arguments, usually constructing less coherent narratives.

Importantly, the stereotypical "characters" listed below do not represent the total narration of argumentation of any given case. In other words, while one defendant might be narrated as "the child killer" by a prosecutor, the main thrust of the argument might be something different, such as "killers must be held accountable." This applies to the defense as well—the defendant might be essentialized as "the mentally ill person" in penalty phase arguments, while the defense contemporaneously makes a more strenuous lingering doubt argument (which has nothing to do with the [stereo]typical character). The point is, this typology of "characters" is a beginning point for analyzing the narratives in these trials. Still, despite the limitations of this typology, it is interesting to delineate at the outset some of the basic characters in the (deregulated) reality constructed through these death penalty stories.

All of these stereotypes rely on *scripts.* Scripts are narrative-like structures that are grounded in stereotypical *expectations* for the behaviors and conditions of "who, what where when, and how" (Amsterdam and Bruner, 2000, p. 121). For example, the "gang-banger" is based on a particular set of ideologically charged expectations—he is a selfish young male person of color lacking in morals who enjoys harming innocent people. Likewise, the "hardworking son" is predicated on a different set of expectations—he was doing what he was supposed to be doing when he got killed: working diligently in his dad's shop. Prosecutor narratives are the result of conflicting scripts—when the gang-banger runs into the hardworking son. The construction of these characters is framed in individualistic terms, and the behaviors of the victim draw on ideological themes including aspects of the American Creed such as egalitarianism (everyone deserves a chance in life, including the upstanding immigrant or the reformed bad guy) or populism (don't believe these over-paid academic experts offering up "the abuse excuse"; use your common sense).

Note also that, in this data set, defenders do not create narratives of victims. Of course, defenders sometimes discussed the victim during

Table 3.12.   (Stereo)types of Victims and Defendants[1]

Prosecution on Victims

(Stereo)typical Character	Victim Characterizations in Data
The Hardworking Average Joe	12
The Pure Woman	10
The Helpless Child	8
The Bad Guy Who Didn't Deserve to Die	7
The Cop Doing His Job	1
The Little Old Lady	1
The Upstanding Immigrant	1

Prosecution on Defendants

(Stereo)typical Character	Defendant Characterizations in Data
The Career Criminal/Dopefiend	9
The Gang-banger/Thug	8
The Lurking Rapist	7
The Depraved Serial Killer	7
The Child Killer	6
The Sociopath	4
The Evil Malingerer	3
No Coherent Character	2
The Racist/White Supremacist	1

Defense on Defendants

(Stereo)typical Character	Defendant Characterizations in Data
The Guy with a Terrible Life	16
The Mentally Ill Person	12
The Addict	9
The Innocent Guy	6
No Coherent Character	5
The Onetime Screwup	3
The Reformed Bad Guy	1

[1]Totals of characterizations are larger than the number of trials because in many cases, attorneys characterized victims and defendants in more than one way.

statements, especially when the victim was involved in crime or appeared somewhat unsympathetic. But generally, defenders rarely mentioned the victim at all, and if so usually only vaguely and in passing. But in none of these cases did the defense construct a coherent and consistent characterization of the victim. Victims are thus narratively constructed solely by prosecutors (at least in these data), equating to a somewhat unchallenged representation of the human beings who died in a violent encounter with the defendant.[19]

CONCLUSION

Despite the goal of discipline imagined in "guided discretion," the death penalty machine operates relatively uncontrolled, especially in California, where penalty phase jury instructions are notably indeterminate. What are the characteristics of contemporary California capital trials under these conditions? In the first place, the defendants in all of the trials during the four years before and after the turn of the century in three large and diverse counties were almost all poor. A disproportionate number of them were African American. In twenty-seven of the thirty-seven cases, there was only one victim, and in the remaining ten cases, seven had three or less victims, suggesting that most of these murders were relatively mundane (although nearly one-third had child victims). In the majority of these cases, the primary special circumstance allowing for a capital charge was "murder committed during another felony," which is conceptually similar to "felony murder" (the doctrine that broadens murder to include victim deaths that are accidental or without the defendant's specific intent during the course of a felony). This also suggests that most of these murders were relatively mundane crime events, although there were a handful of apparently unusual, "egregious" murders in the data set. In all but eight of these cases, the prosecution argued that the defendant had committed prior violent acts, although less than half (seventeen of thirty-seven) had prior felony convictions. Aside from the "catchall" mitigation Factor (K), the defense attorneys in these cases argued almost exclusively along four dimensions of mitigation: Factors D (defendant under emotional disturbance), G (defendant under duress of another person), H (defendant mentally impaired or intoxicated), and I (defendant age). Aside from I, all of these factors describe some form of "diminished autonomy," suggesting (at least to their defenders) that most of the defendants in these cases were impaired in some way when they committed their crimes.

All of this adds up to a picture of dystopia—poor, marginalized, impaired, and often intoxicated people undertaking mundane violence. The death penalty is supposed to be reserved for "the worst of the worst"; and after "guided discretion" is supposed to be imposed in a *non*-arbitrary manner. These data suggest otherwise. They suggest instead that "death deregulated" is still applied mostly to America's outsiders—just as it was prior to *Furman v. Georgia* (1972).

NOTES

1. A mentor once told me that "complicating things" is a bad idea because the goal of social science is to clarify. However, in this case, complication is the

right thing to do precisely because "simple" narratives of murder and execution bracket out and elide the social complexity that drives violence.

2. "Guided discretion" describes the legal rationale for "the penalty phase" of a capital trial that emerged out of the *Gregg v. Georgia* (1976) decision. In essence, the concept of guided discretion is that juror must be able to evaluate aggravating and mitigating evidence; this "weighing" process was supposed to eliminate the bias and arbitrariness in capital case outcomes identified in *Furman v. Georgia* (1972).

3. For a discussion of "repressive formalism" see Milovanovic (2003, p. 21).

4. *Proffitt v. Florida, Jurek v. Texas, Woodson v. North Carolina,* and *Roberts v. Louisiana*, 428 U.S. 153 (1976). These cases reestablished the constitutionality of capital punishment in the United States.

5. *Lockett* removed virtually all limitations on mitigating evidence.

6. However, in the relatively common situation in which the original jury is unable to unanimously decide on a penalty (either LWOP or death), the prosecutor has the option of retrying *only* the penalty phase—with a new jury—or accepting a judge-imposed LWOP penalty. In these "penalty-retrial" cases, the new jury is instructed that the defendant has already been found guilty of capital murder and that their job is simply to decide between a sentence of LWOP or death.

7. At the time of this writing, none of these defendants have been executed.

8. I identified the foreign national defendants by looking up their names on the Death Penalty Information Center website, which maintains a running list of all condemned foreign nationals in the United States

9. These numbers are based on self-reports and obviously include some overlap, which apparently accounts for the total of 114 percent.

10. Although note that Baldus and Woodworth (2004) argue that the empirical evidence "reveals that while the discriminatory application of the death-penalty against black defendants (and defendants whose victims are white) continues to occur in some places, it does not appear to be inherent in the system—in other words, race-of-defendant discrimination is not an inevitable feature of all post-*Furman* death sentencing systems." The bottom line is that the "race effect" in capital punishment systems is quite complex—as evinced by another empirical fact about death penalty demographics, namely that *death eligible* populations include larger percentages of blacks than their respective census populations. However, when the race of the *victim* is factored into the equation, it appears that blacks *are* treated slightly more harshly. Moreover, blacks are often underrepresented in jury pools (Ferrall, 2004). For a detailed discussion of this complex issue see Baldus and Woodworth (2004).

11. At the time of this writing, I have not been able to identify the race demographics of the jurors who adjudicated these trials.

12. Incredibly, the husband and wife had been loudly arguing, after which the husband abruptly left the apartment to buy a hamburger. The defendant in this case attacked the woman at home in the short time the husband was gone. The husband returned not long after eating his hamburger to find his bludgeoned wife. Neighbors had heard their earlier fight and the police assumed he was the killer.

13. Cases with child victims also stand out as shocking or morally offensive, as in the case in which the defendant was convicted of sexually assaulting and killing a twenty-one–month-old girl under the care of his girlfriend.

14. This was the only case in the data set in which the special circumstance was retaliatory murder of a witness.

15. For comparison to other condemned populations on special circumstances charged, I conducted a search for "capital punishment" or "death penalty" and "special circumstances" in the title for all available years for law reviews in Lexis-Nexis Academic; this search yielded no articles. A similar search of criminal justice abstracts yielded two articles. One article showed that in a sample of 115 California homicide cases, those in which the defendant was charged with the specials "robbery" or "sexual assault" tended to lead to capital charges (see Yarvis, 2000). Another article showed that "multiple victims," "prior homicide," and "contemporaneous felony" increased the likelihood of a death charge in a large sample of San Francisco homicides (see Weiss et al., 1996).

16. Note that in some cases, the factual characteristics of the murder and defendant may have seemed to warrant a particular special circumstance that was not charged for some reason—for example, some of the defendants were characterized as gang members by the prosecution, but not formally charged with that special circumstance. It is impossible to know why this is so without interviewing prosecutors about the particulars of each case.

17. Furthermore, arguing Factor I does not necessarily equate to an argument about the mitigating characteristics of youth or old age; in cases where the murder was an isolated incident, some defenders argued that the defendant's mature age was mitigating because it showed he had lived crime-free until committing the murder.

18. Factor H was often conflated with Factor D (the offense was committed while the defendant was under extreme mental or emotional disturbance), or defenders would explain to the jury that they could consider the evidence as either factor H or D, whichever they thought made more sense. This confusing situation again illustrates the indeterminacy of guided discretion.

19. Sociolegal scholars have discussed the politicized manner by which victims have become almost sacrosanct in capital cases (Sarat, 2001, Ch. 2), and also in the criminal justice system generally (Simon, 2007, Ch. 3).

4

• • •

The American Creed in Prosecutor and Defender Narratives

Having now delineated the relevant academic literature on capital punishment, hegemony and resistance, the theory of American Exceptionalism and the U.S. retention debate, and the empirical features of my data set, I now turn to the ideological questions that drive this study.

In this chapter, I undertake tracing the construction and possible subversion of the American Creed's ideologies in capital trial discourses. I achieve this by drawing exhaustively from all the trials in this data set, but sometimes focusing more closely on a particular trial that represents others in the data. I argue that, while glimmers of resistance appear in defense discourses, the hegemonic work of the Creed generally operates to simplify conceptualizations of murder, execution, the human mind, and human agency and thus brackets out alternative, potentially subversive knowledge about murder and the human—even in defendant narratives.

I begin by drawing examples from prosecutor argumentation to show how their discourses draw upon and constitute aspects of the Creed. I next analyze defender arguments to show how, while they sometimes approach challenging the Creed, they often also rely upon and construct aspects of Creed ideologies. I then take up the question of why even defender discourses tend to avoid confrontation with the American Creed. I ask: what are the limits on the potentially subversive narrative? What is it about law and the legal context[1] that limits the possibility of potentially subversive narratives? In investigating these questions, I argue that there is a tension within law that on the one hand recognizes social and environmental influences on human lives, but on the other hand privileges the individualistic value of assigning responsibility to a culpable human agent. In this sense, the law itself *inherently* constitutes and is constituted by the American Creed. Finally, I conclude that the Creed as a racist master frame perpetuates the conditions of oppression that foment the very kinds of violent crime capital punishment is supposed to address.

PROSECUTOR NARRATIVE

Both prosecutors and defenders "narrate" the defendant in all phases of the trial. However, one of the primary goals for prosecutors in the guilt phase is to prove the intent to kill, which inherently involves telling an individualistic story about the defendant's actions that resulted in murder. In this sense, prosecution narratives are often going to be individualistic and seem to draw on and construct aspects of the American Creed. But despite the obviousness of this situation, it is important to point out and discuss it—precisely because it is the law itself (not simply or solely the individual actions of prosecutors) that draws on and perpetuates the American Creed. Put another way, the law *is*, in a sense, the American Creed, and vice versa—just as the Creed consists of individualism and egalitarianism (among its other ideologies), so does the law. Both come from Enlightenment ideals that transformed into "American" versions of the political ideologies of England and Europe that promoted capitalism. Because of this, I try in this project not to conceptualize the Creed and the law as somehow separate but instead as interrelated forces, one of which (the law) is an institution that produces tangible effects on human beings.

A useful way to trace the Creed in the law will be to apply Amsterdam and Bruner's (2000) model of narrative to these particular cases and analyze the ideological "cargo" transmitted in these particular stories. In this section I describe the modal narrative themes and provide examples and narrative fragments from specific trials.

The modal prosecutor narrative followed this form:

- the victim is the protagonist
- the "steady state" is the victim's (stereo)type character's placid world (e.g., the "hardworking son" working hard in his father's business or the "pure woman" peacefully watching television in her apartment)
- the "trouble" is the defendant's violent interruption of this placid world
- the "redress" is the death penalty for the defendant
- the lesson in the "coda" is that retribution (and often also incapacitation) is society's only suitable response to the "trouble" because the victim's family deserves it

For example, in the following case, the prosecutor opens the trial by describing the "steady state" of a nine-year-old victim (and daughter of the murder victim) of sexual and physical assault by the defendant:

> May it please the Court, Ladies and gentlemen of the jury and alternates. December 22nd, three days before Christmas, for a nine-year-old child it's a period of great joy because Christmas is approaching. And for [the victim], who was nine years old at that time in 1990, it was even more joyous because [she] had been out of her home for well over a year. (Trial 20, 2689)[2]

Subsequently, the prosecutor describes his theory of the murder, which in the narrative schema represents the "trouble" caused by the defendant's entrance into the scene:

> [She] remembers going to bed and going to sleep in her mother's bed with her younger sister, Mandy, Friday night. The next thing that she remembers is being carried, taken out of her mother's bed and being carried into her room. And at this time she thought that it was her mother that was carrying her, 'cause she's a nine-year-old kid, half awake, half asleep, probably more asleep than awake. . . . When she was placed in her bed she suddenly became aware that it wasn't her mother who had carried her but it was the defendant, and the reason she knew that was because he told her to take her clothes off and that woke her up. And when she didn't take her clothes off he took them off her. . . . And he removed the pants and the underpants, as well as her top at some point. . . . And the language that she uses to describe what he subjected her to is very graphic and very hard, street hard, because as she describes it, once he got her clothes off he told her to suck his dick. And then after she did that he then laid her out and got on top of her and he tried to force vaginal penetration with his penis. Her term is that he fucked me, and it probably is the best description of what he did to her. Not only did he try to vaginally penetrate her, he tried to put his penis into her anus. And then after that he had her orally copulate him again, suck his penis again. And she says that she could taste the semen and she knew what it was. . . . After that he left her room and she quickly got some pants on, very thin, elastic tight pants, underpants and pants. She didn't get any further dressed because the defendant came walking into her bedroom again for a short period of time, enough for her to quickly get dressed, and he had his hand behind his back and he says, "Now you're not going to tell your mother, are you?" And [she] had been down this road before and she said, "No." But I guess she didn't say no convincingly enough, because from behind his back the defendant pulled out this hammer, and with this hammer this man brought it down squarely on top of [her] head right up here with the pointed end of it. And she started bleeding. And he struck her at least one more time because [she] put her hand up to block the blow and that blow hit the wrist and broke her wrist, broke her arm. And he struck at her a couple more times because she had or has a number of scratches and bruises on her face. . . But he stopped

his attack on her because [her mother] had returned home, whether it was
her car driving up or whether it was hearing the front door being shut and
the latch pulled across, whatever it was that alerted him that [the mother]
had returned home, whether [she] had faked unconsciousness or was really a
bit unconscious, I don't know. But we do know from [her] that the defendant
left her and went into the living room area, and basically confronted [the
mother], because she heard her mother crying out, "Stop it, you're hurting
me." And she heard and saw the defendant strike her mother with the hammer a number of times in the head, the pounding of [her mother, the murder
victim] with this hammer to such a degree that it breaks the handle here,
there's a fracture and you can see it. . . . He pounded [the victim's] head so
forcefully with his hammer it crushes in the bones on the side of the face, the
eye orbit is totally fractured. But he doesn't limit it just to the front of the face,
it's the top of the head where again it looks like he used the point end, the
claw end to strike . . . [the daughter] goes running out the back door. (Trial
20, 2694–2697)

I include this long passage in its near entirety to give the reader a sense
of the tone and content of the prosecution narratives of murder in these
cases—this somewhat cinematic narrative is typical of the descriptions
of murder events constructed by the prosecutors I analyzed. Disturbing
details of sexual abuse and vivid descriptions of lethal violence characterized many of the prosecution narratives in these cases. For prosecutors
the *source* of these kinds of horrifying "troubles" is always solely the defendant himself—in prosecutor narratives, the *cause* of the crime and the
trial resides in the heart, mind and soul of the defendant.

In a different case, the victim, four-year-old Jamie Martinez had been
living with her aunt and uncle, Vera and John Martinez, along with six
cousins in a cramped two-bedroom apartment. According to the testimony of the medical examiner, Jamie's death was caused by burns from
scalding hot water. According to evidence introduced and argued by
the prosecutor, John and Vera murdered their niece by submerging her
in 140-degree bathtub water for several seconds and then neglecting her
for one to two hours while she died slowly of shock and fluid loss. In
separate trials, Vera and John were each found guilty of capital murder
and sentenced to death.[3] The prosecution's narrative theory of the murder
roughly followed the structure delineated by Amsterdam and Bruner. Jamie's "normality" was the very first topic raised by the prosecutor in his
first address to the jury (after voir dire):

She's a normal, little three-and-a-half-year-old girl. Jamie knew how to walk,
was learning how to talk, was learning those things that we associate with a
three-and-a-half-year-old child. She was potty trained. She loved her grandmother. She loved her cousins. She is what we call a toddler. And she looked

up at the world as any three-and-a-half-year-old or any four-year-old does, up; she looked up at the world. (Trial 13, 5848)

This steady state, exemplified by Jamie's innocent and hopeful first steps as a member of human society, was interrupted by the trouble of John's (and his wife Vera's) allegedly ruthless and selfish violence against her. The basic thrust of the prosecutor's argument in the guilt phase was to focus on the result of the "trouble," namely Jamie Martinez's injuries. Much of this argument consisted of graphic descriptions of Jamie's injuries:

They murdered her in the most painful way a human being can be murdered. They threw her into a boiling tub of hot water, so hot, ladies and gentlemen, it degloved her; it took her skin off from her chest down to her little toes. So hot, ladies and gentlemen, it looked as if she was dipped in a vat of acid, so hot that it boiled her toenails off her feet. (Trial 13, 5850)

At the end of his opening statement, the prosecutor briefly returned to the theme of Jamie's (destroyed) "normality," reminding the jury, "She was never going to see her fifth birthday. That wasn't going to happen. She was never going to ride a bicycle" (Trial 13, 5874).

Finally, in his opening statement, the prosecutor twice alluded to the apparently "unimaginable" or "unbelievable" nature of Jamie Martinez's death, a theme he returned to in his closing, and again in the penalty phase arguments: "I mean, how do you ever explain any of their conduct? Does your 'why' work there? No. It can't" (Trial 13, 12768). To encapsulate his rhetorical position, the prosecutor told a fable about a scorpion who tricks a frog into carrying him across a river. "Halfway across, the scorpion stings the frog and both begin to drown. When the frog asks the scorpion why he did it, the scorpion replies, That's the way I am" (Trial 13, 12767). The prosecutor finished the parable by declaring, "That's the way John Martinez is" (Trial 13, 12767). The primary script at work in this prosecution narrative is: *killers are inherently evil.* To say, "That's the way John Martinez is," is to suggest that any contextualization or explanation is unnecessary when it comes to John's life and Jamie's death. The understanding of a killer is that he is inherently evil—*that's* why he killed Jamie. This script precludes or brackets all of the contextual factors that could plausibly assist a juror in understanding the death of Jamie Martinez. This script thus effaces alternative, contextualizing stories that connect the specific (Jamie's death) to the general (the conditions, including poverty and racialized inequality, that may have helped produce it).

Interestingly, this script also reflects a complicated and somewhat counterintuitive conceptualization of individualism. If the defendant is *inherently* evil, unable to choose goodness, then his actions are *determined* by evil—not so much by his volition. There is an important ideological difference between "inherently evil" and "willfully evil." Individualism is predicated on the notion that human beings are entirely able to choose their behavior; the "inherently evil" conceptualization of the killer suggests that some human beings do not possess such an ability to choose. A covert message of the "inherently evil" script is that such defendants are similar to creatures lacking the ability to choose, which is at odds with the individualistic aspect of the American Creed. I discuss the complexities of this framing of individualism in more detail later in this chapter.

Finally, the prosecutor in this case put the jury in a position of making a zero-sum decision, declaring that John "does not deserve to win" (Trial 13, 1283), as if being sentenced to LWOP would be a "victory"; he characterizes LWOP as "safety, happiness, success" (Trial 13, 8954) for John.

In his closing argument in the guilt phase, nearly all of the prosecutor's argument consisted of an enumeration of the direct evidence as it applied to the prosecutor's theory of the murder. Some of this involved ridiculing John's recorded statements to law enforcement, and quite a bit of it involved describing Jamie's injuries and arguing they could only have been the result of intentional torture, which was the special circumstance charged. In the closing, John Martinez Jr., became an important character in the prosecution narrative. John Jr. made statements that were entered into evidence that he witnessed his parents abusing Jamie. For the prosecutor, John Jr. is both a symbol of the *steady state* prior to Jamie's death and a linchpin for the proposed *redress* of the *trouble*:

> And he told everybody what he saw. He's an eight-year-old. He gets on the stand and his feet don't touch the ground. This little kid was subjected to so much. He saw it all going down, he's going to feel protective. His life just got flipped over upside down. He lost his parents, he lost his cousin, he lost his brothers and sisters. "Because I was feeling sad in my heart. I wanted to get it out. I wanted to tell the truth." (Trial 13, 8101)

John Jr. is cast as an innocent yet heroic child who sacrifices his parents in the name of "truth" and "justice" because of knowledge—"in his heart"—that what they did was wrong. If John Jr. (an innocent) says John and Vera tortured Jamie, it must be true, because such a declaration has very bad effects, so goes the prosecutorial logic. Facing up to this "truth" of horrible violence is very difficult, heroic even, and the jury is explicitly exhorted to join John Jr. in doing so:

> You're going to need some courage here because this is not an easy case. It's so despicable, it's so painful, but you're going to have to roll up your sleeves and become involved. You're going to have to analyze these facts.

And it's easy to say nobody could do this to a child. I don't want to hear it. Go for some lesser included offense. I don't want to know about torture. I don't want to deal with evil. But if you look at yourselves, you are the community. I mean, you represent [the community]. And this crime occurred in [the community], and it's going to require certain commitment of you. And it now your responsibility as we turn this case over to you. (Trial 13, 8104)

Like John Jr., the jury is thus representative of normalcy, of a *steady state* ("you are the community"), and the singular agents of *redress* ("it is your responsibility"), and must evince heroism ("you're going to need some courage here"). The scripts at work here mirrored those in the opening argument—John's killing of Jamie was inexplicable and the only redress is retribution against him.

The prosecutor left hanging one powerful theme related to the *redress*, with which he began his closing argument, namely the "only you can speak for the victim" trope:

The enormity and the gravity of this case is astounding, yet you haven't been able to feel, haven't been able to talk, haven't been able to express any emotion about it, whatsoever. And what is ironic about that request for you is that that was Jamie Martinez's life, that this is what she lived through every day of her life at the Martinez house. She couldn't go home and cry to her mother. She couldn't say, "stop." She couldn't say, "I want to just watch TV, quit burning me, quit handcuffing me. Don't put a blow dryer on my face." She couldn't. (Trial 13, 8027–8028)

But *you can,* implied the prosecutor. Here, Jamie Martinez's inability to speak on her own behalf—both during her death and during John's trial—is compared to the *jury's* prohibition from discussing the case prior to deliberations. Moreover, the jury's sudden freedom to discuss the case is implicitly juxtaposed with Jamie's silence. The implication is: *Now is the time to speak for Jamie, and only* you *can do it.*

To preempt the probable defense argument that the codefendant dominated the Martinez household and thus was responsible for Jamie's death,[4] the prosecutor also emphasized John's ability to make decisions and his ability to understand right from wrong, which oddly contradicted his previous analogy between John and a scorpion (which cannot make decisions). In his cross-examinations of defense witnesses, the prosecutor frequently asked them simple yes-or-no questions about whether John was "a stupid person" or "knew right from wrong." Moreover, the prosecutor repeatedly ridiculed the notion that John's autonomy may have been somewhat diminished and argued that John was a sovereign subject, in full control of himself: "[The defense has argued] that he's not responsible for his actions and that he merely stead [*sic*] by, watched as a blob of goo as his wife tortured and mutilated Jamie Martinez. That is a bunch of baloney" (Trial 13, 8934), and later, "even if you are to assume he was paralyzed, that he is a blob of goo and cannot move, how could any father let their child see this?" (Trial 13, 8951). The argument here is that what the defense might have characterized as a limited form of diminished autonomy (Vera's dominance of their relationship) is utter nonsense, the equivalent of erasing all of John's agency and reducing him to "a blob of goo." It is a flat, simplistic, commonsensical rhetoric of individual autonomy: "The defendant is not suffering from any psychiatric illness or disorder, or anything like that. He did his activities and participated in his conduct for the sole reason that he wanted to. He made explicit choices, as you heard throughout his interview, of conduct that he decided to engage in" (Trial 13, 12764).

One interchange between the prosecutor and a defense witness exemplifies the prosecution position that "diminished autonomy" is simply ridiculous.

Q: Okay, He's not dumb, is he?

A: No.

Q: He's not stupid, is he?

A: No.

Q: He can make his own decisions, can't he?

A: Well, that's a good question.

(Trial 13, 7247)

Here the witness struggled because he apparently understood that John was not "stupid" but also believed that John's autonomy was somewhat influenced by his relationship with Vera. In this formulation, it is possible that John could be both intelligent *and* nonautonomous. Faced with this contradictory conceptualization of the human, the best this witness could say was, "Well, that's a good question." This waffling illuminates the hegemony of individualism; even the defense witness struggled with the notion that the defendant's behavior could be determined by something more than his own will.

The prosecutor's rhetorical strategy in the penalty phase was to cast himself as a representative of Jamie Martinez, and to argue that the *only* acceptable redress would be to give John Martinez the death penalty. The decision for the jury thus became a zero-sum question, a status competition. This was most strikingly achieved during a section of the argument in which the prosecutor engaged in a mock examination of a fictional Jamie Martinez, asking himself questions such as, "What happened to your head?" and answering, "They burned my head in the bathtub." In comparison to the other cases in this data set, this prosecutor was unusually histrionic in his argumentation, frequently describing John as a monstrous character such as a "camp commandant of a concentration camp" or an "animal." Perhaps most conspicuous was the prosecutor's practice of "reserving" a seat in the court audience on behalf of Jamie by literally putting a "reserved" sign on an empty chair. His point in doing so was to "remind" the jury that Jamie had no advocates, neither in life nor during her trial: "I had Bob, the bailiff, leave this seat right here empty. It's not a prosecution trick or anything like that. I had Bob leave one seat open. One seat to represent somebody who cares about Jamie Martinez. There isn't anybody" (Trial 13, 8936). The implication here is that *the jury* should be in that chair, and that its only recourse is to punish John with the death penalty.

There are several aspects of the American Creed operating in this narrative. In the first place, it is suffused with *populism*. "Murder is inexplicable" is a simple and narrow conceptualization of homicide that excludes and labels elitist the complex psychological explanations offered by scientific mental health experts. There are tones of *egalitarianism* in the prosecution's construction of the "steady state" of Jamie's world prior to the alleged abuse from John and Vera—the message was that all three-year-old girls, even poor, abandoned, marginalized children deserve a chance. But *individualism* is the central ideological force driving and being driven by the story of John Martinez's murder of Jamie Martinez. The prosecution narrative here was partially constructed through the ridicule of diminished autonomy; recall the prosecution's treatment of the defense expert on autonomy:

Q: Okay, He's not dumb, is he?

A: No.

Q: He's not stupid, is he?

A: No.

Q: He can make his own decisions, can't he?

A: Well, that's a good question.

(Trial 13, 7247)

The prosecutor here implies that it would also be "stupid" to think that the defendant was not in complete command of his will. As with the example from the beginning of this chapter, the *cause* of the violence in the John Martinez case, according to the prosecutor, is solely the will of the defendant.

The Cause of Murder

It is important to point out that this conceptualization of "cause" is borne out through the criminal law's rules of adjudication of guilt or innocence, which frame the trial as a process for proving guilt—*not* as a process for understanding the complex array of social or contextual factors that lead up to any murder. Put another way, the law's rules conceptualize the question of "cause," a priori, as a question of *individual* culpability. Nevertheless, in addition to the legal-structural forces that frame the cause of murder individualistically, prosecutors frequently go beyond the basic legal objective of assigning legal responsibility and explicitly argue that the defendant is the sole "cause" of the murder (and the trial). In a different case, the prosecutor made this point repeatedly:

> He's the one at fault. This is all laid at his doorstep. A lot of tears have been shed in this courtroom, and they all come from one source, him. (Trial 19, 5533)

> There's only one person in this courtroom who has volunteered to be here, and that's the defendant. He volunteered to be here by his conduct and his crimes. (Trial 19, 5549)

> What this case is all about is not what's happened over the last few months here but what he did on those days, on those days he had their lives and the life of [the victim's daughter] and the life of her family and her loved ones in his hands and as well as his own. And on those days he chose to kill. He chose to take life. His situation here has always been in his own hands, and he placed himself here. (Trial 19, 5614)

Over and over in this data set, prosecutors explicitly argue that the defendant is the cause of the "trouble," as these examples from other trials indicate:

> None of us would be here until this man would be here—until this man had made front page news. That is why the Whites are here. That is why we are all here. (Trial 3, 3939)

> All those opportunities to turn off and go somewhere else, he took that long drive, and even when he got to the murder scene, that otherwise beautiful place on top of the hill, he made the choice there, and he made a series of choices there. He chose first to shoot [a victim]. And then he chose to shoot [a victim], keep her from running away, even though she was begging for her life. He chose to ignore those pleas for her life. And then he chose to come back to [a victim] and put the muzzle of that gun next to [the victim's] head. And even then, he chose to go back go [the other victim] and give her the kill shot, too. (Trial 7, 12571)

There is only one reason why all of you are here is because the two people, and two people only, have caused you to be here. . . . These predators chose torment, they chose death, and they chose murder. It is their actions that cause you to be here. (Trial 8, 8444–8445)

So I don't want to hear about this abuse making him turn to a life of crime like he is, you know, one of many who do that. He chose it. (Trial 33, 7003)

The prosecutor in the last quote explicitly challenges the "social determinism" or "diminished autonomy' rhetoric sometimes employed by defenders, portraying it as "the abuse excuse." This rhetorical tactic juxtaposes two visions of the human—one based on individualistic "will" and the other on "the abuse excuse." This juxtaposition invites jurors to make a zero-sum decision about the defendant's process of "choice," thereby forcing them to take sides in the culture war over whether people's behavior can be explained entirely by their will or partially by the influence of social forces. And while the following quotes do not explicitly compare "free will" to "the abuse excuse," they do imply this juxtaposition:

However, I am not going to apologize for the fact that you are here because it is not my conduct that brought you here, and it is not the court's conduct that brought you here. It is not [the defense attorneys]. It is not your conduct that brought you here. What brought you here is the defendant's conduct. That is why you are here. We are not here for any other reason. (Trial 4, 3233)

Why are you here? Who is making you look evil right in the eyes? There's only one person who put you here, only one person who committed these brutal acts and only one person who chose death and chose murder. It is Mr. Keaton's actions that put you here. He chose death, he chose murder, he chose to load that gun with bullets that would kill, he chose to carry that gun, he chose to threaten to kill [the victim's mother] he chose to pull the trigger and shoot a deadly weapon, a deadly bullet at [a victim], he chose to move that baby into the front seat at gunpoint and terrorize her without her mommy there to protect her, to tell her that it was going to be all right. (Trial 15, 8576)

[The defense is] trying to make you feel guilty for the decision you are going to have to make in this case. Nobody should feel guilty. Nobody is responsible for being here, for putting you here other than Mr. Rawls. (Trial 5, 2642)

According to prosecutors, these defendants must be held responsible for causing the violence requiring the jury's participation in the trial. And in the most dramatic version of this rhetorical tactic, the following prosecutor intones "he chose" over and over, like an incantation:

> There is only one person that put you here, only one person that pulled the trigger and committed these brutal acts, only one person that chose death. It is the defendant's actions alone that cause you to be here.
> He chose death over life.
> He chose murder.
> He chose to load that gun with shotgun shells.
> He chose the ammunition that would do the most damage.
> He chose to bring that gun along.
> He chose to gather together a group of predators to go out and stalk innocent citizens in our community.
> He chose his partners in crime.
> He chose [the victim] as the perfect victims.
> He chose to snatch [the victim] off the street when [the victim] offered him his bride's gift.
> He threatened [the victim] with death if he did not get in the van.
> He and his brother . . . chose to strip [the victim] of all of his personal belongings.
> He chose to threaten [the victim] with death again if he did not give him more.
> And he ordered [the victim] to obey him at the ATM or be shot in the back.
> He chose to frighten [the victim] so badly that [the victim] was forced to beg for his life. It was the only thing he had left.
> He chose the dark spot on a deserted street.
> He chose to order [the victim] out of the van.
> He chose to get out of the van himself with a loaded weapon.
> He chose not to let [the victim] go.
> He chose not to listen to his gangster comrades who told him to let [the victim] go.
> He chose to eliminate the witness for his own protection.
> He chose to earn stripes for his own fame.
> He chose to point a sawed-off shotgun directly at [the victim's] beating heart.
> And he chose to make a final display of power. He denied the pleas for mercy from [the victim] telling his comrades: No, he was the man in charge, he was making the decisions. He told them that he was making a deliberate decision to commit first degree deliberate murder. And he watches as [the victim] covered his heart to save his own life.
> In his last act of power, he chose to pull the trigger and send a deadly explosion into [the victim's] heart.
> (Trial 29, 4140–4141)

This last quote is remarkable for its vociferous insistence on an individualistic conceptualization of the cause of murder. This narrative fragment, in which the defendant was a sociopathic "gang-banger" who coldly robbed and killed a "hardworking average Joe," is constitutive of individualism—and is also constituted *of* individualism. In these passages, the "cause" of the crimes (and the trials) is exclusively the will of the defendants. The hidden cargo animating this prosecution narrative involves a stereotypical set of expectations for the behaviors for a particular type of individualistic defendant, namely the sociopathic "gang-banger" who "chooses and chooses" to engage in dangerous, offensive, "gang-banger" behavior.

Similarly, in the following passages, prosecutors relentlessly emphasize the defendant's free will and ability to "choose":

> If you were to ask me, [the prosecutor], give us one word which sort of is the theme of what you want to say about Mr. Williams. . . . The word is "choice." "Choice." In the sense of being able to choose, in the sense of having free agency. (Trial 9, 6355)

> He became this way because of his own free will. Something we all have. There's nothing, nothing he can point to, that the defense has pointed to, that would account for the way he is and what he did except for his own free choice in doing it. (Trial 30, 3924)

This last passage is notable because it illustrates the prosecutor's commitment to a simplistic and purely individualistic conceptualization of the human—for this prosecutor "nothing" outside of the defendant's inherent being and "free choice" can explain his actions.

> This is not somebody who is automatically controlled by his brain. This is a thinking, non-challenged human being that wound up doing this murder for free will. (Trial 10, 6630)

Note this prosecutor's emphasis on the defendant's "nonchallenged" status, arguing that, although some types of behavioral determinism may be possible (e.g., a person "controlled by his brain"), *this particular* defendant is *not* controlled by some external force.

> And the first [thing] I want to talk about is accountability. I would hope that we all would feel that people who commit crimes should be held fully accountable for their actions. This is a bedrock of our system, accountability. That if you—accountability is about choices. See, when you come right down to this, this case is about one thing. Really it comes down to one thing, and that is choices. (Trial 27, 3111)

In this passage, the prosecutor explicitly identifies *the law's* commitment to individualism—"This is a bedrock of our system, accountability

. . . accountability is about choices." In this prosecutor's conceptualization of the law's perspective on human agency, individual choice is "a bedrock" principle. This understanding of the law brackets out the possibility of other explanations for human behavior and violence, and reflects an understanding of the law that limits the possibility for subversion.

In the following passage, the defendant is *not* a "rabid dog," but an agentive, self-authored subject:

> He's able to prey on a child. He's not a rabid dog who's just automatically aggressive and violent who's just turned on—who's just biting and biting and biting. He's able to choose when he wants to be violent. He's able to choose when he wants to satisfy his grotesque, perverse sexual needs. He is able to make that choice. He is not a robot. He's not a rabid dog. (Trial 12, 2701)

Interestingly, the "defendant chose evil" theme in this passage is somewhat at odds with the prosecutor rhetorical technique of comparing defendants to monsters or animals (discussed below); the contrast is especially clear when the prosecutor explicitly points to the difference between a willful human being and a "rabid dog." Like other prosecutor discourses, this contrast is simplistic, black and white, and sets up a simplistic zero-sum conceptualization of the human—he is either 100 percent willful or a "rabid dog" that "bites and bites" uncontrollably.

This juxtaposition resembles other simplifications and "zero-sum games" embodied in death penalty discourses. Sarat (2001), for example, discusses at length the simplistic nature of seeing the death penalty as a seemingly simple answer to complex questions of crime and government control of crime:

> What I have tried to show in this book is that state killing is a distraction or, worse, a force that makes our society neither safer nor saner. At its best, capital punishment may give some temporary satisfaction to the legitimate personal anger of those whose loved ones are killed in senseless acts. But state killing is part of a strategy of governance that makes us fearful and dependant on the illusion of state protection, that divides rather than unites, that promises simple solutions to complex problems. (p. 247)

In a similar way, Zimring (2003), points out how penalty phase proceedings in capital trials have become zero-sum status competitions between the defendant and the victim's family: "It is assumed that there is a 'zero-sum' relationship between the welfare of the victim's relative and that of the offender: the greater the suffering to be inflicted on the offender, the better the victim's loved ones should feel" (p. 55). The juxtaposition between "willfulness" and "determinism" constructed by prosecutors in the passages quoted above is redolent of these previously elucidated sim-plistic formulations found in death penalty discourses.

Sociopathic Killers

Aside from the insistent and explicit valorization of individualism suf-fusing prosecution narratives, one of the other most common rhetorical tactics was to characterize the defendant unequivocally and vividly as a sociopath. In the following case, for example, the prosecutor frequently painted the defendant as an utterly selfish, antisocial character choosing to kill repeatedly to avoid being caught: "And he made a decision. He made a decision that the lives of these people are worth less than his own hide, that his life, his convenience, his comfort is worth more than the lives of these three people. Even if you are a ten-year-old child, you're nothing in his account book" (Trial 19, 5539).

And, like the "willful defendant is the source of violence" trope, the "sociopath" characterization was common in prosecution arguments, sometimes including straightforward name-calling:

> There is nothing wrong with him other than the fact that he is a psychopathic deviate. (Trial 29, 4155)

> You are going to come to the inescapable conclusion that the death penalty for this miserable sociopath is the only proper punishment that exists in the whole world for a man of that ilk. (Trial 17, 4763)

> It's going to be patently obvious to you that the factors in aggravation totally, totally dominate those factors in mitigation that were presented to you by the defense and that death row . . . is the only place to house this miserable sociopath in a single cell, not on the mainline with other prisoners, and house him until he can be executed. (Trial 21, 5902)

> The evidence shows he was thinking about himself. The evidence shows it's meism. He was thinking about me, Rick Tenant. Rick Tenant does what he wants gets what he wants. (Trial 2, 6455)

> What type of malignant heart does it take, what type of cold, calculated per-son does it take to sit here in this hardware store, people buzzing all around you, and you're just lurking for the opportunity to strike? You are casing for that opportunity, waiting for that opportunity. What type of malignant heart does that? (Trial 11, 3117)

> This guy is as cold as they get. Because after you shoot people like this in a parking lot, to turn around six weeks later with the same gun and shoot a

guy who's just doing his job—that is cold, ladies and gentlemen. That is a cold man. (Trial 27, 1681)

Sometimes, prosecutors augmented the "selfish sociopath" characterization with a theme about narcissistic "pleasure":

He showed [the victim] no sympathy. He brutally raped and murdered her in such a fashion to satisfy his sadistic desires. To feel better himself. To make himself feel good and pleasure, he did the things to her he did. And he left her there lying like so much garbage. (Trial 9, 6415)

Sperm has to get in that rectum through an erect penis, doesn't it? That is a pretty good inference. And we can see what handcuffs do to this guy in terms of excitement and pleasure. And that is a rock that nobody can crawl out from under in this case. That is just a fact. Pretty good inference that it was done for pleasure. It is pretty complicated of a crime, isn't it, in terms of all the manipulation of [the victim], isn't it? There is a lot done to her in a period of time, wasn't there? That is pleasure driven. And I will tell you another reason. He killed because he is selfish, killed to eliminate a witness, could have tied her up and gone to the freeway, absolutely he could have. He didn't want to be here in front of you on this case. He didn't want to have a witness. That is another reason, another poor excuse to make this decision that he made that affected so many people's lives. (Trial 10, 6637)

In constructing these sociopathic characters, prosecutors seem to strive for total "otherization" of defendants, marking them as not only deserving of death for their crimes, but virtually nonhuman and terrifyingly dangerous. The scripts underlying these prosecutor narratives evince an expectation about the behavior of a killer, namely that they are utterly selfish and pleasure-seeking—but also utterly willful. Prosecutors thus achieve at least two goals in these types of narratives. Through their characterizations of defendants as totally willful sociopaths, they simultaneously establish *mens rea*, and also thoroughly "otherize" defendants.[5]

Defendants as Animals or Monsters

As introduced in the Martinez case above, prosecutors also sometimes compared defendants to animals or monsters. This labeling is rhetorically complex because, unlike the "sociopath" characterization, an animal's or monster's actions are determined by inherent, nonagentive aggressiveness or violence, not by "willfulness." To be an animal or a dragon or a "creature" is to be unable to prevent oneself from committing violence—a notion that runs counter to scripts related to Creed conceptualizations of the human. For example:

There is a temptation to characterize someone like him as an animal, but the sad reality is the only animals capable of doing such grotesque acts are people such as he. (Trial 19, 5573)

When I say she was thirty-two inches tall, this is exactly the height that this little girl was before she entered the home of those two creatures sitting over there. (Trial 17, 2737)

Ladies and gentlemen, I submit to you, by this evidence, by the law, these two subhumans are guilty as charged.[6] (Trial 17, 4541)

Not to mention that this is the same man they call Dragon. That is what he is known as out on the street, ladies and gentlemen: Dragon, a mythical monster that breathes fire.
    That is what a dragon is. Kind of ironic when you look at the fact that [the victim] died from a slow burning fire. (Trial 4, 2588)

The prosecutor was especially vivid in his depiction of defendant Niles Gladly, who was convicted for raping and killing a twenty-four-year-old woman with whom he was acquainted from having cleaned her carpet:

When this feral pig of a defendant stripped her of her clothing and stripped her of her dignity, what do you think [the victim] was thinking? (Trial 21, 5906)

Don't you just wonder, too, what words this hyena was mouthing to her? (Trial 21, 5906)

Nice conquest, Mr. Reptile. (Trial 21, 5923)

Thanks, Niles. Thanks. You miserable viper. (Trial 21, 5932)

Did you ever hear one word of remorse from that tattooed hyena, one word to his mother or anyone else about remorse? (Trial 21, 5961)

These defendants are "monsters," "hyenas," "feral pigs," "miserable vipers," or returning to the Martinez case, "scorpions" or "tigers"—all beings which cannot, by definition, have a consciousness or conscience or possess human traits such as greed, selfishness, or restraint. Nevertheless, the fact that it would be illogical to *execute* (if not "exterminate") a "feral pig" or other animal for killing a person seems irrelevant. The prosecutors in this set of cases did not appear to be troubled by the illogic of on the one hand asking for a retributive punishment (which could only sensible apply to an agentive human), but on the other hand labeling the defendant as a creature unable to comprehend retribution (or any theory of punishment for that matter). Purportedly rational, liberal societies based on "the rule of law" do not *execute* "feral pigs" or "miserable vipers." Of course, dangerous animals may be *exterminated* in the name of safety, but since the Enlightenment, animals have very rarely been given trials nor been punished for violence against human beings.[7] This contradiction is particularly interesting because it shows how logic is not necessarily important in legal arguments, a situation which seems to contradict rational formalism.

Other sociolegal scholars have noticed this contradiction in portrayals of killers or other purportedly dangerous people. Daniel LaChance (2007) argues that state policies allowing the condemned to request a special "last meal" and also the opportunity to speak special "last words" ironically vivify the condemned man and inscribe him with a kind of last-minute sense of agency, albeit within a structure of total domination. LaChance argues that these fleeting moments of individuality confer just enough of a sense of willfulness on the condemned that they embody something like a "self-made monster," a character that paradoxically both can't help being dangerous (like an animal), but also possesses willfulness (p. 3). LaChance argues that the execution of "self-made monsters" maintains a retributive tone that prevents state killings from seeming like bizarre, ceremonial (and anachronistic) euthanizations of rabid animals (p. 10).

In her recent ethnography of maximum security prisons, Rhodes (2004) similarly describes the characterization of persons as "beasts"—unable to stop themselves from "bad behavior"—in her elucidation of prison workers' attitudes about the concept of "psychopath":

One mental health worker emphasized the characterological[8] basis of predation by telling the story of the scorpion that begs a ride from a turtle and promised not to bite him. When the scorpion does bite after all, he says to the outraged turtle, I couldn't help it! It's my *nature.* For mental health workers, psychopathy—when framed as a discrete disorder signifying an essence or nature—offers the strongest possible terms for resisting exposure to those inmates they feel they cannot affect . . . [Psychopathy] marks some inmates as beyond treatment and suitable only for the tightest control. (p. 179–80, italics in original)

Or, in the capital cases at hand, "psychopathy"[9] marks capital defendants as beyond "treatment"—or any non-lethal state intervention—and suitable only for execution. The notable difference between these two venues for the narrative construction of characters (either inmates or defendants) is that in the law, unlike in a prison, deterministic discourses about "essential psychopathy" contradict the legal prerogative of *mens rea* when deciding punishment. Nevertheless, as Rhodes eloquently describes, the paradoxically individualistic-yet-deterministic character

of the essentialized "psychopath" is concomitant with modernity's (purported) rationalism:

> These diagnostic categories, then—the dangerous individual, moral insan-
> ity, psychopathy—are roughly the same age as the modern prison itself. . . .
> These terms incorporate two great modern inventions. One is the industrial
> machine: the possibility that others may be objects—or even that one may be,
> oneself, an object—circulates through the same loops that make it possible
> for the person to be seen as an element in industrial production. The other is
> the invention of the individual as a repository of hidden motive—the notion
> that character is written into us, remains partially hidden from view, and
> has possibly monstrous dimensions. Seen in terms of what they make it pos-
> sible to say about human nature, these diagnostic categories mark the site of
> a long-running engagement with the outer limits of modern individualism.
> When psychopathy is the term chosen . . . it is used to indicate that at these
> limits we are, as one mental health worker put it, "clear off the end of the
> diagnostic scale." At that end of the scale the instrumental possibilities of
> language crystallize into the notion of a mostly masculine hyperrationality.
> And in a reinforcing and contradictory image, a looping effect with a life
> of its own, the machine shares this stage with the monster and the animal.
> Together they constitute the strongest possible phrasing of individual choice
> as character. (p. 181–82)

Here Rhodes describes how it can be that "the machine" of a rational
(masculine) agentive human can "share the stage" of modernity with "the
monster" or "the animal." From Rhodes's point of view, the deterministic
aspects of an "essential" psychopath are not, after all, in contradiction to
individualistic willfulness, but rather *constitute* hyperindividualism. If
Rhodes is correct, it may be that what I initially marked as a contradiction
in prosecutor narratives—the disjunction between "characterological"
defendants and the legal need for *mens rea*—might instead be an instance
where prosecutors, like prison workers, *construct* individualism through
a narrative of "masculine hyperrationality."

Steady States and Redress

Another common script embedded in prosecutor narratives was a delineation of vividly nonviolent "steady states" preceding murder. For example, in the penalty phase closing argument, the prosecutor constructs
a somewhat fanciful depiction of a serene pre-"trouble" world:

> May it please the court, ladies and gentlemen of the jury and alternates: I
> don't know whether it's the time of year or whether it's the nature of this
> case, but one of the things that I enjoy doing even in the courtroom is look-
> ing outside the windows. And it amazes me how the little things in life give

us so much pleasure. . . . And then there's also the realization the best things in life aren't things at all. To feel the presence of someone you love, to feel their touch, to feel the warmth, comfort, and the love of the embrace of your mother or a mother embracing her child. To bathe in the glow of their presence, to hear the musical sound of their voice or just the contagious smile that they have. It makes you know that you're safe. It makes you know that you're loved. It makes you know that you have meaning in life and you're important. These little things that aren't things that are so important that we frequently overlook or don't fully appreciate until they're taken away. And once they're gone, be ever-lasting agony, especially if it's by violence. (Trial 19, 5528–5529)

This somewhat florid description of premurder beatitude is representative of the other "steady-states" delineated by prosecutors in this data set.

Much prosecutor argumentation in the penalty phase involved describing, in detail, the "trouble's" destruction of the "steady-state," often in the form of asking the jury to imaging being the victim, as evinced by the following series of statements from the same case:

What was her last thought? What was the last image that she saw? Was it his malevolent face? What a great thing to take with you to death. The last thing is the person who is inflicting all this violence upon you. (Trial 19, 5535)

What's going through her mind? You want to live. You desperately want to live. And he's toyed with her. How can you get out of this? How can you see the people that you love? How can you continue to enjoy the little things in life? What do we know about the people that he's brutalized, defaced, and defiled? (Trial 19, 5537)

Constructing arguments in such a way as to place the jury in the position of the victim situates the victim as the clear protagonist in the narrative and has the effect of framing the victim as similar to the jurors and simultaneously "otherizing" the defendant.[10]

Finally, having constructed a vivid filmic narrative in which the sympathetic victim's beatific "steady-state" has been destroyed by the evil, pleasure-seeking, sociopathic defendant's "trouble," many prosecutors argue that *this particular* murder is exactly the type for which the death penalty has been designed: "So I ask you, if this isn't the kind of case that warrants the death penalty, for this kind of situation of one murder victim that occurs in connection with a child molestation, whatever would?" (Trial 19, 5546–5547).

In a related way, this prosecutor, like many others in these data, argues that death is the only appropriate sentence because LWOP is a relatively "easy" punishment and would be "a victory" for the defendant:

It's not that he likes it. It's just that's something that he can adjust to because in prison he'll be on the mainline if he is not on death row. And in that environment, he'll make a life for himself: Play basketball, watch television, meet new friends, find love, take guitar lessons, draw, enjoy music, watch the sky go over with the clouds going overhead and birds, play sports, pump iron, stay in shape, hang out with the guys. It's not a life we would want, but then again we wouldn't do the things that he's done. And if he had his druthers he'd be out. But is that the appropriate punishment for what he did? With these crimes and his background, life without parole isn't just punishment. It isn't justice in this case, isn't just punishment. (Trial 19, 5611)

Somewhat far-fetched descriptions of prison life such as this were not uncommon in this data set, constructing what amounts to another zero-sum decision for jurors—vote for death or let the defendant off the hook. Prosecutors in this data set frequently implied that LWOP would be a lenient penalty or that LWOP would not only be a "victory" for the defendant but would be relatively pleasant:

They have their life in jail, their card games, their basketball games. If they get in trouble, they have to eat the food loaf, the disciplinary loaf, and they get to look forward to when they come off of the punishment and eating regular, nice, hot meals. (Trial 36, 14702)

Whether he is life in prison [sic], able to marry [his friend] and have conjugal visits and recreation and television, or whether he is executed, it [sic] is not coming back. (Trial 5, 1899)

He has got hobbies. Books to read. Keeps himself in good physical condition.[11] His future is incarceration. He has status there. He is a gang member. He controls things. He tells who gets to watch TV, what channel they get to watch. What order people get to read the newspaper in. He gets to be involved with gang training, with making weapons. (Trial 7, 12617)

Is it just that he should be able to wake up each day and look forward to another day to breathe the air, to see the clouds move across the sky, to enjoy listening to his stereo or watching a television or exercising, or seeing his family, or writing letters, or receiving letters, falling in love, being in a relationship, to enjoy sports and exercise, to be out on the yard and feel the sun on his face, to enjoy his memories, to be able to dream and hope, to have his status, and to have his fame. (Trial 29, 4136)

The decision between a "lenient" LWOP and harsh death sentence seems even starker when the prosecutor argues that LWOP will not incapacitate the defendant, as in the following case where the defendant was involved in a fight while in county jail during his trial:

> I mean if he can fly off and hit somebody and punch him a couple of times when he's got this trial, when an incident like this can be used to show he's dangerous in custody and it's in his best interest to behave, once he's doing natural life in prison, what's there to restrain him? He is doing natural life, the prison authorities can't give him one more day's worth of punishment. No harm, no foul. (Trial 19, 5612–5613)

Invocations of the necessity of incapacitation such as this, where an LWOP decision is characterized an ill-advised "victory" for the defendant, were common in this data set:

> About his behavior in custody, I would like you to think about this: If you give him the lesser sentence of life in prison without parole, you are removing him from one population and putting him in another population, all the people who work in the correctional setting, all the other inmates who are held in the correctional setting. (Trial 29, 4185)

> With Cornelius Jones, if you grant him leniency and give him a life sentence, what you're doing is mortgaging the life, the lives, I should say, of all the inmates that he will serve time with. You're mortgaging the lives of the staff that will work around him, with him. (Trial 36, 14688–14689)

> Think about this, too. If you will reward this type of conduct with a verdict of LWOP, what will that mean? It will mean like giving him a platinum VISA card to continue his marauding ways through the state prison system. (Trial 21, 5963–5934)

> Can you, ladies and gentlemen, as representatives of the community, as the conscience of this community, can you take a chance that this defendant is not going to use a weapon when he wants to? That he's going to kill some innocent guard; that he's going to kill some innocent, frankly, inmate. Can you take that chance with this man? Because by giving him life without parole, you are. (Trial 9, 6405)

Generally prosecutors thus narratively constructed defendants as willful, dangerous, unrestrainable sociopaths who purposely destroy "steady-states" simply for their own selfish, greedy and evil reasons, and for whom only a death sentence is appropriate.

For prosecutors, the only acceptable redress for the violent spoilage of "steady-state" by these defendants must be a vengeful execution, as the prosecutor in this case makes clear:

> In our society, the individual has given over the seeking of personal retribution to the community. And it's our responsibility, in order to keep a civi-

lized society and to protect everybody, to make sure that not just the big get justice but the small get justice. And we've turned that responsibility over to this system and to the jury. And if you want to call the imposition of the death penalty on the defendant over there for what he did to [the victims] vengeance, fine. We'll call it vengeance. (Trial 19, 5615)

This prosecutor understands capital punishment as explicitly for the benefit of victims and victims' families, thus clearly manifesting what Zimring (2003) refers to as "vigilante values." Notably, this was the only *explicit* invocation of vengeance in these data. However, other prosecutors often implied that victims and victims' families deserved the (purported) retributive satisfaction of the defendant's execution, sometimes by suggesting that the jury "speak" for the victim, as this same prosecutor does in three different trials:

Now, nothing you do obviously is going to bring or give life back to [the victim]. But you can give her something. You can give her something underneath that tombstone with the big pink heart down in Texas. You can give her a just verdict. You can give her a verdict called for by the evidence. Not because you're mad at anybody. Not because you want revenge. Not for any base thing. You can just say that we've looked at the evidence, what's been presented to us, and what's warranted. What there is reasonable grounds for is the punishment of death [*sic*]. (Trial 33, 7013)

But you can give her something. You can give her something as she lies at rest beneath that cold, marble headstone down at Holy Sepulchre. You can give her a just verdict. That's what you can do for [the victim]. You can give her a verdict called for by the evidence. Not because you're mad at anybody. Not because you're mad. Not because you want revenge. It's not that. It's not for any base thing. (Trial 17, 5115)

You know, I know and I realize—and I know you do, too, that nothing you do is going to bring or give life back to [the victim]. But you can give her something. You can give her something underneath that cold iron tombstone in an icy cemetery in Indiana. You can give her a just verdict. You can give her a verdict called for by the evidence, not because you're mad at anybody—no, that shouldn't enter into it—not because you want revenge—that shouldn't enter into it—not for any base thing. You can just say when you vote for the death penalty that we looked at the evidence that's been presented to us and that's what's warranted. There is reasonable grounds for the imposition of death in this case [*sic*]. (Trial 21, 5965)

These arguments from three different trials are almost identical—and all constructed by the same prosecutor. This suggests that some prosecutors (at least in this county) rely on "boilerplate" or "canned" arguments that can be made to fit most any murder trial, and elucidates the clichéd and simplistic nature of prosecutor arguments. And despite denying the role of vengeance in choosing a death sentence, these passages *imply* a symbolically retributive benefit that the death sentence would provide for the victim.

Prosecutor narratives of the victim, defendant, crime, and purpose of capital punishment become complete when the prosecutor argues for capital punishment—this is the "redress" for the defendant's "trouble." In doing so, the implication is that a death sentence would be "for" the victim and victim's family, which is a straightforwardly retributive understanding of punishment. In the Martinez case, as well as many others (such as the three quoted above), the *reason* for the redress is to act on behalf of the victim and victim's family. The lesson in the codas in these types of narrative is that victims and victim's families have a right to kill their killer, but that this killing must be mediated through the state—or perhaps that the state has an obligation to kill on behalf of the victim.

THE CREED'S INDIVIDUALISM

These narratives, and their lessons about retribution, draw upon and construct aspects of the American Creed. In the first place, prosecution arguments usually speak in the language of individual accountability, specifically assigning the source of the crime and trial to the heart, mind and soul of the defendant exclusively—this is redolent of the individualistic aspects of the Creed.

Importantly, as Rhodes (2004) has pointed out, the concept of "individual will" is complex, but deeply connected to contemporary understandings of what it means to be a human being. First, notions of agency that are central to the ideology of possessive individualism entail certain features:

> There are three layers to the sense of agency I am talking about here. One is simply the capacity to act; the second is self-awareness of one's acts—a feeling of being the person in charge of them; and the third is the question of whether and how much one's felt choices are really submission to the enforced or internalized demands of others. (p. 249)

I argue that the type of individualism narrated by prosecutors mostly contains the first two of these aspects of agency—the third "layer" delineated by Rhodes is more likely to be discussed by defenders (as I discuss in the next section of this chapter).

As I have been arguing throughout this book, individualism (in all its complexity) is central to "modern" institutions, such as the law; Rhodes

(2004) points out how it operates in one of the legal institution's most instrumentally powerful organizations, the prison:

> For the prison to do its work of control, a self capable of responding to and eventually internalizing that control must be assumed for the prisoner. This self is represented as a kind of charmed circle of autonomy and potential self-regulation; the man with a strong personality both owns himself *and* is responsive to circumstances that impose reflection and change on that self. (p. 67, italics in original)

In reading this passage, one could easily replace "prison" with "law," and "prisoner" with "juridical subject." Like its progeny, the prison, the law's "work of control" requires an autonomous, self-authored subject. Rhodes recognizes the inherently ideological nature of this situation, asking rhetorically: "What are the contexts in which certain ideas about self and self-responsibility become useful? What *work* is done, in the kind of practice that engages this man, by regarding himself in such full—not to say murderous—possession of individuality and autonomy?" (p. 68).

The answer is that the "work done" by this ideological construction of self is that it locates responsibility entirely within the monadic self—and brackets out other explanations for behavior that might inculpate systems of control (such as "prison" or "the law" or "society"). The logic of the prison control system, not unlike the logic of the legal system—based on a rational and individualistic understanding of the human—ignores the fact that prisoners (like juridical subjects) sometimes make *apparently* irrational choices that turn out to be unexpectedly rational. In Rhodes's example of prison, this "irrational rationality" might take the form of choosing to "go to the hole" to avoid appearing weak—under the law, it might involve "joining a gang" to obtain a family, or "using drugs" to salve emotional distress.

Moreover, the individualistic logic of the prison control system—like the law—explicitly valorizes individualism by defining the human *as* willful: "I asked Rick whether he felt that to believe that someone has no choice is to diminish him, making him in some fundamental way less than a full person. Yes, he said, that is exactly what I think" (Rhodes, 2004, p. 82).

And beyond the individualistic aspects of the Creed instantiated in prosecutor narratives, we can see how the concept of revenge—even if invoked somewhat covertly—is an idea rooted in the ideological concepts of populism and liberty. Recall that Zimring (2003) argued that prosecutor argumentation framing execution as a service for victim's families draws on "vigilante values," which are rooted in a distrust of the state, which is deeply populist and libertarian. In this sense, Zimring imagines—and these data support—a possible causal relationship between these aspects of the Creed and U.S. retention of capital punishment. But while vengeful prosecutor narratives draw on the Creed, they also *constitute* it. That is to say, when prosecutors propose to jurors that the defendant is solely responsible for the murder and that the only appropriate redress is for him to be killed for the benefit of the victim and victim's family, they are discursively *making a case for* individualism, liberty and populism. These narratives are inherently racist and classist because, as I discussed earlier, the Creed itself was borne out of the racist and classist ideologies of the Enlightment and American slavery (and its abolition).

DIMINISHED AUTONOMIES AND THE POSSIBILITY OF RESISTANCE: DEFENDER NARRATIVES

The aggravating factors are the direct result of the mitigating factors.
(Trial 12, 2797)

As I have tried to make clear, it is not surprising to see prosecution narratives relying on and perpetuating Creed ideologies. However, defendant narratives are also frequently redolent of these same ideologies. In most of the cases in this data set, defendant narratives were constructed through the grammar of the Creed—valorizing individualism, populism, egalitarianism, and libertarianism—even as they aimed to counter the prosecution's goals of conviction and death sentencing. This situation illuminates the mutually constitutive relationship between the law and the Creed—the law talk of potentially subversive legal actors can only approach subversion through alternative versions *of* Creed ideologies, *not* by directly challenging the Creed itself. Put another way, defenders must walk a narrow tightrope when constructing their contextualizing narratives for fear of crossing over into stories that explicitly take on the Creed. Defense narratives aim to show how "context matters," but sometimes turn out to valorize the very Creed ideologies—especially individualism, populism, and egalitarianism—that may be operating to prop up the retention of capital punishment in the first place. This will become clear later in this chapter.

As I have discussed in detail earlier, the capital penalty phase creates a space where crossing the line and taking on the Creed should be possible. Two narratives in these data appear to have come close to doing so. I begin with these two trials in which defenders delineated vivid narratives of troubling social histories, and along the way made rhetorical gestures toward something close to subversion of Creed ideologies.

American Domination of Mexico Leads to Murder:
Covert Subversive Cargo in the Ricardo Arguello Case

Over a few months in 1999, a series of somewhat bizarre assaults took place in a Southern California beach town. In each case, Ricardo Arguello accosted a group of women late at night near the bar strip in the lively tourist section of town. In two of these three assaults, the victims were injured but escaped alive. In the third incident, a woman died as a result of her head striking a brick planter box near the curb on a side street. In one of the assaults, the woman had gotten into her car after leaving a bar with friends and passed out; she was awakened by the defendant smashing a brick through her car window. He then attempted to sexually assault her in the car. After a violent scuffle inside the front seat of the car, he managed to get control of the car and drive away with her inside. He drove away with her in the car and tried to convince her to have sex with him, taking out his erect penis and putting on a condom. Eventually, the woman was able to get out of the car and escape without being raped.

In the murder event, the victim had been drinking heavily all night in bars near the beach. At some point, she left a small group of friends and walked toward her home relatively close to the main drag. The prosecution's theory of the murder was that Arguello encountered her on the street, chased her, assaulted her, and banged her head against the brick planter box to kill her, and then raped her and took a few of her possessions. The defense version of the event was that the two were walking down the street talking about buying marijuana and the victim squatted down near the curb to urinate in the street, but fell back and knocked her head on the planter box, after which Arguello raped and robbed her.

Before addressing the defense's quasisubversive narrative in this case, I briefly note the prosecutor's depictions of the defense's experts because these depictions illuminate prosecutor reliance on populist knowledge about experts. The prosecution narrative in this case, as in most of these cases, followed the general pattern of Amsterdam and Bruner's (2000) theory of narrative, with the victim's "steady state" being interrupted with the defendant's "trouble," with an open-ended demand for "redress." In the penalty phase, the prosecutor spent considerable time attempting to debunk the defense's mental health evidence suggesting the defendant was brain damaged. One of the prosecutor's tactics, in this instance, was to ridicule PhD psychologists and argue that only a "real" doctor with an MD, not a PhD neuropsychologist, could ever detect brain damage. He repeatedly referred to the fees charged by defense experts, calling them professional witnesses:

> Now, Dr. Cunningham, in the realm of professional witnesses, ladies and
> gentlemen, is a gold medal winner. He made $350,000 last year testifying in

court cases. He has—he made $17,000 on this case, and we heard evidence in this case that at one point he charged $34,700—I'm sorry, $34,763.84 on one case. He's made over a million dollars in the last eight years testifying. (Trial 20, 3284)

And we're never going to know why people rape, why people murder. And, you know what, sure as can be, if we ever do, it's not going be these psychologists that tell us. It will be real doctors. If there's anything wrong with his brain, you would have heard from a real doctor. (Trial 20, 3313)

These arguments are written in the grammar of populism. The message is covert but obvious: "common sense" is more important than "elite," scientific knowledge—which can be bought. And the "common sense" on display here is that individual persons are willful, autonomous agents, regardless of any mental illness or intoxication. Instantiation of populism and individualism such as this was common in cases with defense experts testifying about some form of diminished autonomy. The following quotes come from three different cases:

What did he just say? If that wasn't psycho-babble, I don't know what it was. (Trial 8, 7137)

Is she really the expert she holds herself out to be or is this another example of psychobabble being an inexact science? (Trial 17, 5102)

They call James Park next, or should I say Swami Park or Carnac or Ezekiel the Prophet? This guy comes in and gives us the equivalent of voodoo predictions, makes off with about eight or $900 of taxpayer money. Let's just review his cross-examination and see how much this clown really knows or doesn't know. (Trial 21, 5946)

Part of the reason for these prosecutor assaults on defense witnesses in these cases is likely because the defense made relatively serious attempts at presenting complex social history evidence in these particular cases.

This was especially true in Ricardo Arguello's trial. To encapsulate: Arguello was born in Cuernavaca, Mexico, into significant poverty, living in an overcrowded house with a dirt floor. He started working at six or seven years old, and from about ten to twelve years old worked with toxic glue without protection. His father was an alcoholic who abused his wife (but evidently not the children). A collection of mental health professionals, including a neuropsychologist, collectively diagnosed him with having a subtle form of brain damage. The upshot was that parts of his brain did not work like that of normal people, and that alcohol amplified his brain damage, but that he was functional and did not *appear* brain damaged. The defense team went to Mexico and interviewed family members and took photographs of the defendant's childhood house and environs, which were introduced into evidence. A psychologist testified to the effects of poverty and neglect.

The defense explicitly connected the defendant's social history to a fairly clearly articulated notion of diminished autonomy:

> The law says you have to consider not just the crimes, but the big picture of the individual's life who you are going to judge. Because it is not just a question of what happened on three different days in 1999 and 2000, it is what happened throughout the entire life here. And at war here are two competing concepts. And they are not mutually exclusive, although the argument you heard earlier would want you to think that. The two competing philosophical views are basically these. One is that we have complete free choice of what we do, that our past doesn't matter, that our upbringing doesn't matter, that what shaped us and formed us doesn't matter, it is only what you did when you did it, and we shouldn't be concerned with anything else. Now, the other view is that we are a product of everything that has happened to us. Every force for good or ill, everything that shaped us for good or ill. (Trial 20, 3315–3316)

The defense here directly raises the possibility that the actions of some individuals are influenced by social forces outside the boundaries of the individual person. By making this argument, the defense attempts to situate the defendant within a larger social nexus, drawing into the equation questions of racism, poverty and by implication dominant and exploitive American capitalism (although the defense does not explicitly raise these structural themes). A social history narrative such as this inherently addresses and critiques dominant American capitalism as it illuminates the stark poverty of Mexicans in Cuernavaca. When interpreting such a narrative, it is possible—if not especially likely—to interpret that this defendant would never have been forced to work at age seven, been forced to work around neurotoxins, felt compelled to immigrate to the United States, live in a cramped apartment, and take a grueling service job, if the forces of American capitalist domination had not contributed to drastically bad conditions in Mexico.

Not surprisingly, the defense never went so far as to explicitly point out the historical/structural context within which this particular defendant's story takes place. That is to say, the defense never proposed that "American dominant capitalism" was on some level complicit for the death of the victim—to do so would be highly subversive, a profound bit of "cause lawyering."[12] Nevertheless, simply describing this defendant's complexly impoverished life and implying that it should be taken into consideration when trying to understand his violent acts points to discomfiting social problems. Saying it out loud—"Ricardo Arguello

was not fully autonomous because his complexly impoverished background subtly damaged his brain, and he therefore should be spared
execution"—comes close to subverting the individualistic aspects of
the Creed. Moreover, considering the extensive use of elite, scientific
knowledge to explain the notion of diminished autonomy, this narrative
also has the potential to reject the populist aspects of the Creed.

In this narrative, the defense turns the prosecution narrative—with
the protagonist victim's "steady state" interrupted by the defendant's
"trouble"—on its head. Here, the defendant is the protagonist, the "steady
state" is an imagined stable life in an imagined Mexico. The "trouble" is
poverty, and the "redress" would be to spare the defendant's life. The
narrative *logic* is the same as in the prosecutor version of the story, but
the *content* is reversed. In this conceptualization of the Arguello case, a
subversive proposed "coda" might be that "we" cannot take the life of a
man who's social history was profoundly influenced by U.S. domination
of Mexico, a man who fell on the wrong side of the double-edged sword
of the American Creed (a sword that allows "us" to enjoy all the benefits
of middle class U.S. life, at the expense of persons such as this defendant).

Yet this narrative is never actually spoken, nor coherently implied. To do
so might seem elitist and deterministic, starkly contrasting the hegemonic
Creed ideologies of populism and individualism. Indeed, when I asked
one of the attorneys who litigated the Arguello case about his reasons for
delineating the defendant's story of poverty and neglect in Mexico, he
told me that their goal in explicating the social history was to show how
his early exposure to neurotoxins contributed to brain damage—there was
little consciousness about the role of capitalism or globalization in creating
the poverty the defendant suffered (Defender #1).

This situation provides some evidence about "the limits of the law"
to allow for some types of discursive structures, such as the "subversive
stories" described by Ewick and Silbey (1995), and investigated by me in
this study. That is to say, even in the relatively expansive realm of capital
penalty phase proceedings, the law is ultimately a conservative discursive
venue that tends to structurally elide or bracket out—often by deeming
"irrelevant"—talk that might challenge the hegemony of the ideologies
underpinning the law.

The sociolegal concept of "the limits of the law" has been discussed at
length by a number of thoughtful scholars. Jenkins (1980), for example,
argues in *Social Order and the Limits of Law* that many legal analysts
interested in studying the law as an instrument of social change mis-
understand the ontological status of the law, misconstruing its essential
"mode of being" and thus developing flawed conceptualizations of its op-
erational status (see p. x). Jenkins's treatise on the law is comprehensive
and complex, but his essential project is to dispel the notion that the law

exists independent of society as a force of social change—this is the limit to which the title of his book refers:

> Put very briefly, we have been too much beguiled by the doctrine of the sovereignty of law, and we have acted as though this ideal were an accomplished fact. We have thus been led to focus attention too exclusively upon the prescriptions that law issues—the legislative enactment, judicial decision, or executive order—and so we have come to think that a valid legal act must be automatically translated into corresponding social action, just as effect follows cause in nature. In sum, we regard the legal apparatus as autonomous and omnipotent, we believe that we need only manipulate it to achieve the social changes that we seek. (p. 118)

At the risk of simplifying Jenkins's argument, a "merely" semi- or quasiautonomous law cannot be expected to operate very effectively at significantly changing the social conditions of society. This theoretical point of view obviously takes up the question of the law's purportedly rationally formal status—indeed, the fallacy or illogic of rational formalism is precisely the issue that Jenkins wishes to theorize. Jenkins's theory itself is philosophically complex and thorough, entailing too much for a complete review here. For the limited purposes of this chapter, his insight that the law is limited in its capabilities to effect societal changes provides a good starting point on the general sociolegal question of "the limits of the law."[13]

In a more recent example of a sociolegal study of the law's limits, Jamieson (2001) analyzes an abiding conflict in feminist theory over liberty and equality, describing how the "equality" camp delineates the law's limited ability to emancipate:

> [Liberation feminists] were seen to have embraced liberal ideology to a fault—to have bought into the notion that law can emancipate women, that changing laws will change society, that the mere presence of a woman in the boardroom would alter institutional structures. But, according to Audrey Lorde, what these women failed to recognize is that the master's tools cannot be used to dismantle the master's house. (p. 16)

Indeed, Lorde's eminently quotable phrase concisely describes exactly the situation I illuminate in this chapter—subversion *of* the law (or rather, the ideologies underpinning the law) is unlikely to occur *in* the law. These examples of the law's limits are similar to the kind of limitation I elucidate in this chapter—namely the law's hegemonic resistance to the possibility of ideological subversion.

Nevertheless, despite the law's inherent or structural characteristics that generally militate against the possibility of ideological subversion, capital penalty phase proceedings create (as I have previously stated) the possibility for at least a glimmer of resistance. The following case offers just such a challenge to the hegemony of the American Creed.

Society Let Him Down: Cornelius Jones Challenges the Creed

In the most subversive argumentation I found in this data set, the defender explicitly argues that "society failed" his client. The prosecution's theory of the crime was that Jones and his codefendant robbed a marijuana dealer's girlfriend and Jones went out of control and stabbed her to death. He later turned up at a hospital with a gunshot wound. Over a long and complicated series of events, Jones's codefendant also went to trial and got LWOP.

> I was pleased to note that even the District Attorney agrees that [the defendant] has a learning disability, and ADHD. . . . From kindergarten on, this sickness could have been treated, and if it had, in all likelihood we'd have a different Cornelius, and we wouldn't be sitting here, standing here today. The frustration that comes with this kind of personal problem can be treated with Ritalin, and with its calming effects, school work becomes possible. Just think for a minute, think for a moment you're a kindergartner; you're in the first grade; all the other kids can do the work, and you can't. And the terrible frustration in this is that you not only perceive yourself as not being stupid; you are not stupid. You just are not able to do and comprehend what other people can do and comprehend. Little wonder that these youngsters act out. Little wonder that they have terrible personality problems associated with it. Little wonder that borderline personality is right next to ADHD in the book. The fault does not lie with Cornelius. He was a child, and it was his system that failed. To expect his mother, burdened as a single mother with five children, to handle the situation was truly not realistic. From kindergarten on, the record shows that Cornelius was out of control. Yet the system did nothing to aid his mother, to help her, or to give any medication to Cornelius. It just didn't.
>
>   . . . What did society do for Cornelius [the prosecutor] asks where was Cornelius's family in court? The question should be where was Cornelius's family when he was in kindergarten desperately needing help? Ritalin could have helped, and never offered it, nor had you been offered any explanation whatsoever as to why we did not.
>
> Nothing.
>
> Society's failure was the cause of this illness, and it could have been avoided. . . . We don't execute sick people for being sick, nor should we.
>
> People do not set out to have learning disabilities, nor do they set out to have it go untreated. We do not let six-year-olds decide on medication. That's just not the real world. And we should not execute them some years later for our mistake as a society. Because that's what we're talking about. We're not talking about letting him—we're talking about whether we should

kill him or not, and are we going to kill him because we as a society made a mistake? That I find very scary.

We do not execute someone that is sick because they are sick. This is not to say that we should allow them to go free, and for some a prison life without the possibility of parole is perfect. The District Attorney makes much of the fact that Cornelius's behavior is not socially acceptable. It should come as little surprise we hardly socialized him. You do not learn social skills in CYA about whether you tell somebody have you ever thought of having a child or whatnot. This becomes a reason to kill him because we didn't socialize him? These are scary things. . . .

Don't punish someone for being sick. Society did not fill its contract. The contract that society has with us is that firemen will protect us if our houses get on fire, policemen will protect us; teachers will teach us and look after, in particularly the most vulnerable part of society, young kids. They did not look after Cornelius. (Trial 36, 14845–14851)

In this closing argument, the protagonist is the defendant, the "steady state" is the defendant's innocent childhood, the "trouble" is society's failure to address the defendant's mental illness, the "redress" would be to spare the defendant's life, and the proposed lesson in the "coda" is that society needs to better take care of its disadvantaged (the unlucky who fall on the wrong side of the Creed's double-edged sword).

This passage has three themes: it at once attributes the defendant's violence to mental illness and poor socialization, and also explicitly argues against state killing for the mentally ill or poorly socialized, and finally implies that it is immoral for a society to execute a member that "society let down." This is something close to subversive language—it at least challenges the policy of state killing, but also *implies* a critique of social inequality, and challenges the individualistic aspects of the Creed. This trial defender characterized his client as precisely the sort of person that falls on the losing side of the Creed's double-edged sword—and proposes that it would be immoral to execute such a person.[14] For these reasons, this narrative can be interpreted as potentially deconstitutive of the American Creed. It does not draw on nor constitute Creed ideologies, but instead presents alternative, more nuanced explanations of human agency. It is thus a narrative that proposes the idea of what might be called a "liminal man," a character that lives between "structure" and "agency" and as such can be seen as a gesture toward the subversion afforded by the structure of the penalty phase.[15]

But in most of these trials, defenders did not approach even these modest levels of ideological subversion. For the most part, defense discourses tended to be somewhat narrower than the narratives constructed in the Arguello and Jones cases. The following case is a good example because it is more typical of the trials in this data set.

The Jury as Protagonist: The Defense Version of John Martinez

Returning to the John Martinez case, the primary evidence against John was a videotaped interrogation in which he admitted to some acts related to Jamie's death, such as turning on bath water, as well as a videotape of John and Vera's son, John Jr., implicating him. Aside from this evidence, there was little to suggest that John was any more or less responsible for Jamie's death than his wife.

At the outset of their arguments to the jury, John Martinez's defenders put the members of the jury in the position of imagining *themselves* as protagonists in a morally complex narrative. Rather than framing the trial as a venue for retribution against a morally culpable monadic agent, the defenders characterized it as a venue for the jury to evince heroic dedication to "the law." Several phrases in the defender's first few paragraphs in opening arguments demonstrate this framing:

> So I'm asking you folks to keep an open mind in this case until you've heard all the witnesses. You've heard all the evidence. (Trial 13, 5877)

> Folks, I'm not asking you this. And I know how hard this is. I'm not asking you to do something that's easy for anybody, because I know what kind of emotions those photographs can cause in everybody. In everybody. I'm asking you to please judge this case on the evidence that's presented. (Trial 13, 5877)

> That's not easy, I know. I'm not asking you to do something easy, but I'm asking you to do it. (Trial 13, 5878)

The members of the jury are thus implicitly exhorted, from the outset, to see the trial as a story with *themselves* as the protagonist. Reflecting classic narrative themes, the jury becomes a singular character, entering the story (the trial) as a "hero," having been "sworn to duty" (following the law) and presented with a challenging task (adjudicating the case). As Amsterdam and Hertz (1992) have pointed out, this narrative strategy has potential advantages for the defense: "It permits the defendant's activity in killing the victim—an activity which defense counsel is not denying and can hardly tuck under the rug—to be fitted into the narrative without becoming the dominant action of the tale" (p. 9–10).[16] As a rhetorical strategy, this framing urges jurors to mentally rearrange the story of Jamie/John such that *their duty to the law* supersedes their retributive impulses: "Thus the defendant can kill the victim without that action becoming the center of attention if the story line goes: *The jurors, faithful to their oath, acquitted the defendant although he sorely tempted them to do otherwise by killing the victim in a dastardly fashion*" (Amsterdam and Hertz, 1992, p. 10, italics in original). Of course, such an approach requires at least a little ambiguity about the defendant's culpability and character, which was the main focus of the defense's guilt arguments in this case.

Perhaps unfortunately for John Martinez, his defenders did not return to the "jury-as-hero" theme in their guilt phase closing arguments. Rather, the strategy was to raise reasonable doubt in the jurors' minds by simultaneously attacking the prosecution's forensic evidence and arguing that Vera Martinez was primarily responsible for Jamie's death, not John. The form of this latter argument was to argue that, not only was Vera more likely to have actually been the primary abuser of Jamie (e.g., "All the physical evidence in this case points to Vera"), but that she abused and dominated John: "Yes, this case is about domination and control, but it's not of domination and control over little Jamie; it is of domination and control of Vera Martinez over John" (Trial 13, 8133). This, then, is a different type of narrative; it is a story about diminished autonomy. In this narrative, the *steady state* is John Martinez's innocent (if somewhat pathetic) disposition prior to getting mixed up with Vera. The *trouble* is Vera's relentless abuse of John. The possibility of *redress* can be obtained by assigning blame to Vera for Jamie's death. And the *moral* of the story is that some persons, who suffer abuse, are not entirely in command of their autonomy and make poor, if not murderous or evil, decisions.

This narrative is achieved by pointing out what the evidence showed about John's inherently innocent disposition: "John was a very shy, and meek, and timid, and submissive little boy. John grew up into a very shy and meek and timid and submissive man" (Trial 13, 5881), and then pointing out what the evidence demonstrated about Vera's cruel domination of John: "What we have is a description of a completely dysfunctional relationship, verbal abuse, physical abuse and, if that's not enough, extramarital affairs that result in kids" (Trial 13, 8136), and then showing how John's innocent and pathetic disposition, coupled with Vera's abuse, led him to incriminate himself: "When you watch that videotape, you will see that John is very, very protective of Vera. . . . This is a man trying to protect his wife" (Trial 13, 8138), and finally by suggesting that John's autonomy was severely diminished: "John Martinez was a man who had absolutely no control about [sic] what was going on around him" (Trial 13, 8155–8156), the upshot being that jurors should not find him responsible for Jamie's death.

Thus we can see that despite the potential in this case to apply Amsterdam and Hertz's inverted narrative form, the main characters in the story remained John, Jamie, and Vera (not the jury), which brought Jamie's death vividly back as the central action of the tale (rather than the jury's heroic decision to acquit John).

Moreover, while the prosecutor's story bracketed out the "why" question of Jamie's death, the defense did very little to reopen that question.

Rather, the defense reiterated its two primary interrelated guilt phase themes in the penalty phase, namely John's good or apparently harmless character, and John's submissive role in relation to Vera, ultimately arguing that his life should be spared for the sake of his family. For example, the defense listed several "aspects" of John's background and character that were meant to illuminate "the meaning of his life" to his family and children (Trial 13, 8987). First, the defense reminded the jury that every witness, including prosecution witnesses, described John as shy, quiet, and respectful. Second, John's family members uniformly described him as affectionate and loving, never hostile or aggressive, consistently a positive force in family relations. Third, the defense summarized evidence that John had made attempts at self-improvement for much of his life, as evinced by his finishing high school and obtaining an electronic technician certificate from a community college. The reason this was understood as "self-improvement" was that John came from a poor family and apparently lacked high intelligence (although they introduced no evidence of any mental impairment). Fourth, John's relatively consistent work history should have been an important signifier of his worthiness, according to his defenders. This was important because it demonstrated that John could adapt well to prison life (a defense expert had testified previously that work history was an important factor in classifying prisoners). The fifth factor argued by the defense was the rhetorically powerful point that John had no criminal history of any kind. Despite poverty and limited cultural capital (not the defense's terminology), John had never been arrested, and no witnesses testified to any significant violence on his part. As should be clear, many of the themes in the defense's narration of the defendant are redolent of the American Creed. It is precisely by describing the individualistic, egalitarian, libertarian, and populist aspects of Martinez's background that the defense intended to "humanize" him—in this version of the story, "human" *is* the American Creed. Consciously or not, the defense draws heavily on Creed ideologies in hopes of "de-otherizing" him.

But beyond these five mitigating factors, the defense strongly emphasized the effect that John's execution would have on his family and children:

> What about the children? From all the evidence you heard, all the evidence you heard in this case, one thing is absolutely clear; if certain aspects of the guilt phase were not clear, one aspect of the penalty phase is very, very clear, that these children, that these children love their father and that they love him a lot. You heard the descriptions about how they react when there's a telephone call. The father calls, John Martinez calls on a daily basis. You heard from the mother, from Aunt Guadalupe how enthusiastic those chil-

dren are, how enthusiastic they are when they go and visit their father, one at a time, and they put their hands up on the glass. They miss their father. They talk about their father. They miss him desperately. (Trial 13, 8991)

This theme was most dramatically on display when the defense declared, "If John Sr. is executed, it will be the first time in the history of the United States that a boy's testimony was used in a court of law to execute the father" (Trial 13, 9011). Here, the jury is strongly encouraged to spare John for the sake of innocent John Jr. Within this narrative framework, John becomes an important part of a social continuum—a continuum that would be disrupted if he is executed. In this sense, the defense's characterization of John attempts to *connect the specific to the general* (e.g., the "specific facts" about John's role in Jamie's death to the "general context" of John's life within a larger social web), a narrative move that is subtly subversive of the individualistic aspects of the Creed. In this instance, the subversive potential of the argument is that it challenges the script underlying the prosecution narrative, namely that the only thing to be understood is the damage to the victim; all else is irrelevant. Yet at the same time, as I discussed above, this contextualizing is spoken in the individualistic, egalitarian, libertarian, and populist grammar of the Creed. We can thus see how the law tends to orient its discourses away from the possibility of challenging its hegemonic ideologies—these defenders "ended up" invoking individualistic aspects of the Creed, in spite of themselves, even while they attempted to tell a story about the quasideterministic nature of "context."

Vignettes of Dystopia: Incomplete Narratives of Ruined Lives

Unlike the prosecutors in this data set, defenders' arguments rarely fit into a neat, simple, flat, temporally short narrative. For obvious reasons, it is difficult to delineate a nuanced story of diminished autonomy that might span several generations and countries. It is much easier to declare, as nearly all the prosecutors in these data did, that the defendant killed the victim because he felt like it for selfish, sociopathic reasons. For this reason, it was harder to pin down precisely the defense version of the story in every case by reading the arguments and some of the testimony. The examples I discussed immediately preceding this section show some of the most coherent narrative material in the defense arguments in this data set. But while complete and coherent narratives were rare in defender discourses, *components* of narratives about "diminished autonomy" were plentiful throughout these data. In the sections that follow, I discuss the three most common themes of diminished autonomy employed by defenders, what I will call "social dystopia," "drug dystopia," and "mental illness."[17]

First, in many of the cases, defenders briefly described their clients' grim social world, implying that jurors should at least sympathize, and sometimes attribute some amount of cause to the surroundings of their client's youth and pre-crime lives:

> This family has had a history of conflict. The father . . . displaying of weapon in a threatening manner . . . is the same father that . . . caroused, didn't bring money home, blew his check on other women, hung out down on seventh street, beat his wife, beat his children, fired a .22 rifle at Irving. Do you think there might be some reason Irving might have a little apprehension of that dad? (Trial 3, 3965)

> And sadly and tragically, you've heard an awful lot about Lew's use of drugs. The reasons that Lew started using drugs are not clear and involve speculation at best. Did he start using drugs because he had some sort of unresolved personality conflict? Did he start using drugs because at the time he was growing up, 40 percent of all blacks were unemployed in [his city]? Did he start using drugs because the world he lived in was made easier by using drugs? Did he start using drugs because he wanted to be somebody, that he wanted to be the go-to guy? (Trial 15, 8692)

> How could these street people, drug dealers, lesbian thieves and just felons keep this story together all the time or they are so remorseful they have come here to tell you the truth? (Trial 4, 2697)

In these vignettes, defenders depict stereotypically "urban" contexts, rife with violence, crime, drugs, and "street life." These quasinarratives thus briefly allude to the postmodern dystopia that is often thought to characterize what people think of as the American ghetto. In making these allusions, defenders hint at the possibility of diminished autonomy—but never make the rhetorical leap of proposing that these dystopic social conditions are implicated in the production of lethal violence.

In other cases, defenders described dysfunctional family dynamics:

> She will tell us Cynthia used to throw the kid against the wall at her house, and she felt very sorry for Charles because he was treated differently than the girls. Even dressed differently (Trial 7, 10508). . . . What you are seeing here is the tip of the iceberg, these are the kinds of things in our experience and life, we know the dirty little secrets that families have that they minimize or hide (Trial 7, 12660). . . . The district attorney in his opening argument stressed a whole series of things about Charles made choices. Charles made choices. Well, Charles did not choose his parents, and Charles did not choose to be mentally ill. (Trial 7, 12668)

> I don't have a photograph of Norbert Williams at age four with feces all over his chest. I don't have a photograph of the look of humiliation and disgust

on Norbert Williams's face when his father called him shit for brains. I don't have a photograph of Norbert Williams's mouth bleeding after his father struck him in the face and blood was oozing from the hamburger-like flesh of his jaw because of the braces he was wearing. (Trial 9, 6427–6428)

And what you see in this kind of thing that is happening here, you see when he is out of control, as a child he has no control, and he has been totally dominated by a woman and is being sexualized, everything is sex, either pro or negative. Is it such a surprise that out of that sexualization would become the desire for control. That is what happened to this child, the child sexualized as he was, out of control as he was, when he developed as a male, what you see is the sexualization becoming the desire to control. (Trial 10, 6726)

In these vignettes, defenders allude to the influence of stereotypically "bad parents," hinting at the determinism of family dynamics—but again, never making the causal argument explicit, nor even strenuously applied.

Other narratives offered by defense attorneys capitalize on concepts of foreignness and cultural conflict:

[The evidence] shows a life filled with turmoil. Lawrence Tran was brought into the war. There's a communist takeover as a result. There's increase in poverty and a decrease in human rights and freedoms. There was an escape from Vietnam when he was five years old, and a twenty-five foot boat crammed with thirty-two refugees. In other words, this is a pretty crowded boat. You have less than one foot per refugee. Three days and three night journey across a stormy sea. He arrives in Thailand, sick and malnourished. The family is robbed by Thai bandits. They're rescued by police. Confined to refugee camps. The conditions are crowded. There's insufficient food and water. There's rotten vegetables. Stones in their rice. Living in tents and filthy conditions. They finally, after several months of living conditions like that, arrive in the U.S. Still no mom, no dad to provide the guidance and nurturing that's necessary to ensure a proper rearing of a child. Being shuffled between older siblings, and struggling to survive (Trial 23, 5832–5833). . . . There was a lot of family deprivation once they got to the United States. There's a struggle to survive. Bad luck in his associations. He felt isolated and alienated from the mainstream of American culture. Lack of self-esteem. No sense of belonging. No support or safety net. He turns to gangs for support and safety. (Trial 23, 5835)

In this passage, the defendant is characterized as a victim of the political fallout of the Vietnam War—although the defense never makes the explicitly causal connection between that war and the defendant's violence. This argument closely resembles the thesis presented by Vigil (2002) in *A Rainbow of Gangs: Street Culture in the Mega-City* wherein he analyzes various Los Angeles gang cultures—including Vietnamese gangs—showing how sociocultural conflict operates to undermine traditional forces of so-cial control, such as parents and education, leading to "functional" gangs.

And while the defendant described in the following passage, an Egyptian national, was not involved in gangs, his defender delineated a similar quasinarrative about cultural dissonance:

> He attended a Muslim school where he was beat up by Muslims periodically as were his siblings because that is what happens in Said when you are a Christian (Trial 12, 2061). . . . The family dealt with it by chaining him up or beating him up with a chain, tying him up, trying to isolate him, basically old middle ages way of dealing with mental illness (Trial 12, 2062–2063). . . . He was so mentally ill his father took him to doctors, to clinics. He got electric shock treatment. And Gabriel Johnson described for you in great detail what that treatment looked like. And we know from Dr. Girgis that's precisely how they treated psychiatric illness or psychotic illness in Egypt now, and particularly about 10 years ago which is when this illness would have started manifesting itself, in the late '80s and early '90s (Trial 12, 2757). . . . He's a human being who has had a lifetime of illness that was never adequately treated in Egypt, that was completely untreated here. (Trial 12, 2795)

In this nightmarish depiction, the defendant is characterized as a misunderstood and abused mentally ill person marginalized in both his home country and new country. In this depiction, Johnson's treatment in Egypt resembled torture, implying that his schizophrenia must be understood within a complex sociocultural context. Still, these factors are *listed* rather than characterized as *causes* of the defendant's lethal violence.

All of these snapshots of violent, marginalized life in the United States came wedged between rambling passages explaining the law of mitigation and aggravation, passages discussing vague ideas such as "fairness" or "justice," passages discussing all types of evidence, discussions of the death penalty generally, and frank pleadings for mercy, among other things. They lack the coherence of a complete narrative, with protagonist, "steady-state," "trouble," "redress," and "coda," although some parts of the narrative structure are in most of these passages. Moreover, these dystopic vignettes briefly illuminate the conditions of those falling on the losing side of the American Creed's double-edged sword. To that extent, these passages have some measure of subversive potential because they imply complexity and the importance of context rather than simplicity and individualistic autonomy.[18] Yet ultimately these stories lack much subversive potential precisely because they *imply* rather than argue. "Implying" suggests a submission to the hegemony of the Creed's ideologies. Defenders proffering vignettes, which lack both the coherent narrative structure and, more importantly, the *causal* argument, operate within the Creed's hegemony.

Dope's Dystopia: Methamphetamine's Diminishing Damage

As with any book, this study is a product of its time and place. Since before *Gregg v. Georgia* (1976), methamphetamine (meth) abuse has persistently plagued Californian society. Meth use, and especially meth use among persons involved in the criminal justice system is higher in California than any other state (Cartier et al., 2006). And although this project is by no means intended to scientifically measure meth use, meth appeared to be significant in several of these cases. Notably, of fourteen out of thirty-seven cases in which drug or alcohol use was a major theme, only *two* cases involved substances other than methamphetamine.[19] To put it most simply, by a large margin, the most common form of intoxication in this data set was meth intoxication (although sometimes in conjunction with alcohol). This is remarkable both as an indication of meth's apparently deleterious effect on human beings, and also as a measure of its discursive potency—the message is clear: methamphetamine is *bad stuff*, perhaps the worst of all drugs, according to defenders (and sometimes to prosecutors). Defenders usually tried to explain how meth abuse diminished their defendants' autonomy:

If after this trial the combination of the prosecution and defense evidence does not convince you what a god awful thing methamphetamine is, we have all failed for [the victims], and Chuck Langford (Trial 7, 6681). . . . Can you say that these murders would have still happened even without the methamphetamine and/or the mental illness he suffers from. (Trial 7, 12686)

The fact, I think, ladies and gentlemen, is that these defendants were so whacked out on drugs, they were so intent on being wannabe killers, desperados, that they didn't have the insight, the impulse control of a three year old; whatever they wanted, they went after. They didn't think about tomorrow. (Trial 8, 7257)

God, look at those pictures. That is the act of a crazed person, crazed by the malevolence of those drugs. What the killings, if you will, show is that mitigation are that these crimes were the mad acts of a drug crazed, chronic drug abuser (Trial 19, 5626). . . . And Martin Michaels was possessed, possessed by the malevolence that created the evil and the malice in this crazed drug culture of which he was part. And who knows what his real choice in that was (Trial 19, 5627) . . . Your verdict must carry a message: Because we can understand the circumstances of Martin Michaels's life, the fact that he was led into drugs, addiction, instant gratification, possessed by malevolence from outside himself, because he was weak, he killed. (Trial 19, 5630–5631)

Mitchell Velasquez was drugged out. He was doing an 8–ball a day. All he was doing was smoking and scraping, smoking, scraping. (Trial 17, 4551)

The one drug that finally bested him in 1994 was a drug called crystal methamphetamine, and it is one of the most dangerous drugs there are because it
goes to the very issues of your ability to control your behavior and impulses
and aggression and sexuality (Trial 2, 5396). . . .But what I will argue to you
is that the crimes would not have happened without drugs and alcohol (Trial
2, 6584). . . . The decision of an addict, the decision of a person whose life is
under the grips of alcohol or drugs, is not the same as yours or mine. It's not
the same as someone who's not affected like that (Trial 2, 6590). . . . My point
is simple. This was a man driven psychologically and chemically at the end.
He was—his life was out of control, and he was out of control. It's not so
black and white, as the prosecutor paints it. And we'll never know where the
rape impulse came from, whether it came from childhood, whether it came
from the dangerous drug like methamphetamine, crystal methamphetamine
alone, or whether it came from him trying to regain control of his life. (Trial
2, 6592)

These assertions about drug-induced psychosis and its effects again
depict for the jury a chaotic world within which the defendant is partially
at the mercy of forces outside of his own will. Moreover, they again illuminate the shadow-world of the dark side of the American Creed's
sword—these defendants are chronically unemployed addicts living in
the margins of U.S. society. In these examples, the implication is that
some degree of causality for the murder can be attributed to the diminishing influence of drugs. But, again, the ideological upshot of these implications is never addressed—the "drug-induced-diminished-autonomy"
trope stands on its own as an "explanation" for violence, without making
the explicit causal connection between the complex social forces underlying drug abuse and the violence that ensued in a drug induced state.[20]

The Madness of Murder: Mental Illness as a Mitigator

The third primary type or "cause" of diminished autonomy discussed by
defenders, along with traumatic social history and meth intoxication, was
mental illness.[21] Many of these defendants were described, on some level,
as mentally ill by their defenders. As indicated by the quotes below, the
mental-illness-diminished-autonomy argument is tricky to make in the
penalty phase because the defendant has already been found sane and
responsible for murder. This means that defenders must try to explain
the concept of a mitigating *diminished* autonomy due to sometimes subtle
mental illnesses, which is something different than explaining legal insanity. Notoriously, the legal threshold for "insanity," which is *not* a term of
art among mental health professionals, requires a remarkably high level
of mental disease. The doctrine of the California penal code's definition

of insanity, which is based on the law school chestnut "the M'Naughten Rule,"[22] is that the defendant has to either not understand the nature of his actions (e.g., thinking the gun is a banana) or not understand that what he did was "wrong" (e.g., not understanding that shooting someone in the head is morally objectionable). If the defendant cannot convince a judge or jury of either of these "prongs," he will be found "sane."

Of course, as any mental health professional will tell you, this legal definition of insanity has nothing to do with scientific knowledge about the human mind. The fields of psychiatry, psychology, and neuropsychology delineate arrays of mental illnesses, with numerous and varying effects on the mind and behavior. These include thought disorders (such as schizophrenia) to personality disorders (such as obsessive compulsive disorder) to mood disorders (such as clinical depression), many of which significantly debilitate persons who are nonetheless able to "know right from wrong" (which is the vernacular shorthand used by prosecutors to describe sanity). Put simply, for scientists of the human mind, the question of "sanity" is much more complex and nuanced than it is for the law.[23]

This leaves defenders in the unenviable position of attempting to bring into the law discomfiting scientific discourse about a topic the law interprets as already settled. Importantly, the law instructs jurors in the penalty phase that they may consider the defendant's mental state at the time of the crime when contemplating penalty. However, like many aspects of jury instructions, this message is confusing because it comes mixed with the implicit message that culpability is a simple and pure binary for the law. Guilt is like pregnancy for the law—either you are or you aren't. "Sanity," as it is defined by the law, is similarly purely dichotomous.

As prosecutors in this data set have argued in trials and mentioned in interviews to me, "who cares" if the defendant is mentally ill—if he "knew right from wrong," it is irrelevant. This point of view about human consciousness is redolent of the individualism and populism of the American Creed. A yes-or-no understanding of "sanity" relies on a simplistically individualistic and "rational" conceptualization of the mind; it also relies on a populist vision of knowledge because it rejects elite, scientific knowledge about the human mind.

Nevertheless, despite the challenge of interpolating scientific knowledge into the law, the penalty phase once again runs against the grain of the law's simple conceptualization of human agency because it allows for *some* degree of contexualization:

> But whether he truly understood and appreciated his actions in the bigger world and it is not an excuse, it is just whether you feel that Irving fits in the bigger world in terms of his own mental illness. (Trial 3, 3995)

But then–then it starts happening, whatever triggers the happening, whether it's biological, the pressure of the grandmother, god knows what it is, his mental illness begins to emerge and things start spiraling downhill. That's what happens. And with the rare exception, rare exception, we have repeated diagnosis of major mental, major depression recurring. And that is one thing that I need to talk about in terms of mitigating factors. (Trial 7, 12670)

[He has] an IQ of 66. Now, what does that mean, what does that translate? To what does that translate? Out of a hundred people tested, he's the lowest one. He fits into the lowest, the first percentile of those tested. He's abnormal. That's right. He's impaired. (Trial 17, 5148)

   One, they find there is extra, extra activity in the area in the temporal lobe associated with basic emotions, with basic instincts. And included in those are sex and violence. That is an area of his brain which he has no control, which he may not ever understand until we are done Monday, that always activated and always slightly damages and is always working overtime for him in a way that cannot be controlled. (Trial 10, 5821)

I suggest to you that this case lends itself at least to one interpretation, that this murder was not for purposes of a robbery, but this murder was a product of his diseased mental state that caused this emotional explosion from being—because he was rejected, and the young man just sort of ignored him. (Trial 11, 3167)

In each of these passages, the defendant is characterized as having less control than a "normal" person (such as a juror) over his autonomy due to a mental impairment—these passages encapsulate the concept of diminished autonomy. In the following passage, the defender goes to great lengths to explain the subtle complexities of schizophrenia:

But you will also hear from people in that area that people thought when they saw him that he was mentally ill, and this was because of his strange behavior. They would see him begging outside barely speak to people. When he would look at people, he would have a very strange kind of blank expression, blank stare on his face. And the employees at some of these businesses said that they thought he wasn't normal, he was whacked out, and that his behavior when he was there in the stores was very odd (Trial 12, 1272). . . . Schizophrenia is a physical illness, the person who has it–and there are different kinds of schizophrenia, and there are different levels of schizophrenia. But the point of the illness is that it affects your ability to perceive reality. In other words, a person with schizophrenia can see. I mean his organs all work. He can see; he can hear; he can taste. But how those signals get interpreted in his brain is screwed up, and it is screwed up because of chemical things happening in the brain. In other words, it is not something that is controlled. It is treated with medication (Trial 12, 2055). . . . It is going to show that his actions are not the result of a sound mind. Beyond the fact that anyone who commits assaultive-type crimes obviously is not completely normal, the evidence is going to show that he has a physical illness that is not controllable by free will, that was not created by any of his own actions, an illness he was born with and an illness that he can no more overcome without the help of medication and medical attention than somebody can will their way out of Parkinson's disease or epilepsy or diabetes or any other physical ailment that somebody is born with (Trial 12, 2069). . . . It is wrong to treat a mentally ill person the same way you treat a person with a normal brain. It is wrong to kill somebody who acted the way they did, not just because of a bad impulse, but because their brain was broken long before they even knew what a brain was. It is wrong in this case to kill this man who is so very sick for reasons beyond his control, beyond his understanding. The punishment of locking him up for the rest of his life in isolation is the only appropriate punishment in this case, because those mitigating factors that we've discussed in this case, they do outweigh the aggravating factors precisely because of the fact that the aggravating factors are the direct result of the mitigating factors. (Trial 12, 2796–2797)

This last passage is especially notable because the defender makes a clear and logical argument about the diminishing effects mental illness have on the defendant's autonomy. The last clause in this quote is remarkable in its parsimony: "The aggravating factors are the direct result of the mitigating factors." For this defender, the *cause* of the victim's death is the defendant's mental illness, and the consequence of this causal relationship is that the defendant is slightly less culpable than "normal" persons—just less culpable enough to warrant an LWOP sentence. This argument about mental illness and aggravated murder—"the aggravating factors are the direct result of the mitigating factors"—directly, if briefly, challenges the individualistic idea that the cause of murder is simply the will of the defendant; instead the cause is schizophrenia.

THE LIMITS OF LAW AND THE EFFECTS OF HEGEMONY

Yet even potentially or partially subversive passages like those describing the causal role of brutalizing social conditions, meth-induced psychosis, or schizophrenia butt up against the limits of the law. Norms of the legal institution and practice constrict the talk that is produced in all criminal trials, including in the relatively unrestricted (or perhaps *differently* restricted) realm of capital penalty phase proceedings. Jurisprudential rules, embodied in cases such as *Lockett v. Ohio* (1978) or *Payne v. Tennessee* (1991), constrain and shape what legal actors are allowed to say during the penalty phase. And organizations with semiofficial status, particularly the American Bar Association, but also particular prosecutor and defender offices, produce regulations or procedures for their members to follow—all of which operate to limit the logistic and strategic possibilities for practicing attorneys. Beyond these codified rules about law talk, norms around ethics and strategic prerogatives restrain litigators from straying too far from the particular details in their present cases—especially if litigators believe that narratives about diminished autonomy might backfire and cause jurors to resent them or their client. I address this situation in more detail in the next chapter.

Moreover, there are inherent limitations on the law as a venue for ideological subversion. As I discussed earlier in this chapter, scholars such as, for example Jenkins (1980) and Jamieson (2001), have discussed the law's various limitations along many theoretical dimensions, particularly its restricted ability to effect social change. Conley and O'Barr (1998) have analyzed legal micro-discourses to make the argument that the law is fundamentally patriarchal in its preference for "male" speech styles and reluctance to incorporate "female speech" (see chapter 4 generally). Indeed, sociolegal scholars representing a variety of academic perspectives have analyzed and theorized various limitations on the role or function of the law in society.[24] I do not aim to weigh in on the various thoughtful treatments of the law's limits in this study; instead I refer to this situation to help contextualize my primary argument about the law's role in perpetuating hegemonic ideologies. Despite the law's various limitations, capital penalty phases clearly provide *some* level of opportunity to construct arguments beyond the prerogatives of any particular case and toward subversion of ideology. In the limited data analyzed in this chapter, these movements toward subversion—in the relatively rare instances when they appeared—were usually incomplete or tentative.

To again quote a prosecutor I interviewed during the course of this study, "Who cares?" Why should anyone be interested in whether or how arguments made by prosecutors and defenders in capital trials instantiate or challenge the American Creed? For one answer, I return to a common thread in recent major studies of capital punishment in the United States, namely a concern with the *instrumental* effects of ideology on state punishment policies, especially the policy of state killing.

In the first place, recall Austin Sarat's (2001) incisive argument that flat, simple, individualistic narratives of murder and execution bracket out and functionally efface the dystopic social conditions in which murder takes place. By pointing out the *ideological machinery* that causes this bracketing, I push his argument into deeper territory, showing how the foundations of American society are implicated in brushing aside complex social issues in favor of easy answers. But at the same time, I also show the law creates the space for some limited assaults on the bracketing forces of American Creed ideologies.

Recall also that the American Exceptionalism argument taking place among Zimring (2003), Whitman (2003), Poveda (2000), Garland (2005), and to a lesser extent, me (in chapter 2), involves investigating the role of ideology in American retention of the death policy. Although I am not able to make an argument specifically about retention from these data, I do show how the ideologies some theorists believe underlie retention are on display in these California trials. To the extent that these ideologies are *inherently* racist and classist—as I argued in chapter 2—the death penalty narratives in these data generally function to perpetuate these undesirable characteristics of the U.S. law. In the next chapter, I focus more closely on the practices and consciousnesses of capital defense attorneys to investigate further the possibility of ideological subversion available within the milieu of the contemporary U.S. death penalty.

NOTES

1. It is probably true that the presence of the Creed in U.S. culture generally—not just within the law—limits the likelihood of subversive narratives. But for the limited purposes of this book, I restrict my analysis to the law.

2. The victim had recently returned to her mother's home after a traumatic stay in a group home.

3. In John's case, the jury that found him guilty of capital murder was unable to agree on his penalty of either death or LWOP; a mistrial was declared and a second jury gave him the death penalty after one day of deliberation.

4. During evidence, the defense introduced evidence that Vera abused John.

5. Although *mens rea* is only required in the guilt phase, the *notion* of a "guilty mind" pervades most prosecution generated narrations throughout these capital trials.

6. This passage is interesting in its contrast between the formalistic invocation of "the evidence" and "the law," and its highly affective reference to the defendants as "subhumans"; see chapter 6 for a detailed discussion of this contrast in prosecutor narratives.

7. See Evans (1906) for a fascinating description of animal trials and executions, including several in the nineteenth century, and even one in the twentieth century (see especially appendix F).

8. In Rhodes's usage, "characterological" means that the cause of behavior resides in the character of the individual.

9. As Rhodes notes, the concept or meaning of "psychopathy" is contested and ideologically charged. I do not aim to resolve the question of the appropriateness or utility of the concept of "psychopathy," but only intend to show that it is used by capital prosecutors.

10. I return to this theme in chapter 6, in which I discuss the "imagine being the victim" theme as an aspect of highly affective prosecutor discourse.

11. This common depiction of prison inmates "staying in shape" invokes stereotypical images of muscular men lifting weights to build themselves "super bodies" that are powerful and, of course, threatening.

12. Cause lawyering describes the work of attorneys who take up cases specifically to advance a particular "cause," such as civil rights and abolition of capital punishment. I discuss cause lawyering at length in chapter 5.

13. It is not my intention to frame law as a method for social change, but rather to show how the law is implicated in perpetuating hegemonic ideologies.

14. His invocation of the notion of "contract" is notable because it illuminates a tension in the United States between individualism and communitarianism—"contract" implies collectivity but is also a primary tenet of possessive individualism.

15. I discuss the "liminal man" in narratives of diminished autonomy in more detail in the next chapter.

16. Amsterdam and Hertz analyze a homicide case in which the defendant did not dispute shooting the victim, but did dispute *mens rea*. In the Martinez case, the defense did not deny that Martinez was implicated in Jamie's death, only that he was not *primarily* responsible.

17. Not surprisingly, these themes were sometimes intertwined with each other; for clarity, I address each theme independently.

18. Unfortunately, they often do so by appealing to moral traditionalism—the importance of the "father-led family," a moral order that tolerates little deviance—and, in so doing valorizes a need for repressive forms of social control, one of which is the death penalty.

19. In one case, the defendant was high on crack when he committed the murder; in the other case, the defendant was extremely drunk and high on heroin at the time of the murder.

20. Moreover, drug-based explanations for crime always leave the door open for prosecutors and jurors to simply "convert" the evidence and decide that the choice to do drugs was freely willed, and in the case of murder, decide that the homicide was therefore still derived from the unencumbered will of the killer.

21. Aside from these three quasinarratives of diminished autonomy, defenders made plenty of other arguments in the penalty phase, including the arguments that (a) the defendant was not "the worst of the worst," (b) LWOP is a harsher punishment than death, and (c) jurors should have lingering doubt about the defendant's guilt.

22. The doctrine described in the M'Naughten rule comes from a nineteenth-century British homicide case.

23. This disjunction between legal and scientific knowledge about the human mind is an interesting and important instance of the clash of two major institutions in Western society, but it is not the primary focus of this project, so I leave this interesting topic for another day.

24. For a compendium of recent essays covering contemporary issues around law's limits, see Sarat et al., 2005.

5

●●●

Forgetting the Future

Cause Lawyering and the Work of California Capital Trial Defenders

In his (1998) article "Between (the Presence of) Violence and (the Possibility of) Justice," Austin Sarat summarizes the work of legal scholars Drucilla Cornell, Judith Butler, and Robert Cover to succinctly explicate one important tension in the law:

> Law exists both in the "as yet" failure to realize the Good and in the commitment to its realization. In this failure and this commitment law is two things at once: the social organization of violence through which state power is exercised in a partisan, biased and sometimes cruel way, and the arena to which citizens address themselves in the hope that law can, and will, redress the wrongs that are committed in its name. (p. 318)

According to Sarat, the law embodies a tension between a quest for "the Good" (perhaps restated as "Justice") and the violence seemingly necessary to achieve Good (although these scholars see the law as never actually achieving Justice but instead manifesting a kind of perpetual promise of Justice that is never quite fulfilled).

Sarat conceptualizes "cause lawyers" as those attorneys who professionally confront this tension. Cause lawyers, exemplified by abolitionist capital appellate attorneys, specifically and purposefully apply themselves discriminately, using the law as a tool to take on a cause: "Cause lawyers use their professional skills to move law away from the daily reality of violence and toward a particular vision of the Good" (p. 318). This activism toward "the Good" can be understood as taking place along a continuum, from the relatively "professional" cause lawyer who is ("merely") willing to "undertake controversial and politically charged activities and/or [have] a sense of commitment to particular ideals" (Sarat and Schiengold, 1998, p. 7), to the "radical" cause lawyers who:

> challenge established conceptions of professionalism with efforts to decommodify, politicize, and socialize legal practice. While they may be forced by necessity to defend established rights, their real goal is to contribute to the kind of transformative politics that will redistribute political power and material benefits in a more egalitarian fashion. Their primary loyalty is not to clients, to constitutional rights, not to legal process, but to a vision of the good society and to political allies who share that vision. (p. 7)

Cause lawyers, working along this continuum, may work toward a vision of the "good society" that involves a variety of "causes" such as human rights, feminism, environmentalism, or eradicating poverty (see Sarat and Schiengold, 1998, p. 5). In the case of abolitionist death penalty lawyers, as investigated by Sarat (1998), their particular vision of "the good society" is both the elimination of the death penalty and a more equal society.

Given its inherently political nature—even in its most "professional" forms—cause lawyering thus presents a problem for the law in a liberal democracy like the United States that purports to maintain a rational and formal legal system. This is because law systems that maintain (or have the veneer of) rational formalism are not supposed to take up "causes" that could jeopardize their (purported) independence. As Sarat and Schiengold put it: "In order to accomplish anything substantial, cause lawyers must necessarily become embroiled in controversial issues of politics and public policy. In so doing, they put the legitimacy of an independent law at risk and thus subject their project to backlash and to the *force majeure* that is at the disposal of the state" (p. 8).[1]

Cause lawyering's political nature also presents a problem for the "professional project" of the legal profession. This is because cause lawyers embody a kind of professional paradox when they "use" the legal profession to take up a cause (see Sarat and Schiengold, 1998, p. 10). Cause lawyers promote the legal profession as a *mode* for social change—but this view simultaneously contradicts the commitment to morally neutral advocacy valued by the legal profession.[2] Cause lawyers are thus "deviants" within their own profession. Nevertheless, as Sarat and Schiengold (1998) point out:

> The elasticity of professionalism means that it can be appropriated and deployed by lawyers representing a wide range of interests and approaches to practice, including cause lawyers. Ideologies of professionalism, like other ideologies, become meaningful by creating distinctions and turning them into oppositions—for example, the opposition between lawyering for clients

and lawyering for causes. Moreover, those ideologies favor particular views of legal practice by asserting their claim to general respect and allegiance. Each of those ideologies seeks to provide an exclusive, normatively coherent, and authoritative portrait of lawyering; yet in juxtaposition they suggest instability and indeterminacy in the very heart of the legal profession's idea of itself. (p. 11)

Studying cause lawyers can thus be seen as a method for illuminating particular aspects of the law's indeterminacy, particularly the tensions between political lawyering and legal autonomy, social advocacy, and professional neutrality.

THE HEGEMONY OF INDIVIDUALISM

This chapter aims to push the boundaries of Sarat's definition of capital cause lawyering to include a more potentially radical "cause" that accounts for the instrumental goals of abolition and social equality but also takes on individualism. As discussed earlier, individualism signifies an ideology in which notions of personhood and social life are based on a single, bounded subjectivity (an individual person). Individualism is closely associated with the political ideology of *liberalism*. According to political theorist David Johnston (1994):

The first premise of liberal political theory is that only individuals count. Individuals formulate projects. Individuals conceive values. When values and projects come to fruition, individuals experience the joy of their attainment; when they fail, individuals feel the frustration that results. Liberal individualism—the claim that only individuals count—is the substance and strength of the liberal tradition. (p. 191)

Groups may "count" to some extent in liberalism, but as Johnston makes clear, the central organizing idea in liberalism is the individual:

The liberal view that only individuals count does not require liberals to be blind to the fact that group membership and shared cultural practices are important to individuals and play a significant role in helping many people to build valuable lives. . . . Individuals may and often do make plans together, share aspirations and goals. But the aspirations and hopes associated with these projects and goals are *individuals'* aspirations and hopes. The satisfactions of success and the disappointments of failure are individuals' satisfactions and disappointments. Only individuals can be miserable and can suffer. These are some of the reasons why liberals hold the view that only individuals count (p. 20–21).

In this chapter, I attempt to improve understanding of how this hegemony is maintained by studying whether and how capital defense trial lawyers—who are, as we know, a set of actors unusually well-positioned to challenge ideologies—take up a "radical" cause by subverting individualism.

DEREGULATED DEATH

As discussed in previous chapters, the penalty phase of a capital trial appears, at first blush, to be an ideal legal location for ideologically subversive acts such as cause lawyering. However, the omnipresence of individualism seems to prevent this from taking place, although as I show below, trial defense narratives do sometimes move in the direction of subversion when explaining their clients' crimes. An interesting puzzle thus emerges—the law formally allows for ideologically subversive cause lawyering, but the hegemony of individualism apparently hinders this possible subversion from taking place.

This is not to say that capital trial lawyers do not make strong cases to abolish the death penalty or to expose racial and socioeconomic inequality during their trials. Sometimes they do. However, it is likely that most capital defense attorneys do not view "subverting individualism" as a "cause" in the first place. But this is exactly the point. Individualism is hegemonic, meaning that its oppressive qualities are invisible to the oppressed.[3] There can be little doubt that the hyperindividualism of contemporary American society contributed to the marginalization of the defendants in the cases addressed in this study. The fact that these defendants and their defenders do not recognize this or see the point as irrelevant—and would perhaps scoff at the proposition—demonstrates my point. To draw a simplistic analogy, the capital defender who doesn't see individualism as a "cause"—in both senses; a reason for their client's oppression and an ideology to attack—is akin to the low wage worker who sees credit card purchases as a good thing.

This chapter draws on semistructured interviews with fourteen capital trial defenders.[4] The interviews were quasiethnographic to the extent that I came to each interview with a set of open-ended questions with the goal of initiating a conversation rather than administering a questionnaire. Each interview lasted between one and three hours; some interviews were recorded and some were not because recording inhibited some interviewees. I analyzed the interview transcripts similarly to the trial transcripts, coding for some predetermined themes and developing new ones as I went along. Confidentiality has been maintained throughout the process.

THE CONTEXT OF CAPITAL CAUSE LAWYERING

According to Sarat (1998), capital cause lawyers swim upstream against an overwhelmingly hostile tide in the legal system. At the time of his essay, death penalty jurisprudence looked very bleak to opponents of capital punishment. Congress had recently limited the *habeas corpus* rights of condemned prisoners—primarily in the form of the Antiterrorism and Effective Death Penalty Act of 1996—and the tone of judicial opinions rejecting condemned prisoners' habeas claims for relief was openly hostile to capital defenders.[5]

This situation has changed somewhat after the turn of the century, with the notable decisions in *Roper v. Simmons* (2005) (which banned the execution of offenders who were juveniles at the time of the crime) and *Atkins v. Virginia* (2002) (which banned the execution of the mentally retarded). Furthermore, due to the prominence of wrongful capital convictions and some controversy related to the constitutionality of lethal injection,[6] the political climate also seems slightly more receptive to the possibility of abolishing the death penalty than it did in 1998. Indeed, abolitions in New Jersey, New York, New Mexico, and Illinois between 2007 and 2011 show that the tide has turned in at least some parts of the United States on this question.

Nevertheless, the important point made by Sarat is that the legal system presents not only a generally hostile environment for attorneys representing condemned prisoners, but also a difficult venue for advocating abolition of capital punishment (see p. 322). This becomes especially clear when looking at the Supreme Court decisions in *Gregg v. Georgia* (1976) and *McCleskey v. Kemp* (1987). The doctrines in these cases preclude legal attacks on the death penalty based on either an Eighth Amendment argument about the cruel and unusual nature of arbitrariness or an argument about systemic racial disproportionality. Despite the limited "chipping away" at capital punishment represented by *Roper* and *Atkins* (and perhaps to a lesser extent, *Ring v. Arizona* [2002], which made it unconstitutional for judges to assign death sentences), it still seems unlikely, for the moment, that capital punishment is likely to be abolished by way of a legal attack on its fundamental constitutionality.

Given the difficulty of achieving abolition through a legal decision, capital cause lawyers, the argument goes, are engaged in something that transcends both the necessary prerogatives of litigating particular cases and also the abolition of capital punishment. According to Sarat, this other thing is essentially an act of testimony about larger questions of social justice—the "cause" of capital cause lawyers is to testify publicly about the relationships between the "immediate" and "small" injustices of their particular case to larger social injustices: "[cause] lawyers broaden the scope of inquiry by linking the particular injustices to which they are opposed with broader patterns of injustice and institutional practice" (Sarat, 1998, p. 324). Again drawing on Drucilla Cornell, Sarat refers to this act of testifying as "remembering the future" (324) because these lawyers make a record of the presently unjust situation for the benefit of history: "Due process guarantees an opportunity to be heard by, and an opportunity to speak to, the future. It is the guarantee that legal institutions can be turned into museums of unnecessary, unjust, undeserved pain and death" (Sarat, 1998, p. 323).

The picture Sarat paints for abolitionist death penalty post-conviction and appellate attorneys[7] in "Between Violence and Justice" is bleak— and it is precisely this bleakness that situates these legal practitioners as cause lawyers. According to Sarat's conceptualization, cause lawyering is defined by the somewhat pyrrhic character of the work. The post-trial attorneys he interviewed describe themselves as "being hammered" by public opinion and the legal institution and developing a "bunker mentality" among themselves to ward off the negativity coming at them from the adversaries, courts, the public and sometimes their own clients. Under these conditions, capital cause lawyers hardened their ideological commitments to abolition and began to redefine success in terms of delaying executions and "testifying" for a future when capital punishment has become an unpleasant memory (Sarat, 1998, see p. 331). Anthony Amsterdam (2007) practiced something like "remembering the future" when he recently argued that significant *moderation* of capital punishment in the form of restrictions on death-eligible murders "will not end the death penalty or racial discrimination or their symbiosis in this country soon. But will lessen somewhat the terrible cost of both and the mortgage of shame that our generation is incurring to history on that account" (p. 8).

Sarat limits his conceptualization of death penalty cause lawyers to those working post-trial. One of the obvious reasons for Sarat's focus on the post-trial area is that trial lawyers are inherently less able, by virtue of the contingencies of trial processes (such as rules of evidence, the overwhelming financial and time pressures of capital trials, or even simply the vicissitudes of the judge), to do much more than keep their heads above water when trying a death penalty case. Unlike their colleagues working post-trial, trial lawyers have to go to court most days and negotiate the complex everyday milieu of the so-called "courtroom workgroup" (the social network in court consisting of attorneys, the judge, clerks, bailiffs, etc.) This situation equates to less reading, writing, discussing, and thinking—less hours to contemplate or even formulate a consciousness about any particular cause.

Another obvious reason to focus on post-trial is that trial lawyers who handle death penalty trials do not always limit their practice to only capital trials, whereas post-trial capital lawyers often work in resource centers devoted exclusively to death penalty appeals and habeas petitions. This means that whereas post-trial lawyers are embedded in and constitute a culture of resistance to the state killing, capital trial lawyers are often public defenders with experience on a variety of felony trials. This raises the questions of whether or not trial defenders (a) conceptualize themselves as cause lawyers and/or (b) evince characteristics of cause-lawyering, whether or not they think of themselves as such.

The objective of this chapter is to investigate how and why, if at all, capital *trial* defenders are involved in a "cause," whether it be abolition or testimony about social injustice, or perhaps "historical testifying" about hegemonic ideologies. And while I have just identified some obvious reasons why capital trial lawyers may *not* be cause lawyers, there are aspects of the death penalty trial that create unique legal opportunities for "testifying." Most important, as I have already suggested, the penalty phase provides one of the few legal spaces wherein precisely the kinds of "testimonial" narratives described by Sarat are explicitly allowed—where the practice of capital punishment is especially "deregulated." It is in the penalty phase that, for the first time, defenders are legally allowed to "publicly testify" about the *relationship* between the particular injustices of the defendant's life and broader questions of justice. One measure of trial defenders' status as cause lawyers is whether or not they actually make this "relationship" argument when provided the chance. That is to say: it is one thing to point out to the jury the specific injustices of the defendant's inevitably grim social history; it is quite another to make explicit the relationship between these and larger patterns of injustice in society. To do the former, as elucidated in the previous chapter, is to list the sad details of a ruined life with the hope that jurors will develop sympathy. To do the latter is to identify the *causes* of these sad details and to imply that, in a sense, all of U.S. society is implicated in these causes. The implication of such an argument would be that "we" should not execute someone who's sad, ruined life is partially attributable to social forces in which "we" all participate. Jeffrey Reiman made this point years ago:

> If people are subjected to remediable unjust social circumstances beyond their control, and if harmful actions are a predictable response to those conditions, then those who benefit from the unjust conditions and refuse to remedy them share responsibility for the harmful acts—and thus neither their doing nor their cost can be assigned fully to the offenders alone. . . . Since I believe that the vast majority of murders in America are a predictable response to the frustrations and disabilities of impoverished social circumstances, and since I believe that that impoverishment is a remediable injustice from which others in America benefit, I believe that we have no right to exact the full cost of murders from our murderers until we have

done everything possible to rectify the conditions that produce their crimes. (Reiman, 1985, p. 131–32)

However, this is not a strategically viable argument to make explicitly, and trial defenders know this. The interesting question, of course, is *why* is it not strategically viable? Why would such an argument lack verisimilitude? My argument here is that the "connecting-small-to-large" argument fails *strategically* because it is threatening to individualism. Individualism's hegemony presents the most powerful reason why trial defenders may not be cause lawyers—because "testifying" about the "cause" (again, in both senses) would most likely lead to a death sentence for their client.

This raises the question of what exactly is the "cause" for death penalty cause lawyers. Is it abolition? This is part of the equation. But is it also, as Sarat argues, historical testimony about social injustice? The latter of these causes is subversive to the extent that it can challenge the notion that human beings are monadic willful agents. The vague sense of "social determinism" that underlies the "social injustice" argument opposes the individualism that underlying prosecution depictions of the "selfish, willful killer." Following Sarat's work on cause lawyering, I now take up the specific question of whether or how capital *trial* attorneys are involved in "testifying" about the relationship between the "small" injustices of their own client's world to the "larger" injustices partially engendered by American individualism.

TRIAL DEFENDERS

As mentioned earlier, death penalty research using qualitative methods such as transcript analysis or interviews (as opposed to quantitative studies, such as tests of racial disparity or deterrence) has focused on the practices of elite defense attorneys (see, for example, Sarat, 2001). This approach has the advantage of offering insight about the "state of the art" in capital litigation, but has the disadvantage of overlooking the everyday world of mundane death penalty trials. Note that capital trials are relatively common in California (although executions are not).[8] It is important to interview and observe experienced, prominent capital litigators, but it is also important to see how the average trial defender handles the average capital trial. The defense attorneys I interviewed were mostly public defenders who had worked on three or fewer capital trials. Many of them had attended death penalty conferences and had undergone special training, and most are well respected for their dedication and competence, but none were high-profile members of the elite guild in the death penalty defense bar.

THE SUBVERSIVE NATURE OF
HISTORICAL TESTIFYING

As briefly discussed earlier, one basic aspect of the "historical testifying" described by Sarat is a process of connecting the "small" narrative of the particular defendant's case to a "big" narrative about injustice (see Sarat, 1998, p. 324). This process is similar to Ewick and Silbey's (1995) notion of subversion wherein some narratives have the counterhegemonic potential to unmask relations between the individual and his or her social world: "Subversive stories recount particular experiences as *rooted* in and part of an encompassing cultural, material, and political world that extends beyond the local" (p. 219, emphasis in original).

What might death penalty narratives be subversive *of?* In the context of capital trials, the narrative battleground is often over causality or volition. In the penalty phase, after guilt has been decided, competing versions of the violence of the murder and the social history of the defendant tend to focus on the autonomy of the defendant. As we have seen, capital prosecutors tend to construct simplistic narratives of individual responsibility while defenders tend to tell stories about the influence of social forces on the defendant's actions. Of course, in particular trials, both sides sometimes stray from this overly simplistic binary—in reality, the "agency-versus-structure" dichotomy is never as simple as it is in academic discourse. Scholars from many disciplines have addressed this conceptual binary in exhaustive theoretical detail, and some have proposed theories that bridge the gap to conceive of humans as agents, but acting within particular sociohistorical contexts that limit perceived and material possibilities for action (Ortner, 2003; see also Dunn and Kaplan, 2009, for a discussion of this theoretical issue). Despite the complexity of the *reality* of the agency-structure nexus, in death penalty trials, lawyers tend to weave their respective narratives of responsibility in somewhat simplistic terms; especially prosecutors, as we shall see in the next chapter. Moreover, the theoretical agency-structure binary serves as a useful heuristic tool for analyzing actual trial narratives.

Given the focus on social forces in capital defense narratives, it seems likely that these stories might potentially be subversive of the individualism articulated in prosecution narratives. Indeed, the prototypical or "generic" defense narrative in penalty phases is temporally long, sometimes spanning generations, situating the defendant within a complex social world wherein his specific violent actions are partially determined by forces outside of himself. Such a narrative would appear to be classically subversive (per Ewick and Silbey [1995])—especially if the relationship between larger forces of injustice and the defendant's actions are made explicit. If this connection is made, capital defenders are trying to tell the jury that human action is partially caused by social forces—something close to "social determinism"—and thus are engaged in a type of cause that transcends not only abolition of capital punishment but also transcends general injustices, such as racism, inequality, and unfairness.

Of course, it would be a major piece of "historical testifying" to argue that individualism is the root of the violence of a particular murder. Rarely do we hear in the nonacademic death penalty conversation something resembling the "social determinism" narrative: "American society cooperatively produces the conditions that sometimes foment violence and that therefore it would be illogical and immoral to execute violent persons because the *cause* of the violence cannot reside exclusively and solely within the mind or heart of the violent person, and indeed resides, to some extent, in all of us." To put it crudely, the argument would be: if "society let him down" then it would wrong for society to execute him. Such an understanding of violence would challenge individualism and simultaneously resist the law's "blind-justice" tendency to bracket out the role of individualism in producing the oppressive, dystopic conditions of life for many of America's poor. To make such an argument would be another form of "remembering the future," one that goes beyond a protest against state killing or racial inequality and to a recording of individualism's hegemonic role in producing violence.

DIMINISHED AUTONOMY REVISITED

The taken-for-granted, "comes without saying" dominance of individualism in the United States makes it strategically risky for trial defenders to engage in cause lawyering. In the trials discussed in the previous chapter, both sides tend to frame the defendant's actions causally in individualistic terms. Trial defenders usually delineated some contextual factors and sometimes attributed some degree of causality to those factors, implying the possibility of something in between pure individual free will and "social determinism." But rarely did any trial defender connect the "small" injustices of the particular defendant's life to the "big" injustices in society, nor did they describe the ideological upshot of this argumentation, that individualism is partially implicated in violence.

Rather, defenders aim to construct narratives that portray a "liminal man," a character instantiating a conceptualization of the influence of social forces on human free will, namely the aforementioned concept of "diminished autonomy." In a sense, diminished autonomy bridges the gap between the overused and simplistic dichotomy of "agency" and "structure," suggesting that the indeterminacy of free will is not quite as radical as most people believe. Stetler's diminished autonomy thus represents a *conceptualization of subjectivity* that is similar to Ortner's (2005), which includes "the ensemble of modes of perception, affect, thought, desire, fear and so forth that animate acting subjects . . . as well [as] the cultural and social formations that shape, organize, and provoke those modes of affect, thought, etc." (p. 31). This nuanced vision of human subjectivity is supposed to be the stock-in-trade of state of the art capital mitigation.[9]

But when defenders do take up something like a diminished autonomy argument, it is usually implicit or tentative. For example, this trial defender dances around the possibility that his client's free will was limited and influenced by social forces in a penalty phase argument:[10]

> What does childhood matter? You know that old contest between what is our basic nature: Is it determined by nature, or is it determined by nurture? . . . Nature versus nurture. Does childhood matter? Is human nature inherently good and then it's spoiled by something, or is it inherently evil? Or is it both? Or is it neither? And where does free will come into this thing? Obviously, we have to assume in the guilt phase that everybody has a choice. Everybody has free will because we have to protect ourselves. Safety comes first. And so we can't be engaged in the causes and in these philosophical and religious concerns because we have to protect each other. That is done . . . What do you really think about free will? Remember during voir dire when [an attorney] brought up that staircase versus the elevator and how every day when he comes to work he has a choice, take that elevator or take the stairs? I guess he has a choice . . . And he also brought up cigarettes. I mean I notice that some of you smoke. I know you have a choice, but it's a tough one. It's not something that, you know—that you need to say, well, every time I light a cigarette, I've got a choice. I think it has to do with the drop in the nicotine level of your blood more than anything is when you get that idea that you've got to light up. These are religious and philosophical concerns. They aren't legal. We've already decided where he is going to die. He is going to die in prison. What you have to decide is whether we need to decide when or to leave it to nature or God. (Trial 33, 7039–7041)

Cleverly, the defender here attempts to draw a parallel between the quasideterministic aspects of his client's social history and an addiction to nicotine. But as should be clear by his emphasis on the jury's choice and the jury's opinion about free will, his argumentation never moves beyond a vague implication that free will is slightly more complex than prosecutors make it out to be, and certainly does not explicitly address the role of state policies or marginalizing individualism in creating his client's social history. This becomes clearer as he somewhat strangely equates an assumption of total free will with public safety: "Obviously, we have to assume in the guilt phase that everybody has a choice. Everybody has free will because we have to protect ourselves. Safety comes first. And

so we can't be engaged in the causes and in these philosophical and religious concerns because we have to protect each other" (Trial 33, 7039).
The implication here is that the safety purportedly provided by the law
is too important to jeopardize by threatening its formalist foundations
with "philosophical concerns" about degrees or a continuum of free will.
Indeed, one way to read this passage is an *instantiation* of individualism.
The trial defender here is speaking individualism's hegemony—even as
individualism oppresses his client, he extols its necessity.[11]

Most defense narratives lacked even the limited sense of diminished
autonomy hinted at in the long quote above. Instead, if the defenders
introduced the idea that social forces matter at all, most did so gingerly,
often in the midst of valorizations of individualism. In the following
passage, the defender proposes the idea of diminished autonomy while
simultaneously acknowledging the primacy of free will:

> [The prosecutor] talked about choices a minute ago. And it's always a theme
> that arises in cases like this. And we will present that evidence to you to
> show not that he didn't have free will, not that he couldn't exercise free will,
> but that the ability to exercise that free will would be more limited than you,
> for example, or most people—you know—that his view of choices and his
> ability to control himself within those choices would be a little less than most
> people. (Trial 2, 5395–5396)

Similarly, this passage suggests the possibility of diminished autonomy, but also defers to the primacy of individual free will:

> I just have a note on free choice that relates up to that diagram. Yes, there
> was free choice. That is clear. And we will not deny that. The ultimate issue
> is, you have, just like there was free choice for everybody else that commits
> these terrible crimes. The question you have to decide whether the free
> choice is of such a quality that maybe you can find some reason and un-
> derstanding in it. And that is where I ask you to go back to those particular
> stressors on him and that particular model which is him and his coping skills
> and his childhood all erupting at that particular time. (Trial 10, 6745)

Here the defender makes a causal argument about childhood trauma
and adult autonomy, but does so while contemporaneously "not denying" that the defendant chose to murder the victim. These penalty phase
arguments exemplify the common practice among capital defenders of
"explaining but not excusing" their client's murders; of walking a tightrope with total free will on one side and social determinism on the other.

In most of these cases, defenders did not explicitly discuss "free will,"
but instead listed childhood (or at least precrime) traumas and either
implied or explicitly argued that these earlier traumas had a causal relationship with the murder, often implying or declaring that the trauma is

not an excuse but an explanation. For example, in this case, the defender vividly describes a series of traumatic events and suggests that these events can explain (but not excuse) the defendant's crimes:

> I wonder what a child learns at age four when he's forced by his father to rub excrement on his chest. I wonder what that child learns that becomes a part of him and that he carries with him the rest of his life. I wonder what a child learns from he's called shit for brains and he's unequivocally rejected by his father. I wonder what a child learns when his father hits his face and his cheek, strikes his braces and oozes blood. And then he still has to go to school that day, suffering the pain and the humiliation. Is it any wonder that [the defendant] turned to drugs and alcohol to escape the pain that he experienced? I don't offer this as the so-called abuse excuse, but it certainly sheds a lot of light on how [the defendant] came to sit in this courtroom in the chair he's in. (Trial 9, 6448–6449)

To the extent that this passage catalogs abuse, it is representative of many passages in the penalty phase arguments I analyzed in this project. But unlike in this passage, most others often did not include the causal rhetoric and simply listed traumatic events and explained to the jury that they "can consider" them when rendering their decision. With few exceptions, the trial narratives in these data rarely went beyond citing defendants' life traumas to make an explicit argument about how traumatic experiences diminish persons' autonomy.

THE POTENTIAL LETHALITY OF SUBVERSION

When asked about the possibility of including potentially subversive themes in trial stories, defenders made clear that such a "cause" risked offending jurors and resulting in a death sentence. For example, one mitigation specialist told me about a recent case in which the defendant was accused of ordering several murders to enforce his control over drug markets in a Midwestern city. The defendant is originally from California, and allegedly a major gang leader who brought his crack cocaine operation to a state in the Midwest. According to the mitigation specialist I interviewed, this defendant wanted to put on a defense that explicitly challenged capitalism and the U.S. government. His line of argument, according to my interviewee, was that government policies and extreme poverty created the conditions in his community that spawned the notorious drug markets of the 1980s and 1990s. His argument was essentially that "the government kept us poor and brought the crack into the community to keep us down," (Mitigation Specialist #1), which is quite an explicit and potentially subversive critique of capitalism and the government. This defendant demanded of his defense team that this argument be used in court during his trial.

This discussion reminded me of a case I worked on myself in my previous career as a mitigation investigator. In that case, my client also wished to use his capital trial as a forum of protest—in this case against a nebulous "modern society" that the defendant believed oppressed all people. In both cases, the defendant's legal team steered him away from such a "cause" and instead assembled a more standard and presumably jury-palatable social history narrative for the penalty phase.[12] The standard social history narrative constructed in each of these cases included some of the aspects of poverty and dystopia that each defendant attributed to their "causes" (capitalism and government conspiracies for the former and "modern society" for the latter), but cast the defendant as a victim of trauma rather than as a subversive "Robin Hood" or "revolutionary" type rebel. The following exchange between me and the mitigation specialist on the "drug kingpin" case is a good example of the attitude I encountered when bringing up the idea of the cause lawyering with trial caseworkers:

Q: On that note, I've always wondered why, why do you think it is that the kind of ideological arguments that I'm talking about right now aren't made in trials or post convictions?

A: They are too scary

Q: For who?

A: For our clients.

Q: They would lose.

A: Yeah I think you would lose. Plus, as a community it's hard to try these things. You got to stick with what works, and even if you stick with what works, it doesn't work. Also, maybe it's me not having too much faith in our jurors or our peers, but it's hard enough to present simple arguments to our juries.

Q: It goes over their heads . . .

A: Yeah, it makes them responsible, we're kind of making them responsible always, it makes all of us responsible, but pointing that out could be the wrong move

Q: Strategic disaster. It is. I've always thought that it always means that the death of this guy . . .

A: Is it worth it?

Q: I don't know, what do you think?

A: I think no. I mean, if you could tell me, for sure, I would still think no. It sounds horrible.

Q: I think what I said sounds horrible, it's really cold. What I'm trying to say is, you and I know, and we don't have to talk about any specifics, we have worked on two cases where the guy had some interest in making some ideological argument for himself. Right? One is the big federal trial we both worked on, and the one you're working on now. Am I right? Why not let him?

A: Because it's scary, because of these messages. One is the message that right now, the way our country is, the jurors wouldn't be able to handle . . . this case is in [the Midwest] . . .

Q: I should ask a juror this and not you . . . but why do you think it's so scary then?

A: I think people over there especially, the majority of people in the country, but people in [the Midwest], for certain, are more fear based than the rest of us. And will fear someone who is perceived as a terrorist, or someone who sympathizes with people who have been called terrorists. That's really scary. We're trying to get our client away from that.

Q: What if he's right?

A: It doesn't matter, unfortunately. A lot of the stuff he says and writes about, he is right. He has become a product of what we have made him.

Q: A real capitalist society.

A: Yeah, he grew up in [the ghetto], where we brought in the crack. He became a crack dealer. We made him this, and he's saying, "Look, you can't punish me for making me do this . . . you made me do it." I agree with that. Jurors in [the Midwest] are not going to buy that, and they're not going to care. It's going to actually piss them off.

Q: It's insulting to them, because they are like, "Hey man you got to take responsibility for yourself."

A: Exactly, how dare you put that ideology, how do you put that on me. I didn't go out and kill all those people, I didn't make those choices. It's easy to sit and talk about choices we might have made, if we were in those situations. Well, you're not in those situations, you don't know what choices you have, you don't understand choice, a lot of these people . . . it's all you have (Mitigation Specialist #1).

For this caseworker, critiquing the state's (or "society's") role in creating the violent crack markets of the 1980s and 1990s might equate to "terrorism" in the minds of jurors, at least in the Midwest. As such, it is strategically *verboten*—precisely because such a critique has the effect of animating or vivifying the relationship between the jurors' participation in U.S. society's individualistic capitalism and the violence it (individualistic capitalism) produces. Put simply, such a narrative points the finger at the jurors and declares, "You are partially responsible for the murders this man committed." This situation brings jurors and the defendant together—but in the inverse direction as "humanizing"; instead of characterizing the defendant as "like" jurors, it implicates jurors in the defendant's violence, characterizing them as "more like" him. Using a capital trial to advocate a "cause" such as those desired by these defendants would thus represent subversion. Cause lawyering of this type, however, seems to be precluded by the hegemony of individualism because challenging ideologies is understood by capital defenders as lethal for their clients.

HUMANIZING V. OTHERIZING

In order to learn about their potential roles as cause lawyers, I studied the *processes* by which defenders construct narratives in their trials. In doing so, I undertook conversations with trial defenders about their general impressions of working on a death penalty case, their goals at the various parts of the trial, their preparations, their understanding of stories or narratives in court, the objectives of these stories, the process of constructing the stories, their sense of whether or not their stories "rang true" for jurors (if their stories had "verisimilitude"), constraints on their stories and storytelling, their opinions about how these stories related to larger discourses in society about free will and responsibility, their opinion about the death penalty's role in society, and their opinion about retention. In addition, I asked questions specifically about purposes of their advocacy work that might transcend the particulars of any given case.

Although most defenders told me it is difficult to generalize about their approaches to capital cases, it became clear that several key themes related to cause-lawyering resonate for many of them. Most of the defenders I interviewed said that their primary goal when handling a death penalty case is to save their client's life. As one defender put it: "Ordinarily guilt or innocence is never much of an issue. The goal is to try and save the guy's life" (Defender #1).[13]

For a different defender, the life-saving goal is bittersweet:

Q: So then, when you're doing these cases what do you think of as your primary goal? I could imagine someone saying, "I follow the law."

A: The end goal has to be to save the client's life and there are times that that bothers me. Having that as a goal means that if the prosecutor lets your client plead to life without the possibility of parole then it satisfies your goal. The case I had last year shouldn't have been a death case, it should have been a first degree murder case and maybe even a second degree murder case. . . . But there was enough hue and cry out in the hinterlands about protecting the people out in the remote areas I guess that's why the DA decided to seek death. My client's record was not that bad and it certainly wasn't the worst. . . . So when I was able to bring the DA around to agree to life without the possibility of parole it was something that we had to consider. I had to convince my client about the wisdom of it. That was hard. Those are hard discussions. . . . The end goal has to be to preserve the client's life. (Defender #5)

This defender expresses the frustration that many defenders feel when obtaining LWOP for their clients—LWOP certainly satisfies the goal of preserving the defendant's life, but doesn't feel much like victory. In ordinary criminal trials, the goal is usually to aim for significantly reduced punishment or acquittal; a life sentence is normally seen as a dismal failure for defense attorneys. But the possibility of a death sentence drastically changes their perspective, prerogatives, and strategies. Saving a life eclipses all other considerations, ironically creating a sense of *narrowness* to capital trials that should, in light of the openness of penalty phase proceedings, have a sense of broadness or deregulation. Put another way, despite the law's deregulation of the death penalty trial, defender norms create a different sort of regulation, one based on the primary goal of saving a life.

Most defenders I interviewed understood their life-saving narratives as having two primary interrelated objectives, "humanizing" the defendant, and "explaining" (but not excusing) the murder.

I have to have the jury know that my client is human. A case that I had last year that settled, my client, an undocumented alien who was in the United States, killed a woman. He kind of burglarized this house, the woman was away, and he was staying there, and he was desperate to get back to Los Angeles where he used to live. Where he has a life, a common law wife, where he has a child that was born while he was in prison. He has been in prison for not the most serious of offenses, for threatening someone with a gun, and got probation for that, and then was involved in a domestic dispute with his wife and they revoked his probation and sent him back to prison. He goes to prison. His son is born while he is in prison. He is illegal, as many clients are. He gets deported to Mexico from prison. Well all he wants to do is get back to L.A. He was working. He is a good worker, all of those things. All he wants is to get back to L.A., so he enters illegally and the border patrol catches him and sends him back. And a couple of days later he enters illegally and the border patrol catches him and throws him back. And this happens, in a month, at least three times he gets caught and sent back. And he is calling his wife in L.A. saying, "I'm trying to get there." And finally he gets in [a rural area], a very isolated area. He gets to a phone and calls. "Can somebody come pick me up? Can somebody come give me a ride?" But nobody can. And so he is in this house and this woman comes over to feed the animals and he asks her for a ride, this is according to him, she picked up a gun and started threatening him. It was a starter pistol, but he didn't know that. So he threw something and then hit her in the head and beat her and killed her. So that was the case. There is a story there about him. If I compare him to Jeffrey Dahmer he sounds better than Jeffrey Dahmer. (Defender #5)

In a similar way as the defense narrative in the Ricardo Arguello case discussed in the previous chapter, this passage provides a good example of the relationship between "explaining" and "humanizing" because it shows how it is through the process of "explaining" the murder that the defendant becomes "human." This synopsized tale of desperate border crossing resembles those of countless Latinos in California. This "explanation"—that the defendant ended up killing the victim in the midst of what appears to be a desperate struggle for survival—is supposed to vivify him, rendering him not unlike persons known to jurors. In this sense, "humanizing" may be too imprecise a term to describe the rhetoric of "explanation." To argue "he is human" is tautological—every person is human. What "humanizing" really signifies here is the idea that murder defendants are not "alien" humans, but characters familiar to and normal to jurors. This narrative demonstrates individualism's hegemony—jurors are meant to empathize with the bootstrapping aspects of the story that call to mind a Horatio Alger novel. According to the defender, his client is an oppressed working immigrant trying to support his family, striving to join the "American Dream" of work and stability. Indeed, this is precisely what is meant to convey his humanity. "Humanity" equates to an underdog striving to attain the American Dream.[14]

Another trial defender discusses the importance of "humanizing":

Q: Okay so how do you develop those arguments? I know there's the facts, but are there other factors that go into your coming up with the argument?

A: Sure. My jurors. I know a lot of my jurors at that point, and I try to fashion an argument. Sometimes I'm successful and other times I'm not, but I try to fashion an argument that will appeal to one or more of the jurors. How do I do it? I always try to humanize my client. That's what I try to do. I often try to think of it as there is a circle of humanity that the prosecution is trying to put my client out of and virtually in every case I've ever tried I know this person. I feel like he is very much like me, because of circumstances of growing up or whatever, I try to convey to the jury that this person is not outside our circle of humanity and here are the parts about him or her that make them worth living. (Defender #4)

In this instance, the defender speaks generally about humanizing, not drawing a connection between explaining and humanizing. Yet this passage reveals her consciousness about the processes of "otherizing"—and her job to fend it off—that takes place in capital trials.[15] From the perspective of prosecutors, capital defendants are not "one of us" but one of *them*, something alien and monstrous. Defenders work to recharacterize their clients as "us," as "human."[16]

How do jurors respond to humanizing and explaining-but-not-excusing? Due to the limitations of my data set, which consists entirely of death sentence cases, I cannot empirically answer this question because I do not have a control group. This study is not an investigation into the effect of narratives on trial outcomes. But investigating trial defenders' attitudes about the verisimilitude of such narratives is important because it reveals defenders' consciousness of ideology in the law; defender use of individualistic stories reveals a knowledge—perhaps unconscious—that individualism seems truthful and more likely to convince jurors. This situation sheds light on the question of the broader definition of cause lawyering that I have discussed in this chapter. If trial defenders are thinking about the verisimilitude of their narratives primarily in terms of *outcomes* it suggests that they are engaged in something less than cause lawyering.

ARE CAPITAL TRIAL DEFENDERS CAUSE LAWYERS?

To the extent that they oppose state killing and sometimes illuminate social inequality, the defenders studied in this project are engaging in something beyond the parameters of their particular trials, and thus fall on the relatively "professional" side of the continuum of cause lawyering delineated by Sarat and Schiengold (1998). However, considering that they are unaware of, avoid, or suppress subversive arguments within the expansive discursive space afforded by penalty phase proceedings, they may be "forgetting the future" precisely so that their clients may avoid a death sentence. As Sarat and Schiengold (1998) point out in their introductory essay on cause lawyering, discussing Luban: "The politically motivated lawyer acts ethically not by evading the essentially political character of relationships but by responsibly representing the political aims of her entire client constituency even at the price of wronging individual clients" (p. 4). At least in these limited data, this political action does not take place.

I have argued in this chapter that this partial "forgetting of the future" can be explained by the hegemony of individualism. In a society where "only individuals count," the attorneys working in perhaps *the* principal institution governing that society (the law) inhale and exhale individualism whether it helps or hurts their "entire client base." Individualism is hegemonic, in the classic, Gramscian sense of invisible power. The hegemony of individualism is so profound, I argue, that it rarely occurs to capital trial lawyers to contemplate how to challenge it.

However, as scholars of resistance narratives have shown, rarely is hegemonic domination a simple, one-way-street dynamic. Rather, hegemony is perpetuated dialectically:

> Finding expression and being refashioned within the stories of countless individuals may lead to a polyvocality that inoculates and protects the master narrative from critique. The hegemonic strength of a master narrative derives, Brinkly Messick (1988: 657) writes, from "its textual, and lived heteroglassia . . . , [s]ubverting and dissimulating itself at every . . . turn"; thus ideologies that are encoded in particular stories are "effectively protected from sustained critique" by the fact that they are constituted through variety and contradiction. (Ewick and Silbey, 1995, p. 212)

The concept of diminished autonomy inherently challenges the notion that "only individuals count." As I have claimed in this chapter, diminished autonomy can be understood as a liminal state, something like a bridge between "agency" and "structure" to explain events (such as homicide). As such, it casts a suspicious (if not truly or entirely subversive) light on the veracity of a liberal, rational-formal legal system that usually precludes discourses that assign blame outside of the individual. In this sense, diminished autonomy is, perhaps, a step toward ideological cause lawyering, although—following Ewick and Silbey—it might also be seen as a temporary antithesis in the dialectical reproduction of individualism's hegemonic power.

Is it possible to subvert individualism during legal proceedings? Under what conditions might lawyers who believe that individualism itself (beyond racism, unfairness or the other normative complaints of capital defense attorneys) harms their "entire client base" be able to say something about it without risking death?

Recall that Ewick and Silbey (1995) argue that several conditions are probably necessary for subversive narratives to emerge. First, the narrator must be socially marginalized because it is "the marginal whose lives and experiences are least likely to find expression in the culturally available plots and characters" (p. 220). Second, the narrator must have an awareness of the structural or institutional plausibility of creating a subversive story: "Knowing the rules and perceiving a concealed agenda enhance the possibilities of intervention and resistance" (p. 221). Finally, the venue for the potentially subversive story must "create both a common opportunity to narrate and a common content to the narrative, thus revealing the collective organization of personal life" (p. 221). As explained earlier in this book, each of these characteristics is on display in the context of capital trials. Defendants are almost always marginalized, their defenders understand the institutional parameters the law provides for telling their story, and the capital penalty phase furnishes one of the few venues in the

American legal system where these types of stories are at least theoretically possible.

Nevertheless, as this study suggests, it may be impossible to employ subversive story telling in capital *trials* precisely because of the ironic narrowness created by the life-saving prerogative discussed above—although the rules governing penalty phase proceedings provide a venue for just about any kind of evidence or argument, the life-saving norm straightjackets trial defenders into telling "jury-friendly" stories that won't upset the ideological apple cart.

I began this chapter discussing Austin Sarat's (1998) study of cause lawyering among *posttrial* capital defenders, and I return to it now because while capital *trials* seem to largely preclude ideological cause lawyering, the jury-free, temporally long context of postconviction proceedings seem to leave more room for taking on ideologies. As Sarat convincingly shows, many posttrial death penalty lawyers "remember the future" and see their work as ideological protest in the form of testimonial. This may be simply because posttrial lawyers have more time—death penalty appeals are measured in years, trials in days.

We might search for subversive stories farther along in the process of state killing to include clemency hearings. Perhaps those advocates begging for their client's lives in the short days or weeks prior to an execution date are able to "remember the future" and make a record of protest against individualism's harms. This seems unlikely to me, however, precisely because of the near totally one-way relation of power in clemency hearings. As Sarat (2005) makes clear in a different text, the possibility of *mercy* created by clemency is directly related to the total discretion of an executive of the state (usually a governor) (see p. 69; see also Whitman, 2003, chapter 3). Only those with near-monarchical power are in a position to grant mercy. In such a context, resistance narratives seem exceedingly unlikely unless the resistor has resigned himself to a Pyrrhic and ultimately self-immolating victory. My choice of the word "begging" when describing the discourses of lawyers representing the condemned at clemency hearings was not offhand. When one is a beggar, it is usually rather difficult to challenge the hegemony of the beggee.

Finally, the work of Avi Brisman suggests that the potential for resistance to hegemony may be found, or at least searched for, at every step of the death penalty process—even the very last steps. Brisman (2009) proposes that certain forms of "volunteering" (the waiver or withdrawal of appeals by the condemned) might be understood as an individual form of agency and protest against state power (see p. 3). This is quite a controversial argument, and one that is fervently resisted by many in the capital defense bar because of the lethal result and what some perceive to be a naïve and overly abstract orientation to state killing. Nevertheless,

Brisman's argument is worth considering in light of his suggestion that such an approach might function to consolidate resistors by connecting the condemned with others involved in different, unrelated protests against state power (p. 19).

Recall from chapter 4, LaChance's (2007) somewhat similar argument about the sense of individual agency inscribed on the condemned through their "last meals" and "last words." The difference between LaChance and Brisman on these final moments of the condemned person's life is that Brisman explicitly views condemned agency as potentially resistant of the state, while LaChance sees the dead-man-walking's last moments of individuality as a kind of faux agency. Indeed, LaChance argues that "last meals" and "last words" simply offer *the veneer* of agency for doomed prisoners; just enough of a veneer as to retain the retribution that keeps the death penalty popular:

> Executions cannot be retributive and thus cannot produce the experience of catharsis, social solidarity, or pleasure that retribution brings, unless they are informed by discursive constructions of the offender as both self-controlled and out of control, calculating and calculable, agentic and inert. . . . The persistence in contemporary executions of unpredictable last words and customized last meals can be understood, then, not in opposition to rational practices [of execution] but rather as part of those forces. Ultimately, rationalization demands optimization, the attainment of that ideal balance between meeting a goal as completely and successfully as possible while expending the least amount of time, energy, and resources possible. . . . Successful rationalization, then, must ultimately involve the minimization of the expressive elements of executions to the lowest level necessary to meet the expectations set by retributive public discourses on crime and punishment, not the total elimination of those elements. (p. 10)

For LaChance, then, the agency of the condemned man is literally co-opted by the state. Resistance by any of these measures—cause lawyering, volunteering, or making rebellious "last words"—seems futile.

In conclusion, the simple question of whether or not capital trial defenders are cause lawyers is, in a sense, beside the point. The point I wish to make in this chapter is that the capital trial, which seems to offer the best legal venue for resistance, turns out to be quite restrictive. This is so, in part because capital trial lawyers, like most everyone else in contemporary U.S. society, live and breathe individualism.

NOTES

1. Sometimes the state's response can have dire consequences for cause lawyers, as in the example of Lynne F. Stewart, a defender of unpopular political

defendants including members of the Weather Underground and most important convicted terrorist Sheikh Omar Abdel-Rahman. In 2005, Stewart was convicted of "aiding terrorism" by conveying messages for Abdel-Rahman and sentenced to federal prison (see Reinholz, 2005).

2. Jenkins (1980) points out the law's inherent limitations as a mode for social change.

3. This Gramscian notion of hegemony focuses on the invisibility of power processes. Colloquial uses of "hegemony" often exclude consideration of power's visibility, rendering "hegemony" a synonym for "domination" or "repression." I explicitly employ the original meaning of the word.

4. I also informally interviewed several mitigation specialists.

5. See Zimring (2003) p. 146–49 for an excellent discussion of the judiciary's dissatisfaction with the practices of capital defense attorneys.

6. Although the U.S. Supreme Court ruled that lethal injection is basically constitutional in *Baze v. Rees* (2008), local jurisdictions are still attending to various technical and legal issues surrounding the actual practice of lethal injection executions (see Furillo, 2008).

7. Technically, "postconviction attorney" refers to an attorney working on claims *outside* the record—essentially a habeas attorney—while "appellate attorney" refers to a lawyer working on claims based on the record of the trial. Most death penalty lawyers working on cases posttrial work on both aspects, although many certainly specialize in either "legal" issues (from the record) or "habeas issues" (often complex social history evidence). Although it might be interesting to investigate differences between habeas and direct-appeal specialists vis-à-vis the question of cause lawyering, I do not take up that question in this article. Hereafter, I use the term "posttrial" to include both.

8. It is hard to know precisely why executions are so rare in California, but one likely explanation is the slow and contentious postconviction process. The recently convened California Commission on the Fair Administration of Justice has gone as far as to declare that "the backlogs in post-conviction proceedings will continue to grow until the system falls of its own weight" (p. 4).

9. The "liminal man" can be interestingly contrasted with LaChance's (2007) notion of the "self-made monster"; both characters are driven by individual agency along with something else. In the case of the "liminal man" that something else is the influence of complex social forces; in the case of the "self-made monster" that something else is "evil."

10. This defendant was convicted of capital murder and sentenced to death for participating in the kidnapping, rape, robbery, and lethal shooting of one woman. His codefendant got LWOP; each defendant claimed the other pulled the trigger.

11. This trial defender later makes one of the more strenuous arguments in this data set about the diminishing effects childhood trauma has on adult autonomy.

12. In both cases, the defendant received a sentence of LWOP.

13. Notably, as discussed in the next chapter, no prosecutor said that her goal in a capital trial is to kill the defendant. Rather, they tend to describe their goals in terms of following the law and fairness.

14. Perhaps not surprisingly, prosecutors tend to construct negative mirror image narrations of defendants, emphasizing the details that oppose defense versions

of "humanity," such as laziness, irresponsibility, and antisocial violence. Of course, these attributes are just as human as the "good" ones delineated by defenders. Concepts of "human" and "humanizing" are complex, subtle, and suffused with ideological meaning—something rarely consciously reflected upon by trial defenders and prosecutors.

15. Fleury-Steiner's (2004) book *Jurors Stories of Death* is a good source on "otherizing" in capital trials.

16. However, defenders' consciousness about jurors is complex, and also evidently influenced by individualism. When defenders recast jurors as benevolent heroes who can take pity on the condemned and vote for LWOP, it is not because they hope that jurors will identify with the condemned's depravity, but because they want jurors to see themselves as merciful *individuals*. This strategy aims to make individualism work on behalf of the defendant rather than against him. But true subversion would involve a leveling down of the juror to the level of the defendant, of getting the jurors to see blood on their own hands. True subversion would "deindividualize" the juror in ways that might preclude the possibility of "mercy" because mercy can only be granted by a sovereign individual. In this sense, we can see how individualism drives defenders' beliefs about both defendants and jurors, in different ways. Thanks to Daniel LaChance for pointing this out to me.

6

● ● ●

Facts and Furies

The Antinomies of Facts, Law, and Retribution in the Work of Capital Prosecutors

Having now analyzed capital trials and capital trial defense attorneys, I turn in this final chapter to the work of prosecutors, revisiting the investigative theme that partially drives any study of the death penalty in the United States—the question of retention of capital punishment.

As I have discussed throughout this book, many factors suggest that the death penalty's days may be numbered in the United States. However, state lawmakers in some jurisdictions have advocated—or actually passed—new laws *expanding* the use of capital punishment to include death sentences for defendants convicted of sexually assaulting children (see Hart, 2006).[1] These conflicting trends raise, once again, the question of whether or when the United States is going to cease the practice of state killing.

One way of investigating capital punishment's life or death in the United States is to examine the practices and consciousnesses of persons who work professionally to inflict the death penalty on particular persons—capital prosecutors. In this chapter, I analyze the work of California capital prosecutors. The results show that prosecutor discourses and attitudes evince a paradox of sorts—while instantiating powerful ideological themes that may underlie state killing (such as retribution and individualism) in trial discourses and also interviews, prosecutors also assert the primacy of "facts" and "law." Why is this paradoxical? It is firstly because there is a tension between the formally rational, bureaucratic *process* through which prosecutors narratively construct reality and the profoundly affective *content* of that constructed reality. Secondly, prosecutors' commitment to and valorization of the formally rational "law" is at odds with their belief that the law's *purpose* is to provide retribution on the behalf of the families of murder victims and also society in general. While this tension does not represent a strict measure of capital punishment's lifespan, its enduring presence in the operation of the law suggests that these types of tensions are not enough to change the law, thereby hinting that while the death penalty may be weakened and may well continue to be whittled down in the United States, it is not close to dying.

CAPITAL PUNISHMENT'S INDELIBILITY

The source of capital punishment's (possible) indelibility in the United States is a complex and difficult to measure question—one taken up by several prominent death penalty scholars, and discussed at length in earlier chapters of this book. Briefly reviewing, some have argued that "American Exceptionalism," in various forms, explains U.S. retention of the death penalty. The arguments range from Zimring's (2003) proposal that a commitment to vigilantism is the operative variable, to Whitman's (2003) suggestion that American harsh punishment can counter-intuitively be explained by a uniquely American commitment to egalitarianism, to Poveda's argument that an individualistic American Creed creates an "executable class" of persons in the United States. I have added to these theories of U.S. retention that a key force underlying the death penalty, beyond vigilantism, egalitarianism, or individualism, is racialized inequality (see Kaplan, 2006). Executees in the United States almost never look anything like executioners—the "race effect" of murder victims and the disproportionate representation of poor persons of color among the condemned and executed is well established, and nearly all prosecutors in death penalty states are white (Dieter, 1998).

However, another branch of what might be termed the "culturist" literature on capital punishment finds that the death penalty may be abolished relatively soon in the United States due to changing norms. Sarat (2001), for example, argues that a "new abolitionism" has been emerging in the United States that invokes "evolving standards of decency" and constitutional due process protections in taking on capital punishment's *legal* (rather than moral) standing (see p. 252). The essence of this new abolitionism is a valorization *of* the law—rather than a challenge *to* the law:

> The new abolitionism that Blackmun championed presents itself as a reluctant abolitionism, one rooted in acknowledgment of the damage that capital punishment does to central legal values and to the legitimacy of the law itself. It finds its home in an embrace, not a critique, of those values. Those

who love the law, in Blackmun's view, must hate the death penalty for the damage it does to the object of that love. (Sarat, 2001, p. 253)

In Sarat's analysis of capital punishment, a different set of cultural commitments—based on legality and fairness—is required to achieve abolition rather than the familiar moral or religious ideals that have long been associated with abolitionism.[2]

As discussed earlier, Garland (2005, 2010) has more explicitly challenged the "American Exceptionalist" theories of retention by proposing that retention is related not to longstanding cultural forces but instead to the recent crime control policies of late modernity coupled with America's radically local polity. Recall that from Garland's perspective, it is likely that the United States is simply lagging behind its European peers in abolishing the death penalty. After all, according to Garland's logic, if the *Furman v. Georgia* (1972) decision had never been reversed, the U.S. version of abolition would have taken place during the same approximate time as France.

In this chapter, I return to the debate that focuses alternatively on deep and longstanding "American" ideologies or more recent cultural-penal developments, and aim to show how a commitment to affective retribution in the practice of capital punishment operates against the prospect of abolition (albeit in contradiction to the law's rational and formal impulses). This argument is consistent with classic treatments of law and punishment that have long recognized the inherent tension in law between vengeful impulses and a "modern" need for formal rationality.

This chapter also adds to the discussion in death penalty research on *contradictions* of capital punishment. Recall from earlier chapters that many scholars have pointed to various legal tensions brought about by the use of capital punishment. One of the most prominent of these tensions is the problem of the use of an *irrational* punishment in a (purportedly) *rational* society. I do not hope to adjudicate these competing explanations for the presence of an affective death penalty in a purportedly rationally formal legal system. Instead, I argue throughout this chapter that the sometimes vexing concomitance of emotion and rationality in death penalty discourses may itself offer a hint about its persistence—to the extent that the law can continue to abide both "facts" and "furies," it is not, after all, an especially "logical" institution, and thus perhaps not susceptible to the disciplining forces of *rational* arguments against legal state killing (such as a "new abolition").

Beyond the complex and perhaps unresolved sense of contradiction between enlightenment ideals and state killing, capital punishment illuminates a number of other conflicts in American criminal law, such as the competing values of retribution and due process (see Zimring, 2003), the paradox of distinguishing state violence from illegal violence (see Sarat,

2001), as well as other major legal tensions such as the competing values of rationality (nonarbitrariness) and individualization, and the contradictory doctrines of individual culpability and "diminished autonomy."

Aside from these contradictions embodied by the death penalty, I describe in this chapter other legal tensions presented by capital punishment, namely the presence of illogical storytelling in prosecution narratives, and a disjunction between the purportedly neutral and self-evident *facts* and *law* valorized by prosecutors, and the *fury* of the content their arguments about facts and within the law.

FACTS

A noteworthy tension in these data involves an unsettling disjunction in prosecutor discourse and consciousness between the seemingly objective "facts" of the crime and also the purportedly neutral "law," and the florid, affective, and sometimes perhaps hyperbolic nature of the arguments *about* facts and law.

The prosecutors I interviewed for this project all privileged "the facts" as foremost in shaping the contours of the narratives they constructed in trials. For prosecutors, the most important thing to know when putting on a capital case is "the facts" of the crime, which they understand to mean the details of the violent events that caused the death of the victim. The word "fact" in the legal context is something of an idiom, a legal term of art, defined in a popular law dictionary as follows:

> Fact: An event that has occurred or circumstances that exist, events whose actual occurrence or existence is to be determined by the evidence. In deciding a case, a court will find facts on the basis of evidence presented to it, and then apply the law to those facts. In a jury trial, the judge will instruct the jury how to apply the law to the facts, and the jury will then find the facts and render a verdict. (Gifis, 2003)

In my interviews with prosecutors, the relevant "events and circumstances" that guided their process of trying a capital case were limited to the temporally short details about the crime and the key characters involved, and were organized around three inter-related factual dimensions:

1. the circumstances of the crime
2. the background of the defendant, and
3. the victim's profile

Prosecutors told me that their respective departments' policy was to bring cases to an internal committee that would consider these factors and make a recommendation for or against seeking the death penalty to the district attorney.[3] None of the prosecutors I interviewed believed that all three factual dimensions had to seem "death worthy" in order to bring a capital charge, but most believed that something like a rough guide of "two out of the three" dimensions had to have certain characteristics in order to ask for the death penalty. Specifically, some combination of "heinous" facts, a "sympathetic" victim, and a "threatening" defendant would prompt prosecutors to go for death.[4] For example, a crime where the victim was tortured by a defendant with a history of violence was enough, even though the lone victim was not particularly sympathetic, by conventional standards (a drug abusing prostitute). In this case, two of the three dimensions—"heinousness" and a "bad" defendant—were satisfactory for the prosecutor to pursue a death sentence.

One of the notable things about this charging rubric is that prosecutors explicitly consider the *status* of the victim when deciding how to charge persons accused of homicide.[5] This runs contrary to the formally rational law's egalitarian foundations and also suggests that prosecutors may act as personal advocates for victims rather than representatives of the state. Indeed, in these data, prosecutors sometimes represented themselves explicitly as advocates for the dead victim, as in the following quote: "I have a client too. The chair next to me appears to be empty, but his name is [the victim]. And I would like to introduce you to him" (Trial 29, 1556).

In a similar way, a different prosecutor constructed part of her penalty phase argument as a "letter" to the victim: "[The victim] will not be forgotten. We promise that you will not die in vain. We promise that you will always be in our hearts, in our souls. We choose, we collectively choose to adopt you and to care for you" (Trial 14, 12037).

As critics of the adversarial system, such as Givelber (2001) have pointed out, prosecutor advocacy for the victims of crime contributes to a general problem of indeterminate or contested "truths" about the facts of particular cases. In an adversarial system, "The Truth" is negotiated between competing knowledge-producing actors, a process that can, at the least, increase the likelihood of wrongful conviction of the innocent (see Givelber, 2001), and perhaps also result in a misleading or simplistic record of the crime, victim, and defendant.

But despite the adversarial nature of their arguments, prosecutors in interviews consistently emphasized the importance of a *seemingly* neutral "truth" deriving from impartial "facts," as the following quote from an interview indicates:

A: Well in any case I think our primary goal is, as a prosecutor, is to expose the truth. Our system, although it's the best in the world, is slanted towards not telling juries the whole truth . . .

Q: So your goal is to uncover the truth or display the truth for the jury? How do you do that?

A: Well it begins in the very beginning of the assignment. You gather discovery. You make discovery available to the defense. You make all discovery available to the defense under the guidelines of either statutory requirements or Brady material. If it hurts you, it hurts you. If it helps you, it helps you. That's not the purpose of discovery. The purpose of discovery is to say here are the facts. This is what we know about this case and related facts. Then I think you have to be quite candid when you place things for a jury. You don't sugarcoat things. You don't try to give things an aura of truth rather that they don't deserve. You don't make arguments that are disingenuous. Not as a prosecutor, that's not our job. You can expect those things from the defense of the defendant but prosecutors have one duty. That is to do a factual expose of a scenario so the jury can make a decision. (Prosecutor #1)

For this prosecutor, the "truth" is the prosecutor's (and not the defender's) "not disingenuous" narrative of the "relevant" events and circumstances. For prosecutors, the "relevant" events and characteristics tend to have to do with the forensic details of the crime. Other events and characteristics—"facts" brought up by defenders and deemed irrelevant by prosecutors—are red herrings, misleading and "disingenuous."

The "relevant events and circumstances" for prosecutors in the trials in this data set tended to be temporally very short, referring to the events causing the victim's death—except in cases where the defendant had a history of crime or violence, in which cases the relevant events and circumstances tended to equate to a temporally long narrative beginning with and including the forensic details of the defendant's earliest crimes or violent acts, but excluding other events and circumstances that might mitigate the defendant's "bad" behavior. In this sense, the "facts" of the defendant's background are only relevant for prosecutors to the extent that they fit into a narrative schema that corresponds to their conceptualization of the defendant as one of a set of stock stereotypical characters such as "the gang-banger" or "the lurking rapist," or, in the following case, "the child killer":

Q: What I'm curious about are the stories that lawyers tell in these cases. So in asking for death in this penalty phase I'm wondering how you put together . . . how you went about deciding what to say?

A: The facts of the crime were big because this particular defendant did not have a criminal record other than a DUI, and so she was . . . to walk into her house and see the pictures and achievements on the walls, framed, if you didn't know what she was like you'd say she was the mother of the year. So I was able to bring in some acts of violence against previous boyfriends. The main thing in this case was the crime itself. (Prosecutor #2)

For this prosecutor, the "crime itself" equates to "the facts." As this same prosecutor points out later in the interview, the important facts are those involved in the violence that caused the victim's death: "Well I have to look at everything. I have to look for mitigating factors. I anticipated the poor little girl had a miserable upbringing and have to cut her some slack thing. But sometimes the facts are just so overwhelmingly premeditated and moving from one room to the other and reloading" (Prosecutor #2).

This defendant was classified by the prosecutor as a self-involved psychopathic mother who murdered her children to spite the children's father—these were "the facts," the only relevant events and circumstances.

And while the following prosecutor recognized the defense's discretion to tell a longer story, he explains how he emphasizes the defendant's background when it includes prior crimes or violence:

> We're gonna play the hand that we're dealt. And you may have a horrible crime that was done in a short period of time. Then we're going to emphasize that. You may have someone who has a series of crimes in which case we would emphasize that. You would have a longer story. But then the defense would tend to make it even longer. Outside these crimes, no matter what the period is, what happened to make this guy act this way. You see how it's phrased. What happened to make this guy act this way? (Prosecutor #6)

Another prosecutor, who did not wish to be recorded, told me that the notion that public pressure on capital prosecutors might lead to over-zealousness is "Hollywood stuff," and that prosecutors in his office always "go by the facts," meaning that they take whatever events constitute the crime and straightforwardly and impartially deliver these to the jury (Prosecutor #3).

One lesson we can take away from these glimpses into the consciousnesses of prosecutors is that despite their invocation of the neutrality of "facts," they see themselves as vigorously engaged in a tough adversarial battle. That is to say, while their version of "the facts" seem to speak for themselves for prosecutors, prosecutors are excising or ignoring other events and circumstances that, according to others (such as defenders) might seem also to speak for themselves, such as traumatic childhood abuse and neglect of the defendant. In my interviews, there was a sense of exasperation running through prosecutors' commentary, as if the "facts" of the victim's death made it self-evident that the defendant deserved a death sentence. This sense of exasperation might help explain the affective and vociferous tone of their arguments in trials.

Another prosecutor explained the primacy of facts this way:

> Q: How do you go about developing your opening statement and your arguments? In guilt and in penalty?

A: Fact driven. Fact driven on the case. Guilt argument is no different than any other argument in any other case. Is there a murder? Is he the guy that did it? And you try to explain to them what murder is and the various elements are. Then you pull in the various facts and say you've proven this you've proven that. I tell them, on occasion, the guilt decision is brain driven. (Prosecutor #5)

For this prosecutor, guilt phase arguments are *rational* and based on his interpretation of "the facts." Interestingly, however, this same prosecutor conceptualizes the penalty phase differently—as "gut driven":

The penalty decision is gut driven. It's a morality decision. You look at what is right and what is wrong. Is he deserving of the ultimate punishment or a lesser punishment? What is he all about? How bad is this crime? How vulnerable was the victim? What has he made of his life? Where did he come from? What did he have? What didn't he have? (Prosecutor #5)

This commentary on the penalty phase is notable partly because it acknowledges the significance of the victim's status. But it is also interesting because this particular prosecutor seems to understand the significance of the defendant's social history when developing a perspective on the suitability of the death penalty. Of course, his own answers to the questions he poses in his comments—What has he made of his life? Where did he come from? What did he have? What didn't he have?—may reflect an individualistic conceptualization of human beings, which might differ for defenders, or perhaps jurors.

LAW

Sometimes, prosecutors invoked the primacy of law rather than facts:

Q: One of the things I'm interested in learning is what are the factors that shape the argument in the penalty phase? So I mean one could imagine that there's the facts, the evidence. But one could also imagine that there are legal constraints on what you can or can't say in sort of developing this story or argument, but also you've already mentioned sort a strategic decision where you choose to ask them. How do you go about shaping that argument? What are the factors that influence it?

A: Legally, obviously, is the first place you start. And the law has changed a lot since I came to the DA's office. What you could argue. Victim impact was never appropriate. In the legal world it is relatively new. Obviously the only thing that was important in the penalty phase is that it always focused on the defendant. The arguments you could use for killing a defendant were always things like his prior record, the likelihood, this is new too, that he would be violent in the future even if locked up without the possibility of parole. (Prosecutor #1)

This prosecutor thinks of penalty phases as disciplined by the law's rules. Similarly, in the following quote, we can see how the formally rational discipline of the law is an important feature for this different prosecutor in developing his arguments:

> And I think from a prosecutor's standpoint they do what we started this conversation with, they expose the truth and they make the logical arguments about why they believe the death penalty is appropriate for this case. And as you know we are not hanging out in this abyss, there are rules and regulations for the jury to consider. They have very specific directions. You may assign whatever weight you want to them, but these are the rules, the K factors that you can consider. So it varies. I would say that in this case that I just finished I would say that my final argument is ten minutes. Because I believe that it was my goal to say to this jury that these are the facts, here is what you heard in the way of evidence and this is why the death penalty applies. Here is what your social responsibility is in considering the death penalty. Then sit down and shut up. (Prosecutor #4)

In these quotes prosecutors are reflecting a commitment to the Enlightenment ideal of formal rationality that is supposed to control the law in a modern liberal legal state, as discussed throughout this book. But despite these prosecutors' emphasis on the predominance of the rigors of a disciplining law (as well as apparently neutral or self-evident facts), much of the tenor of prosecutor argumentation in the trials analyzed in this study was anything but neutral and rational.

FURIES

I now return to some of the passages quoted in chapter 4 to demonstrate how prosecutor arguments in these trials were often floridly emotional when describing defendants and their violent acts:

> Now after and during this nightmare then at the rape scene, she is taken by these two hyenas on the Bataan Death March, as I like to state it, fifty-five yards up from the rape scene where she was hogtied like a rodeo animal— you can see that very plainly in the series five pieces of —and then she is executed. (Trial 33, 6092)

> Don't you just wonder, too, what words this hyena was mouthing to her? What terms of endearment do you think he was telling her once he spilled

his seed of lust into her now damaged anal cavity? What do you think he was saying to her? Can't you just imagine? (Trial 21, 5906)

But when you put in the context of Tara's account of what happened, he stuck it in her anus. Then he made her suck his penis, and then he ejaculates on her. She said that she could taste the ejaculate in her mouth, and it's all over the front of her sweatshirt, and down here there's something that looks like fecal material and could be a combination of fecal material and saliva, her saliva, her fecal material, his semen. (Trial 19, 4738)

There was trauma to her breasts. At the site of the autopsy X-rays were taken. And it was discovered by X-ray that this mousse can—this is Loreal freehold styling mousse—this item was found inside of [the victim's] stomach, her abdomen. It had got there by being rammed up through her rectum and through the wall that separates the rectal area from the stomach and left within her rectal area—excuse me, in her abdominal area. (Trial 9, 1963)

In each of these graphic descriptions, the prosecutor depicted filmic vignettes of terrifying, gruesome violence, all delivered in the sanctimonious grammar of indignation. These "facts" speak for themselves—but are spoken furiously—and declare that the defendant is utterly Other, an inhuman threat to the sanctity of the victim, and by implication to society.

Sometimes these frightening vignettes invited the jury to imagine being the victim:

Imagine, imagine what that child was thinking about the last thirty minutes, those torturous minutes of her life. Imagine the indescribable terror of having a gun in your face and seeing the finger on the trigger and seeing everyone around you trying to save you, unable to bargain for your life no matter how much they pleaded and no matter how hard you hoped; the absolute fear of knowing that you would never run to your mommy again, you would never feel her arms around you, knowing that your mommy isn't with you to make you safe and that your big brothers aren't there to protect you, that you're aunties and your uncles and your cousins are all gone, you're all alone, all alone, a helpless little vulnerable girl with this very mean man who keeps pushing this gun in your cheek and he won't let you go, no matter how hard anyone asks him. And even though everyone is telling him to let you go, even people who are begging him for your life, every time they did that, he just pushed that gun harder into your cheek. That soft little cheek and that cold hard metal. And he was so mean and you were so afraid. Your precious little eyes showed us the terror that you felt. And it was those same eyes that begged you, begged all of us, to save you. But he wouldn't let us save you. Imagine knowing that no one can save you, that he's not going to let them. (Trial 15, 6873)

As she realized she was being caught by this guy capable of karate and manhandling someone, imagine the terror when she realized she was caught.

Imagine the helplessness she felt as the handcuffs went on her. Imagine the fear and the terror that she had when she was taped. Imagine the feeling of impending doom as that gag went in her mouth. "I can't scream anymore, even." It is out of this world. It is unimaginable. Where did her thoughts turn at the end? Maybe her dead [*sic*]. Maybe she can't help. I don't know. Imagine the impact on her not only physically but spiritually when she was beat those thirty-one times. (Trial 10, 6640)

What does it feel like to be a victim like that? How does it feel to have your skin come off? How does it feel to see your red body with your skin ripped off your body and know that you don't stand a chance to live; to be hung, to be stuffed in a box, to be shoved behind a door? How does that last second of agony feel before death mercifully takes over? (Trial 14, 12047)

Regardless of whether or not these passages may violate legal norms about appropriate arguments they seem to push the boundaries of the (purportedly) rational law's limits on "inflaming the passions" and possibly prejudicing the jury.

Beyond colorful descriptions of the crimes and florid invitations for jurors to imagine being the victim, prosecutors occasionally invoked explicitly retributive rationales to support giving a death sentence. These sections of arguments are notable because they illuminate prosecutors' attitudes about the concept of retribution as a theory of capital punishment:

A pronouncement of death to Irving White says: the intolerable nature of the evil acts you have perpetrated, based on the quality of man that you are, must be punished to the maximum. It is a cleansing and it is a catharsis that restores in some vital sense, order and continuity to what we have. (Trial 3, 3916)

And when I say "necessary," I mean morally necessary. I mean that justice requires a verdict of death in this case. (Trial 8, 8442)

A late social philosopher, Robert Nesbitt, says: until catharsis has been effected [*sic*] through a trial, through a finding of guilt and a punishment, the community is anxious, fearful, apprehensive and above all, contaminated. (Trial 8, 8524)

The whole notion of the death penalty as punishment is a way that is our certainty and our community, that we express this denunciation of a wrongdoing. It's a way that we maintain order for the law. And it's essential that this punishment be reserved for the gravest of crimes and that it should adequately reflect not only your outrage but your revulsion at this crime, a revulsion that is felt by the great majority of citizens when they witness the murder of an innocent child. (Trial 15, 8677)

But one of the concepts that we kept was this concept of punishment. And punishment is necessary. Those of you who have raised children and those of you who are raising children and those of you who will raise children in the future, punishment is an important part of a family, and it is an important part of society. And the death penalty is an acceptable punishment. There comes a point in time where a person has crossed the line, and the only appropriate punishment is death. (Trial 6, 16470)

And what you are doing by choosing this punishment is you are stating the level of moral outrage that you feel at these crimes and at this defendant. When you choose the death penalty, you are stating the level of outrage that you have for kidnapping and terrorizing and then murdering a perfectly innocent little child. (Trial 15, 8577)

These rationales for state killing are explicitly retributive, and contrast other, more rational and utilitarian theories of punishment, such as deterrence, and incapacitation. Retribution is fundamentally *irrational*, predicated on emotion and an unpredictable logic of vengeance—indeed, explanations of retribution border on the tautological. To argue that "we must give him death because he deserves it," is circular in its logic. But as I have pointed out, logical coherence is not a necessary ingredient for the production of trial arguments.

And while it is perhaps unsurprising that capital prosecutors used vividly affective and retributive rhetoric in their trial arguments, they also display similar illogics in interviews:

Q: Opening up the frame here, as somebody who has conducted a capital case, what do you think the role of the death penalty is?

A: Well I would hope it was deterrence, mostly. But I think that it is the appropriate punishment for certain people. I think that the death penalty should be extended to more crimes. But I think there are certain cases where there is no better punishment than death. Granted they sit around forever, the appellate process is very lengthy. Who knows if I'll even see [the defendant] executed. Deterrence it doesn't really deter people. I have a lot of job security because I keep seeing people come through the system over and over again.

Q: From my academic research on that issue and from talking to some judges, prosecutors, defense attorneys, most people agree with you that it doesn't have a strong deterrent effect but its main function to be this sense of justice. What do you mean by that? What is it about doing that that equates to justice?

A: If someone is given LWOP they are still given the opportunity to read magazines and watch TV and to basically go on with their life in this confined environment. I don't think that's appropriate for some people. I don't think it should apply to all murders, but I think it's something that should be reserved for the worst of the worst. And that one I prosecuted falls within that category. I've had other cases where it wasn't even a question, we didn't have special circumstance, but I'm just saying, it wouldn't apply to all people. Someone who kills a child by shaking will get twenty-five to life. Yes they deserve to go to prison and hopefully not get out. But it's not necessarily a death penalty case. But if you have torture, a special circumstance, have you talked to Judge Smith [a pseudonym]? He prosecuted an aunt and uncle who tortured [a victim]. Horrible. They are the poster children for the death penalty. To me that's justice. (Prosecutor #2)

For this prosecutor, the death penalty is "appropriate" for certain "worst of the worst" defendants. The "worst of the worst," of course, is a subjective construct, akin to pornography—it is hard to define but you know it when you see it, depending on your perspective on "it."

The following prosecutor struggles somewhat with the *purpose* of the death penalty as he delineates a rationale that resembles retribution:

A: It's obviously tough to decide what the death penalty does. All the death penalty does for sure is ensure that that defendant does not ever commit another crime or kill someone else. Whether or not someone says, "I think I won't kill this person because I don't want to get death," there is no way of knowing because you can't prove the negative. I also believe that that's probably not likely anyway, that people who are willing to commit capital crimes aren't probably thinking of the consequences of death.

Q: Not weighing carefully, "Should I shoot the guy in the liquor store or not?"

A: Right. I don't think that's part of it. I think in California and in the United States the idea of the death penalty is that there are some crimes that are so horrific to the public in general that they don't believe that any other penalty is appropriate. Of course, in California that's kind of an odd comment anyway since they never die.

Q: So I'm going to use the sort of sociological terminology now. It sounds to me like you're saying that there's an incapacitory effect, meaning that this guy isn't going to be able to hurt anybody because he is not going to be alive anymore. And there's something some kind of symbolic message effect that we, as a society, have decided that some crimes are bad or heinous enough that they deserve the most harsh punishment that we as a society can give.

A: I think it's cathartic for the public at some point, even though the death may never be carried out, or something happens that it is postponed for fifteen to twenty years, even though it is expensive and it is more expensive to put somebody to death in California, only because of the appellate process, but it feels cathartic somehow to say that, "You will die for killing [a young female victim]." That cute-little-girl kind of thing. I think it serves a purpose even if it's not carried out. (Prosecutor, #1)

This prosecutor envisions lethal retribution as cathartic and symbolic, a necessary act that provides a cleansing for a society soiled by the murder of a sympathetic victim such as a female child. This commentary is notable because it invokes a particular theory of the state's role in managing violence—namely that the state's job is to intervene *after* the violence and enact retribution upon the perpetrator for symbolic reasons. This rather Durkheimian way of conceptualizing state punishment fits with the general trend in death penalty discourse of bracketing out social causes of violence and focusing instead on a sort of ex post facto "easy solution" to the complex problem of racialized inequality that is involved in producing violent and impoverished communities and persons.

For another prosecutor, retribution is "simply" appropriate:

Q: So this is just a big open-ended question, but as a person who has participated in capital trials, what do you think is the role of the death penalty in the U.S.? What is its function or purpose?

A: The role of the death penalty is to serve as the appropriate punishment for certain crimes.

Q: That's it?

A: That's it.

Q: Okay. When you have done these capital trials . . . let me ask you to elaborate on that response a little bit. Because what I assume you mean by that is that you don't see it as having a great deterrent effect? But you think of it as a just punishment and that's essentially its role.

A: It has a tremendous deterrent effect on the perpetrator.

Q: On the guy. The one guy?

A: Right. The recidivism rate amongst people who are on death row is zero. Deterrence regarding whether or not other people are deterred by the fact that someone else received the death penalty for their conduct, in my view, is not a factor. It's not relevant. Frankly, I think it's a diversionary tactic. As if the existence or the nonexistence of deterrence is somehow for or against support for the death penalty.

Q: Why do you think it's a distraction?

A: Because I think it's very difficult for people to argue the nuts and bolts aspect of the punishment. Some people just don't like the thought that the government is going to take someone's life. And they don't want to or can't argue whether that's appropriate. So instead it becomes a diversionary tactic of let's talk about something else. Because in no other type of crime do we talk about punishment being a diversion to others. I can't think of any other type of crime where we talk about deterrence. The nature of the punishment, certainly the fact that you might be caught and punished might have some deterrent effect on someone who is thinking about committing a crime, but the specific nature of the punishment, whether it's two years in state prison or three years in state prison. (Prosecutor #4)

For this prosecutor, deterrence is a red herring because, for him, it is irrelevant to the real question of capital punishment's appropriateness. For him, the death penalty is simply "the appropriate punishment for certain crimes," although he also believes it manifests specific deterrence on the defendant.

These affective "furies"—vivid descriptions of violent deaths, invitations to imagine being murdered, and invocations of affective retribution—are constructed within the formally rational context of "facts" and "law." This situation presents yet another paradox in U.S. capital punishment, a paradox that can be partially explained by the social rules of the legal institution, yet may also shed light on the question of U.S. retention of the death penalty.

INSTITUTIONAL NORMS

It is important to note that the contradictory predicaments I have described in this chapter can be partially understood as the product of legal-institutional norms that operate to filter or discipline emotionally driven actions such as prosecuting a capital trial. Prosecutors are taught to "play by the book" and "uphold justice" no matter how angry they become over the particulars of any given case. These values are embedded in jurisprudential rules prohibiting "emotional" or "inappropriate" rhetoric in closing arguments (such as *Darden v. Wainwright* [1986]), as well as quasiregulatory documents such as the American Bar Association's Standards for Criminal Justice (see American Bar Association, 2007, Standard 3–5.8).[6]

These institutional conditions help explain, to a certain extent, the legal antinomies elucidated in this chapter. There is an inherent tension in contemporary criminal legal processes between the affective urge toward retribution that arises in human beings when confronted with a terrifying and offensive killing, and the law's (purported) necessity for formal rationality. Durkheim alluded to this tension long ago when he argued that "[modern] punishment constitutes a reaction of passionate feeling, graduated in intensity, which society exerts through the mediation of an organized body over those of its members who have violated certain rules of conduct" (Durkheim, 1984, p. 52).[7] When prosecutors tell their vivid horror stories in the grammar of bureau-speak, they *embody* this tension.

CONCLUSION: THE VEIL OF FACTS AND LAW

Prosecutor reliance on the purportedly neutral and self-evident "facts" and the purportedly formally rational law operates like a veil covering the affective spirit of their retributive arguments. This situation represents yet another contradictory aspect of state killing. While prosecutors shrug and point to the seemingly obvious, straightforward and neutral "facts" and "law" when making their arguments and describing their processes of constructing their arguments, they do so in the emotional grammar of sanctimonious outrage—all toward a goal of irrational retribution. This situation suggests that, while there appear to be societal trends that cast a suspicious light on the retention of capital punishment in the United States, (at least some) practitioners of state killing are deeply and emotionally committed to its symbolic necessity.

Can this commitment be a measure of the death penalty's life or death? The contradiction in prosecution discourses between "facts" and "furies" suggests that not only is logical coherence not especially important in legal discourse, but also that the (purportedly) formally rational law in the United States has *not* disciplined the urge toward vengeance described by Durkheim (and others). If this is so, it may indicate that, in spite of some trends against state killing, the law itself seems to be enduringly comfortable with the tension-riddled "Frankenstein's monster" of what the death penalty has become in the United States, and is not likely to abandon it any time soon.

NOTES

1. Such statutes have been invalidated by the United States Supreme Court (see *Kennedy v. Louisiana*, 2008).

2. More recently, Sarat (2005) has analyzed an empirical instance of "new abolitionism" in Illinois governor George Ryan's (in)famous mass commutation of Illinois' condemned that was principled *not* on "mercy" but on ideals of legality and fairness.

3. I was told that prosecutors usually invite the defendant's lawyers to these meetings to make an argument about why the case at hand should not be a death penalty case. Ultimately, the decision is up to the district attorney.

4. I put these terms in scare quotes because their meaning is indeterminate—different for prosecutors and defenders, and probably also different for judges, jurors, and the public.

5. Status here means "social standing" in terms of race, class, and gender; but it also refers to the victim's role in the killing, whether he or she was "totally innocent" (e.g., a sleeping child) or "implicated" (e.g., a drug dealer).

6. Although *Darden v. Wainwright* (1986) delineates the conditions of inappropriate prosecutor argument, the court found that the prosecutor involved in this

case did *not* cross the boundaries into inappropriate argument. Indeed, courts often find that inflammatory prosecutor argument is "harmless error."

7. Durkheim's arguments about law and punishment in "primitive" societies with "mechanical solidarity" and "modern" societies with "organic solidarity" are open to criticism, particularly to the extent that "modern" societies have turned out to be as harsh or harsher than "primitive" societies. Nevertheless, Durkheim's insight about the tension between "passionate feeling" and "the mediation of an organized body" resonates well with the argument in this chapter about "facts" and "furies."

Epilogue

Perhaps too much has already been said about the death penalty in the United States. Given the abundance of scholarship on capital punishment, especially in the thirty-five years since *Gregg v. Georgia* (1976), what more can we possibly learn about the topic? In concluding this book, I recall a comment made to me by the eminent legal scholar Franklin Zimring when I explained this project to him. He said something like, "So, you want to throw your hat into the death penalty ring, eh?" I think he meant to express that undertaking to contribute something intelligent to the death penalty discussion is a risky proposition due to the abundance of thoughtful discourse on the subject. Benjamin Fleury-Steiner echoed this sentiment in the introduction to his (2004) book on capital jurors, and David Garland makes similar comments in *Peculiar Institution* (2010).

Yet not enough of this abundant and thoughtful discourse on capital punishment has focused on the question of the *ideological* nature of capital punishment—especially its ideologically charged *process*. The books and articles written about the death penalty over the last three decades have focused on everything from the normative question of its morality (Bedau, 1987; Bedau, 1997; Sarat, 2001; Steffan, 1998) to its history in the United States (Banner, 2002) to the cultural values or other factors leading to its continued use in the United States (Garland, 2010; Whitman, 2003; Zimring, 2003) to cultural representations of state killing (Sarat, 2001) to comparative studies of the use of capital punishment in the United States and around the world (Hood, 2002; Johnson and Zimring, 2009; Whitman, 2003) to portraits of the condemned (Von Drehle, 1995) to accounts of wrongful conviction and execution (Bedau and Radalet, 1987; Prejean,

2005) to analyses of constitutionality and fairness (Paternoster, 1991) to thick descriptions of capital jurors' experiences (Fleury-Steiner, 2004).

Of these works, only two (Sarat 2001; Fleury-Steiner, 2004) contend with the deeply ideological nature of death penalty discourses and processes. This is not to suggest that some of the other treatments listed above fail to address or acknowledge that understanding ideology is necessary to understanding capital punishment. Zimring (2003), for example, proposes that the ideology of vigilantism underlies the use of capital punishment; similarly, Whitman (2003) posits that a commitment to the ideology of egalitarianism props up state killing in the United States. However, these analyses conceptualize ideology as somewhat static or inert—they conceive of it as a structural force girding or supporting the practice of capital punishment. They do not address the transitional "life" of ideologies as they are constructed and subverted through legal *processes*. Fleury-Steiner, on the other hand, shows how the narratives produced by jurors in their decision-making process construct racist and classist ideologies of the human, particularly in their process of "otherizing" defendants as *subhuman* threats to the white middle class. In this sense, we can see how Fleury-Steiner has contributed to understanding how the discourses produced in the death penalty process are involved in creating ideologies—not just how ideologies operate as a sort of base upon which the superstructure of the death penalty stands.

Likewise, in this study I have attempted to trace the ideological cargo carried within the stories told by everyday practitioners of death in the United States. This project thus follows in the tradition of Fleury-Steiner's work, except that I analyzed the *producers* of death penalty narratives (attorneys) rather than the *interpreters* of them (jurors). The goal has been to uncover the ideological work done by these stories—how these stories are constitutive and deconstitutive of the American Creed's ideologies—individualism, populism, egalitarianism, laissez-faire, and liberty.

I began this undertaking by discussing theories of capital punishment, theories of narrative, and theories of hegemony and resistance. In this introduction, I discussed in detail the various theories of retention of the death penalty in the United States, and also the numerous theoretical treatments of capital punishment's many contradictions (such as vigilantism versus due process, and illegal killing versus state killing). I also addressed the sociolegal scholarship on "the narrative construction of reality," arguing that investigating how capital defendants are narratively constructed in trials can teach us something important about both the processes of capital punishment and also the ideological "cargo" embedded in death penalty discourses. I also discussed some of the key sociolegal treatments of hegemony and also the possibility of *resistance* to hegemony. This discussion focused on Ewick and Silbey's (1995) groundbreaking theory of narrative resistance to hegemony, particularly on their notion that connecting the *specific* details of an event (such as a murder or crime) to the *general* structure of the social world that is implicated in the production of the event. One of the important points to emerge through this literature review was that penalty phase processes create an unusual legal opportunity for exactly the type of resistance proposed by Ewick and Silbey because they provide the structure to tell stories that explicitly connect the specific to the general. Put another way, the rules of evidence in penalty phase proceedings structurally open up legal discourses to the possibility of connecting up the "proximate causes" (e.g., the defendant's will) to the "distant causes" (e.g., the social world that influenced the defendant). I argued further that this unusual legal opening for potential subversion creates the opportunity for law stories to explicitly take on the very ideological underpinnings that are probably implicated in propping up the death penalty in the United States (e.g., the American Creed). Investigating if or how actual trial narratives undertook this potential subversion became the primary focus of this book.

I then described the theory of the "American Creed," and how it is related to the contemporary American death penalty. This description entailed a discussion of the contemporary academic debate around "American Exceptionalism" and the question of U.S. retention of capital punishment. I organized this discussion around the recent works of Zimring (2003) and Whitman (2003), who make explicitly "exceptionalist" arguments about uniquely "American" ideologies that explain retention (for Zimring, it is "vigilantism," and for Whitman it is "egalitarianism"), and also Garland (2005, 2010) who disputes the notion that there is something ideologically and abidingly unique about the United States that explains retention, and instead points to the more recent politics of crime control. I elaborate on this debate by proposing that the current "American Exceptionalism" theories are deficient in their somewhat conspicuous neglect of the role of racialized inequality in the American Creed and its relation to retention of capital punishment. These points framed the remainder of the book as I proceeded to analyze how actual death penalty narratives are constitutive of and resistant to the American Creed.

Next I described in detail the "anatomy" of capital trials in general, and also the characteristics of the specific trials analyzed in this study. This entailed first noting how landmark capital jurisprudence has structured the phases and evidentiary rules of capital trials. I then described the various demographic characteristics of the particular trials in this data set, including the race and socioeconomic status of defendants (with comparisons to the demographics of the relevant counties), the various "special circumstances" charged by prosecutors in each case, and the aggravating and mitigating factors invoked by prosecutors and defenders during each penalty phase. Finally, I developed a typology of (stereo)typical victim and defendant "characters" constructed by prosecutors and defenders in trial narratives, noting the ideological implications of these portrayals, namely that these characters drew upon scripts related to aspects of the American Creed, such as individualism, egalitarianism, or populism.

I then undertook to show how the narratives produced in these data operated to construct and subvert the "American Creed." I began this section by showing how the arguments constructed by prosecutors tended to conform to the model of narrative theorized by Amsterdam and Bruner (2000), in which the story begins with a "steady-state" which is interrupted by a conflict or "trouble" which in turn calls for a form of "redress," and which concludes with a "coda" expressing some kind of "moral of the story." The modal prosecutor narrative followed this form: the protagonist is the victim, the "steady state" is the victim's placid world, the "trouble" is the defendant's violent interruption of this placid world, the "redress" is the death penalty for the defendant, the lesson in the "coda" is that retribution (and often also incapacitation) is society's only suitable response to the trouble because the victim's family deserves it.

Not surprisingly, these prosecution narratives and their "lessons" about retribution, instantiate aspects of the American Creed. Firstly, the prosecution stories were almost always constructed in the language of individual accountability, specifically assigning the source of the crime and trial to the heart, mind and soul of the defendant exclusively. These narratives drew on scripts that "expect" characters to behave in specific ways—usually in ways that reflect a belief in the primacy of individualism, liberty, and populism. Moreover, revenge, which was often invoked by prosecutors (albeit usually rather covertly), is an idea rooted in the ideological concepts of populism and liberty. Recall that Zimring (2003) argued that prosecutor argumentation framing execution as a service for victim's families draws on "vigilante values," which are rooted in a distrust of the state, which is deeply populist and libertarian.

But while vengeful prosecutor narratives draw on individualism, populism and liberty—key aspects of the American Creed—they also *constitute* these ideologies. That is to say, when prosecutors propose to jurors that the defendant is solely responsible for the murder and that the only appropriate redress is for him to be killed for the benefit of the victim and victim's family, they are not only drawing on scripts about individualism, liberty, and populism, but also discursively *making a case for* these Creed ideologies.

Defender narratives were significantly less in line with Amsterdam and Bruner's model of narrative. Instead, defenders tended to rather incoherently propose a series of factors for jurors to consider in weighing their penalty decision, without organizing these factors into a narrative structure. In a few examples from these data, defenders did construct relatively coherent narratives, with the *defendant* constructed as the protagonist rather than the victim, but this was the exception to the rule. In two of the trials in this data set, the defense explicitly challenged the hegemony of the Creed by clearly connecting the defendant's social history to his diminished autonomy—and implying that the *cause* of the crime could be found in the social forces that shaped the defendant (and not simply his will to attack the victim).

Generally, however, defenders tended to list thematic factors or influences on the defendant and urged the jury to consider them when deciding their client's fate, without making the rhetorical move to frame the *cause* of the murder as these factors, nor to organize these factors into a narrative structure. Three "factors" stood out in defender arguments, namely the effects of the defendant's turbulent social world, the effects of drugs, and the effects of mental illness.

One of the key findings from this section was that the narratives constructed by *both* prosecutors and defenders tend to instantiate the ideological tenets of the American Creed. This was somewhat surprising because while I began this project with the expectation that prosecutor narratives would embody the Creed, I suspected that defender narratives would challenge it, due to the evidentiary latitude offered by the penalty phase. This is not to suggest that defenders never made "social determinism" arguments, framing the cause of the killing as at least partially related to social forces outside the boundaries of the defendant's will. But, *generally*, these quasideterministic arguments were relatively incoherent and included among a laundry list of other arguments to the jury about why they should spare the defendant (such as "lingering doubt" or the vague notion of "mercy").

This finding led me to ponder the question of *why* defender narratives rarely approached subversion, given the evidentiary latitude afforded by the penalty phase. In contending with this question, I argued that the limitations of the defenders' potentially subversive stories are related to inherent limits in the law's capability to take into consideration the influence of social and environmental forces on the behavior of legal subjects. That is to say, there are *inherent* limits of the law—it is fundamentally a conservative institution that, by its nature, tends to perpetuate hegemony. This is partially due to the rationally formal law's commitment to "relevance," and also to norms of the legal profession. But, as scholars such as Jamieson (2001), have shown, the law is fundamentally an institution of the conventional power-wielders in U.S. society—it is "the master's tool," not well suited to dismantle "the master's house."

The final two chapters then investigated the practices and consciousnesses of the producers of these narratives—capital defenders and capital prosecutors. In the former, I examined defender practice and conscious-ness vis-á-vis the question of whether and how they might be engaged in "cause lawyering." I concluded that the defenders in this data set were generally *not* engaging in cause lawyering, despite the opportunity provided by the penalty phase. I made this argument because defenders never explicitly took on the ideological hegemony of the American Creed, and indeed often tended to instantiate aspects of the Creed in their narra-tives by, for example, "humanizing" the defendant through a valorization of individualistic and populist characteristics.

Finally, in the last chapter, I described contradictions and tensions in the law demonstrated by capital prosecutors' practices and conscious-nesses as a way of investigating the death penalty's "life or death." This investigation led to the insight that prosecutor discourses evince a para-dox between a commitment to "facts" and law, and a demonstration of "furies," or affective, hyperbolic narratives of killing. In a return to the theme of U.S. retention of capital punishment, I finally argued in this chapter that this contradiction's presence in the law indicates that the formally rational law in the United States has not yet resolved its abiding tension between "vengeance" and "rationality"—which I argue suggests that the death penalty is probably here for the time being.

I began this book by describing two versions of the story of one murder in a small town in California from a case I worked on prior to graduate school as a mitigation investigator. These competing narratives of the murder of a twelve-year-old girl and her killer—like most of the trials I analyzed in this study—represent two conflicting ideological positions.

The first version of the story of murder, the prosecution narrative, delineates the forensic details of killing, in this case a terrifying strangu-lation and mutilation of a young girl. In the prosecution narrative, the defendant simply decided to selfishly destroy the peaceful "steady state" of the protagonist victim because he felt like it. Moreover, in this version, the only acceptable means of rectifying the ruined "steady state" is to destroy the killer in the name of retribution on behalf of the victim. This narrative is temporally short, simplistic, and coherent—it is a cut-and-dried explanation of violence.

As I have tried to point out throughout this book, this type of narrative instantiates ideologies constituting the American Creed. This conceptu-alization of the defendant's actions reflects an understanding of human agency as inherently and straightforwardly individualistic. Likewise, framing the social world as a place in which individuals have the freedom to act according to their will—but must accept responsibility for their actions—represents a deeply libertarian conceptualization of American society. This individualistic and libertarian construction of the human and his social world is thus aligned with the classically liberal ideologies of egalitarianism and laissez-faire. Moreover, notion that explanations for murder should be un-complex and "commonsensical" evinces a commitment to populism—a rejection of "elite knowledge" that could explain the violence in a more nuanced way.[1]

The second version of the story, the defense narrative, delineates the complex social conditions partially implicated in determining the defendant's violent actions. In the defense narrative, the defendant was driven to attack the victim partially due to a sort of overdetermination—he literally could not help himself because of complicated and overwhelming forces that go far beyond his simple will. In this version of the story, the protagonist is the defendant, rather than the victim, and his "steady state" was destroyed by a confluence of external forces—from parental abuse and neglect, to exposure to neurotoxins, to marginalization in the social world of schools and public infrastructure. These external forces are understood in the defender narrative as partially implicated as *causes* of the violence that led to the death of the victim—these are the forces of overdetermination. In this narrative, the appropriate mode of redress for the injustice of the defendant's ruined "steady state" is to bestow mercy upon him by sparing the death penalty. The unspoken implication or upshot of this version of the story is that the influence of social forces on the defendant transform him into a "liminal man," a person in between structure and agency, and it would be inappropriate for the state—for "us"—to execute him.

As I have argued throughout this study, this second type of narrative has the *potential* to subvert or challenge the hegemony of the ideologies comprising the American Creed. Essentially, this quasideterministic version of the story of killing and the killer challenges the individualistic aspects of the American Creed (individualism, liberty, and laissez-faire), while also privileging "elite knowledge"—the grammar of medicine and social science—in explaining human behavior, thus challenging the "commonsensical" nature of populism. However, as I have also argued, this potential subversion of the hegemony of the Creed is quite tentative, and when present, usually implicit in the actual legal narratives produced by the defenders in the data that I analyzed.

Moreover, while I began this research with the expectation that defender narratives would conform relatively closely to the theory of subversion proposed by Ewick and Silbey (e.g., explicitly making connections between the *specific* details of the crime and the *general* influence of the larger social world), I found that this was generally not the case. Instead, defenders constructed incoherent narratives that sometimes included potentially subversive themes, but rarely directly took up a thoroughly deterministic viewpoint, and thus rarely took on the hegemony of the Creed.

This book contributes both to contemporary scholarship on capital punishment and also to the more general field of sociolegal studies. Firstly, the primary finding here—that capital narratives (including from the defense) generally tend to draw upon and construct Creed ideologies— adds to the scholarship on retention of capital punishment. This research thus provides some empirical support for the claim that deep "American" ideologies (such as those constituting the Creed) are implicated in retention, at least to the extent that it illustrates the deeply hegemonic nature of those ideologies. Further, the data here suggest that the law's longstanding tension between impulses toward, on the one hand revenge, and on the other hand, rationality, is not close to being resolved—which suggests that the vengefulness underlying the retributive use of capital punishment has not diminished enough to effect abolition.

More generally, this research adds to the sociolegal scholarship on narrativity, hegemony, and resistance to hegemony. This project elucidates the process of constructing narratives in capital trials, and along the way shows how the hegemony of Creed ideologies tends to overpower the possibility for resistance offered by penalty phase proceedings. Finally, the descriptive findings from this research lend empirical support to some of the truisms about the American death penalty, namely that it is used against marginalized persons of color who are often intoxicated.

Ultimately, this study is about the elusive yet powerful role of ideology in legal discourses. Through analyzing the content and processes of death penalty narratives, this research illuminates the mysterious and covert life of the ideologies of individualism, egalitarianism, liberty, populism, and laissez-faire in the law.

A final reiteration about generalizability is in order. The data for this project is limited to a handful of cases and interviews from three large and diverse California counties. I believe these counties are representative of other locales in California, and probably many parts of the United States—this collection of cases is, after all, the full set of death sentence resulting cases for the years 1996 to 2004 for three of the largest counties in California. Still, caution should be taken in drawing general conclusions from these relatively limited data.

NOTE

1. Of course, as I have alluded to elsewhere, the law itself—which structures the prosecution narratives—also inherently embodies the ideologies of the American Creed. That is to say, the rules of the purportedly rational/formal U.S. legal system constrain the contours of legal narratives to fit within demarcations of individualistic conceptualizations of the human. Rules of evidence and bedrock American jurisprudential concepts such as *mens rea* inherently instantiate the American Creed.

References

American Bar Association (2007). "Criminal Justice Section Standards." http:// www.abanet.org/crimjust/standards/pfunc_blk.html#5.8

Amsterdam, Anthony (2007). "Race and the Death Penalty Before and After McCleskey." *Columbia Human Rights Law Review, 39,* 34.

Amsterdam, Anthony G. and Jerome Bruner (2000). *Minding the Law.* Cambridge, MA: Harvard University Press.

Amsterdam, Anthony G., and Randy Hertz (1992). "An Analysis of Closing Argument to a Jury." *New York Law School Law Review, 37,* 55.

Associated Press (2009). "New Mexico Repeals Death Penalty." *Los Angeles Times* web page. http://www.latimes.com/news/nationworld/nation/la-na-new mexico-death19–2009mar19,0,5497063.story

Bakan, Steven E., and Steven F. Cohn (1994). "Racial Prejudice and Support for the Death Penalty by Whites." *Journal of Research in Crime and Delinquency, 31,* 202–9.

Baldus, David and George Woodworth (2004). "Race Discrimination and the Legitimacy of Capital Punishment: Reflections on the Interaction of Fact and Perception." *Depaul Law Review.* Summer. *53,* 1411.

Baldus, David V. and George Woodworth (1998). "Race Discrimination and the Death Penalty." *America's Experiment with Capital Punishment: Reflections on the Past, Present, and Future of the Ultimate Penal Sanction.* Edited by James R. Acker, Robert M. Bohm, and Charles S. Lanier. Durham, NC: Carolina Academic Press.

Baldus, David, C. Pulaski, and G. Woodworth (1990). *Equal Justice and the Death Penalty.* Boston: Northeastern University Press.

Banner, Stuart (2005). Personal communication with the author.

Banner, Stuart (2002). *The Death Penalty: An American History.* Cambridge, MA: Harvard University Press.

Bedau, Hugo Adam (1987). *Death is Different: Studies in the Morality, Law, and Politics of Capital Punishment.* Boston: Northeastern University Press.

Bedau, Hugo Adam (1997). *The Death Penalty in America: Current Controversies.* Edited by Hugo Adam Bedau. New York: Oxford University Press.

Bedau, H. A. and M. L. Radelet (1987). "Miscarriages of Justice in Capital and Potentially Capital Cases." *Stanford Law Review, 40*, 21.

Braithwaite, John (1989). *Crime, Shame and Reintegration.* New York: Cambridge University Press.

Bright, Stephen B. (1994). "Counsel for the Poor: The Death Sentence Not for the Worst Crime but for the Worst Lawyer." *Yale Law Journal, 103*, 1835.

Brisman, Avi (2009). *The Waiver and Withdrawal of Death Penalty Appeals as "Extreme Communicative Acts.* Unpublished manuscript, available from the author.

Bowers, William J., Marla Sandys, and Benjamin D. Steiner (1998). "Foreclosed Impartiality in Capital Sentencing: Jurors Predispositions, Guilt –Trial Experience, and Premature Decision Making." *Cornell Law Review, 83*(6).

Brown, Michael K., Martin Carnoy, Elliott Currie, Troy Duster, David B. Oppenheimer, Marjorie M. Shultz, and David Wellman (2003). *Whitewashing Race: The Myth of a Color-Blind Society.* Berkeley: University of California Press.

Bruner, Jerome (1991). "The Narrative Construction of Reality." *Critical Inquiry, 18.*

Burns, Robert P. (1999). *A Theory of the Trial.* Princeton: Princeton University Press.

California Penal Code 190. 2

CALCRIM (2008). Judicial Council of California Advisory Committee on Criminal Jury Instructions. http://www.courtinfo.ca.gov/jury/criminaljuryinstructions/calcrim_juryins.pdf

CNN (2005). "Train Collision Near Los Angeles Kills 11." http://www.cnn.com/2005/US/01/26/train.derailment/

California Commission on the Fair Administration of Justice (2008). *Report and Recommendations on the Administration of the Death Penalty in California.*

California Department of Corrections and Rehabilitation (2011). "Condemned Inmate Summary List." http://www.cdcr.ca. gov/Reports_Research/docs/CondemnedInmateSummary. pdf

Cartier, Jerome, David Farabee, and Michael L. Prendergast (2006). "Methamphetamine Use, Self-Reported Violent Crime, and Recidivism Among Offenders in California Who Abuse Substances." *Journal of Interpersonal Violence, 21*(4), 435–45.

Chatman, Seymour (1981). "What Novels Can Do That Films Can't (and Vice Versa)." In *On Narrative.* Edited by W. J. T. Mitchell. Chicago: University of Chicago Press.

Cole, David (1999). *No Equal Justice: Race and Class in the American Criminal Justice System.* New York: The New Press.

Comaroff, Jean and John Comaroff (1991). *Of Revelation and Revolution.* Chicago: University of Chicago Press.

Conley John M. and William M. O'Barr (1998). *Just Words: Law, Language, and Power.* Chicago: The University of Chicago Press.

Costanzo, Mark and Julie Peterson (1994). "Attorney Persuasion in the Capital Penalty Phase: A Content Analysis of Closing Arguments." *Journal of Social Issues, 50*(2), 125–47.

Cotton, Allison M. (2008). *Effigy: Images of Capital Defendants*. Lanham, MD: Lexington Books.

Coutin, Susan Bibler (2000). *Legalizing Moves: Salvadoran Immigrants' Struggle for U.S. Residency*. University of Michigan Press.

Cover, Robert (1992). "Violence and the Word." In Minow, Martha, Michael Ryan and Austin Sarat, Eds. *Narrative, Violence and the Law: The Essays of Robert Cover*. Ann Arbor: The University of Michigan Press.

Coyne, Kate (2004). Personal communication.

Death Penalty Information Center (2011). http://www.deathpenaltyinfo.org/

Death Penalty Information Center (2009). http://www.deathpenaltyinfo.org/

Death Penalty Information Center (2008). http://www.deathpenaltyinfo.org/

Death Penalty Information Center (DPIC) (2005). http://www.deathpenaltyinfo.org/

Death Penalty Information Center (2006). http://www.deathpenaltyinfo.org/

Dieter, Richard C. (1998). *The Death Penalty in Black and White: Who Lives, Who Dies, Who Decides*. http://www.deathpenaltyinfo.org/article.php?scid=45&did=539

Dumm, Thomas L (2000). "Death, Modernity and Enlightenment." *Punishment and Society*, 2(4), 471–76.

Dunn, Kerry and Paul J. Kaplan (2009). "The Ironies of Helping: Projects of Social Improvement and Executable Subjects." *Law & Society Review*, 43(2).

Durkheim, Emile (1984). *The Division of Labor in Society*. Translated by W. D. Halls. London: Macmillan.

Evans, E. P. (1906). *The Criminal Prosecution and Capital Punishment of Animals*. London: Faber and Faber.

Ewick, Patricia and Susan S. Silbey (1998). *The Common Place of Law: Stories of Everyday Life*. Chicago: The University of Chicago Press.

Ewick, Patricia and Susan S. Silbey (1995). "Subversive Stories and Hegemonic Tales: Toward a Sociology of Narrative." *Law and Society Review*, 29(2).

Farber, Daniel A. and Suzanna Sherry (1996). "Legal Storytelling and Constitutional Law: The Medium and the Message." In *Law's Stories: Narrative and Rhetoric in the Law*. Edited by Peter Brooks and Paul Gewirtz. New Haven, CT: Yale University Press.

Ferrall, Bard R. (2004). "Capital Punishment: Hugo Bedau & Paul Cassell eds., Debating the Death Penalty: Should American have Capital Punishment? The Experts from Both Sides Make Their Case." Review essay. *Journal of Criminal Law and Criminology*, 95(365).

Fine, Robert and Daniel Chernilo (2004) *Studies in Law, Politics and Society, Volume 31*, Edited by Austin Sarat and Patricia Ewick. Amsterdam: Elsevier.

Fitzpatrick, Peter (1992). *The Mythology of Modern Law*. New York: Routledge.

Fleury-Steiner, Benjamin (2004). *Jurors Stories of Death: How America's Death Penalty Invests in Inequality*. Ann Arbor: University of Michigan Press.

Fleury-Steiner, Benjamin (2002). "Narratives of the Death Sentence: Toward a Theory of Legal Narrativity." *Law and Society Review*, 36(3).

Fleury-Steiner, Benjamin and Victor Argothy (2004). "Lethal 'Borders': Elucidating Jurors' Racialized Discipline to Punish in Latino Defendant Death Cases." *Punishment and Society*, 6(1), 67–84.

Foucault, Michel (1977). *Discipline and Punish: The Birth of the Prison*. New York: Vintage.

Franzosi, Roberto (1998). "Narrative Analysis—or why (and how) Sociologists Should be Interested in Narrative." *Annual Review of Sociology, 24*, 517–54.

Furillo, Andy (2008). "California Still has Legal Issues on Lethal Injection Executions," *Sacramento Bee*. April 20, 2008, Main News Section, page A1.

Garland, David (2010). *Peculiar Institution: America's Death Penalty in an Age of Abolition*. Cambridge, MA: Belknap-Harvard University Press.

Garland, David (2005). "Capital punishment and American Culture." *Punishment & Society, 7*, 347–76

Garland, David (2005). *Capital Punishment and American Culture: Some Critical Reflections*. http://research.yale.edu/ccs/papers/garland_cappunishment.pdf

Garland, David (2001). *The Culture of Control: Crime and Social Order in Contemporary Society*. Oxford: Oxford University Press.

Garland, David (1990). *Punishment and Modern Society: A Study in Social Theory*. Chicago: University of Chicago Press.

Gates, E. Nathanial. (1997). "Volume Introduction." *Critical Race Theory: Essays on the Social Construction of "Race."* Edited by E. Nathiel Gates. New York: Garland.

Gerstle, Gary (2001). *American Crucible: Race and Nation in the Twentieth Century*. Princeton: Princeton University Press.

Gerwitz, Paul (1996). "Narrative and Rhetoric in the Law." *In Law's Stories: Narrative and Rhetoric in the Law*. Edited by Peter Brooks and Paul Gerwitz. New Haven: Yale University Press.

Gifis, Steven (2003). *Barron's Law Dictionary*. Hauppauge, New York: Barron's

Givelber, Daniel (2001). "The Adversary System and Historical Accuracy: Can We Do Better?" in *Wrongly Convicted: Perspectives on Failed Justice*. Edited by Saundra D. Westervelt and John A. Humphrey. New Brunswick: Rutgers University Press.

Hajjar, Lisa (2004). *Studies in Law, Politics and Society, Volume 31*. Edited by Austin Sarat and Patricia Ewick. Amsterdam: Elsevier, 2004.

Haney, Craig (2005) *Death by Design: Capital Punishment as a Social Psychological System*. New York: Oxford University Press.

Haney, Craig (1997). "Violence and the Capital Jury: Mechanisms of Moral Disengagement and the Impulse to Condemn to Death." *Stanford Law Review. 49 Stan. L. Rev. 1447.*

Haney, Craig (1995). "The Social Context of Capital Murder: Social Histories and the Logic of Mitigation." *Santa Clara Law Review, 35.*

Haney, Craig, Lorelei Sontag, and Sally Costanzo (1994). "Deciding to Take a Life: Capital Juries, Sentencing Instructions, and the Jurisprudence of Death." *Journal of Social Issues, 50*(2), 149–76.

Hart, Lienne (2006). "More Calls for Death Penalty in Child Rapes." *Los Angeles Times*. October 10, 2006, p. A15.

Holdman, Scharlette (2007). "The Nature and Role of Mitigating Evidence in Capital Cases." http://www.capitalethnographyproject.com/pdfs/Natureand RoleofMitigatingEvidence.pdf

Hood, Roger (2002). *The Death Penalty: A Worldwide Perspective*. Oxford: Oxford University Press.

Innocenceproject.org (2005). *Mistaken ID.* http://www.innocenceproject.org/causes/mistakenid.php

Jamieson, Beth Kiyoko (2001). *Real Choices: Feminism, Freedom, and the Limits of Law.* University Park: The Pennsylvania State University Press.

Jenkins, Iredell (1980). *Social Order and the Limits of Law: A Theoretical Essay.* Princeton: Princeton University Press.

Johnston, David (1994). *The Idea of a Liberal Theory: A Critique and Reconstruction.* Princeton: Princeton University Press.

Johnson, David T. and Franklin E. Zimring (2009). *The Next Frontier: National Development, Political Change, and the Death Penalty in Asia.* Oxford: Oxford University Press.

Lauerman, Kerry (2001). "Killing as Closure." Salon.com. http://dir.salon.com/news/feature/2001/04/14/mcveigh/index.html

Kaplan, Paul J. (2008). "Facts and Furies: The Antinomies of Facts and Law, and Retribution in the Work of Capital Prosecutors." *Studies in Law, Politics and Society. Special Issue: Is the Death Penalty Dying?* 42, 135–59.

Kaplan, Paul J. (2006) "American Exceptionalism and Racialized Inequality in American Capital Punishment." *Law and Social Inquiry,* 31(1).

Kaufman-Osborn, Timothy K. (2002). *From Noose to Needle: Capital Punishment and the Late Liberal State.* Ann Arbor: The University of Michigan Press.

LaChance, Daniel (2007). "Last Words, Last Meals, and Last Stands: Agency and Individuality in the Modern Execution Process." *Law and Social Inquiry,* 32, 701.

Lauerman, Kerry (2001). "Killing as Closure." *Salon.com,* at http://dir.salon.com/news/feature/2001/04/14/mcveigh/index.html.

Lipset, Seymour Martin (1996). *American Exceptionalism: A Double-Edged Sword.* New York: W. W. Norton and Co.

Lynch, Mona and Craig Haney (2000). "Discrimination and Instructional Comprehension: Guided Discretion, Racial Bias, and the Death Penalty." *Law & Human Behavior,* 24(3), 337–58.

Lynch, Mona and Craig Haney (2007). "Impelling/Impeding Momentum Toward Death: An Analysis of Attorneys" Final Arguments in California Capital Penalty Phase Trials." Unpublished Manuscript, available from the author.

Lynch, Mona (2003). "Capital Punishment as Moral Imperative: Pro-death Penalty Discourse on the Internet." *Punishment & Society,* 4(2).

MacPherson, C. B. (1962). *The Political Theory of Possessive Individualism.* Oxford: Oxford University Press.

Madsen, Deborah (1998). *American Exceptionalism.* Edinburgh: Edinburgh University Press.

Messner, Steven F., Eric P. Baumer, and Richard Rosenfeld (2006). "Distrust of Government, the Vigilante Tradition, and Support for Capital Punishment." *Law & Society Review,* 40, 559.

Mauer, Marc (1999). *Race to Incarcerate.* New York: The New Press.

Maynard, Douglas W. (1990). "Narratives and Narrative Structure in Plea Bargaining." In *Language in the Judicial Process.* Edited by Judith N. Levi and Anne Graham Walker. New York: Plenum Press.

Meranze, Michael (2005). *The Peculiarities of the Americans.* Paper presented at the Annual Meeting of the Law and Society Association. Las Vegas.

Milovanovic, Dragan (1994). *A Primer in the Sociology of Law*, Second Edition. New York: Harrow and Heston.

Olson, Susan M. and Christina Batjer (1999). "Competing Narratives in a Judicial Retention Election: Feminism versus Judicial Independence." *Law and Society Review, 33.*

Ortner, Sherry (2003) *New Jersey dreaming: Capital, Culture, and the Class of '58.* Durham, NC: Duke University Press.

Ortner, Sherry (2005). "Subjectivity and Cultural Critique." *Anthropological Theory,* 5(1), 31–52.

Oxford (2002). *Oxford Pocket American Dictionary of Current Usage.* Oxford: Oxford University Press.

Paternoster, Raymond (1991). *Capital Punishment in America.* New York: Lexington Books.

Pierce, Glenn L. and Michael L. Radalet (2005). "Empirical Analysis: The Impact of Legally Inappropriate Factors on Death Sentencing for California Homicides, 1990–1999." *Santa Clara Law Review,* 46(1).

Poveda, Tony (2000). "American Exceptionalism and the Death Penalty," *Social Justice 27, 252.*

Prejean, Helen (2005). *The Death of Innocents: An Eyewitness Account of Wrongful Executions.* New York: Random House.

Reinholz, Mary (2005). "Lynne Stewart Still Combative After Terror Verdict." *The Villager,* 74(41). February 16–22, 2005. http://www.thevillager.com/vil_94/lynnestewart.html

Rhodes, Lorna A. (2004). *Total Confinement: Madness and Reason in the Maximum Security Prison.* Berkeley: University of California Press.

Reiman, Jeffrey H. (1985). "Justice, Civilization, and the Death Penalty: Answering van den Haag." *Philosophy and Public Affairs,* 14(2) (Spring, 1985), 115–48.

Richman, Kimberly (2002). "Lovers, Legal Strangers, and Parents: Negotiating Parental and Sexual Identity in Family Law." *Law & Society Review,* 36(2), 285–324.

Riessman, Catherine Kohler (1993). *Narrative Analysis.* Newbury Park, CA: Sage Publications.

Rubin, Paul (2006). "Capital Punishment and Deterrence." Testimony before the Senate Judiciary Committee. Feb. 1, 2006.

Sanger, Robert M. (2003). "Comparison of the Illinois Commission Report on Capital Punishment with the Capital Punishment System in California." *Santa Clara Law Review,* 44 (101).

Sarat, Austin (2005). *Mercy on Trial: What it Means to Stop an Execution.* Princeton, NJ: Princeton University Press.

Sarat, Austin, Lawrence Douglas, and Martha Merrill Umphrey, (eds.) (2005). *The Limits of Law.* Stanford: Stanford University Press.

Sarat, Austin (2001). *When the State Kills: Capital Punishment and the American Condition.* Princeton: Princeton University Press.

Sarat, Austin (1998). "Between (the Presence of) Violence and (the Possibility of) Justice: Lawyering Against Capital Punishment." In *Cause Lawyering: Political Commitments and Professional Responsibilities.* Edited by Austin Sarat and Stuart Schiengold. Oxford: Oxford University Press.

Sarat, Austin and Stuart Schiengold (1998). "Cause Lawyering and the Reproduction of Professional Authority: An Introduction." In *Cause Lawyering: Political Commitments and Professional Responsibilities*. Edited by Austin Sarat and Stuart Schiengold. Oxford: Oxford University Press.

Simon, Jonathan (2007). *Governing Through Crime: How the War on Crime Transformed American Democracy and Created a Culture of Fear*. Oxford: Oxford University Press.

Smith, Philip (1996). "Executing Executions: Aesthetics, Identity, and the Problematic Narratives of Capital Punishment Ritual." *Theory and Society, 25*. 235–61.

Smith, Phillip (2003). "Narrating the Guillotine: Punishment Technology as Myth and Symbol" *Theory, Culture and Society, 20*(5), 27–51.

Soss, Joe, Laura Langbein, and Alan R. Metelko (2003). "Why Do White Americans Support the Death Penalty?" *Journal of Politics, 65*, 397–421.

Spivak, Gayatri Chakravorty (1996). "Subaltern Studies: Deconstructing Historiography." *The Spivak Reader: Selected Works of Gayatri Chakravorty Spivak*. Donald Landry and Gerald MacLean, editors. New York: Routledge.

Steffen, Lloyd (1998). *Executing Justice: The Moral Meaning of the Death Penalty*. Cleveland: The Pilgrim Press.

Steiker, Carol (2002). "Capital Punishment and American Exceptionalism." *Oregon Law Review, 81*, 1.

Stetler, Russel (1999). *Capital Cases*. http://www.nacdl.org/public.nsf/941a6d5b3 ad55cd485256b05008143fd/bee3ff4450880bb485256704006793eb?OpenDocument

Stevens, John Paul (2010). "Book Review: Peculiar Institution." *The New York Review of Books*. http://www.nybooks.com/articles/archives/2010/dec/23/ death-sentence/

Soss, Joe, Laura Langbein, and Alan R. Metelko. (2003). "Why Do White Americans Support the Death Penalty?"*Journal of Politics 65*(2), 397–421.

Times Wire Report (2006). "Executions Put on Hold Until Review." *Los Angeles Times*. December 20, 2006, A26.

Tonry, Michael (1996). *Malign Neglect: Race, Crime, and Punishment in America*. Oxford: Oxford University Press.

Toobin, Jeffrey (2004). "A Bad Thing." *The New Yorker*. Mar, 22.

U.S. Census Bureau (2006). http://quickfacts.census.gov/qfd/states/06000.html

U.S. General Accounting Office (1990). "Death Penalty Sentencing: Research Indicates Pattern of Racial Disparities." Reprinted in *The Death Penalty in America: Current Controversies*. (1997) Edited by Hugo Adam Bedau. Oxford: Oxford University Press.

Vigil, James Diego (2002). *A Rainbow of Gangs: Street Cultures in the Mega-City*. Austin: University of Texas Press.

Von Drehle, David (1995). *Among the Lowest of the Dead: The Culture of Death Row*. New York: Random House.

Wacquant, Loic (2000). "The New Peculiar Institution." *Theoretical Criminology, 4*(3), 377–89.

Weisberg, Robert (1984). "Deregulating Death." *The Supreme Court Review, 1983*, (1983), 305–95. The University of Chicago Press.

Weiss, Robert E., Richard A. Berk, and Catherine Y. Lee (1996). "Assessing Capriciousness of Death Penalty Charging." *Law & Society Review, 30* (3).

Western, Bruce, Becky Pettit, and Josh Guetzkow (2002). "Black Economic Progress in the Era of Mass Imprisonment." In *Invisible Punishment: The Collateral Consequences of Mass Imprisonment*. Edited by Marc Mauer and Meda Chesney-Lind. New York: The New Press

White, Hayden (1981). "The Value of Narrativity in the Representation of Reality." *On Narrative*. Edited by W. J. T. Mitchell. Chicago: University of Chicago Press.

Whitman, James Q. (2003). *Harsh Justice: Criminal Punishment and the Widening Divide between America and Europe*. Oxford: Oxford University Press.

Yarvis, Richard M. (2000). "Homicide, psychopathology, prosecutorial and jury Discretion and the Death Penalty." *Criminal Behavior and Mental Health*, 10(4); 256, 13.

Yen, Hope (2005). "O'Connor Dismisses International Law Controversy as 'Much Ado About Nothing.' http://www.law.com/jsp/article.jsp?id=1114160707182.

Zimring, Franklin E. (2003). *The Contradictions of American Capital Punishment*. Oxford: Oxford University Press.

Zimring, Franklin E. and Gordon Hawkins (1986). *Capital Punishment and the American Agenda*. Cambridge: Cambridge University Press.

CASES CITED

Atkins v. Virginia, 536 U.S. 304 (2002)

Baze v. Rees, 553, U.S. 35 (2008)

Darden v. Wainwright, 477 U.S. 168 (1986)

Dobbs v. Zant, 720 F. Supp. 1566 (N. D. Ga. 1989), *aff'd*, 963 F. 2d 1403 (11th Cir. 1991). *Rev'd and remanded on other grounds*, 506 U.S. 357 (1997).

Eddings v. Oklahoma, 455 U.S. 104 (1982)

Furman v. Georgia, 408 U.S. 238 (1972)

Gideon v. Wainwright, 372 U.S. 335 (1963)

Gregg v. Georgia, 428 U.S. 153 (1976)

Kennedy v. Louisiana 554 U.S. (2008)

Lockett v. Ohio, 438 U.S. 586 (1978)

McCleskey v. Kemp, 481 U.S. 279 (1987)

Payne v. Tennessee, 501 U.S. 808 (1991)

Ring v. Arizona, 536 U.S. 584 (2002)

Roe v. Wade, 410 U.S. 113 (1973).

Roper v. Simmons, 543 U.S., (2005)

Strickland v. Washington, 466 U.S. 668 (1984)

Woodson v. North Carolina, 428 U.S. 280 (1976)

CALIFORNIA TRIAL TRANSCRIPTS CITED (CODED)

Actual defendant names, counties, case numbers and transcripts are available from the author:

Trial 1
Trial 2
Trial 3
Trial 4
Trial 5
Trial 6
Trial 7
Trial 8
Trial 9
Trial 10
Trial 11
Trial 12
Trial 13
Trial 14
Trial 15
Trial 17
Trial 19
Trial 20
Trial 21
Trial 23
Trial 27
Trial 29
Trial 30
Trial 33
Trial 36

INTERVIEWS CITED (CODED)

Anonymous transcripts of interviews available from the author:

Defender # 1
Defender # 2
Defender # 4
Defender # 5
Mitigation Specialist # 1
Prosecutor #1
Prosecutor #2
Prosecutor #3
Prosecutor #4
Prosecutor #5
Prosecutor #6
Prosecutor #7

Index

About the Author

Paul Kaplan is associate professor of criminal justice in the School of Public Affairs at San Diego State University. He received his PhD in criminology, law, and society from the University of California, Irvine. Prior to graduate school, Professor Kaplan worked for several years as a capital mitigation investigator. Professor Kaplan's primary research area is the sociology of capital punishment, but he also works on projects involving sociolegal theory, cultural criminology, and comparative law. His work has appeared in journals such as the *Law & Society Review*, *Theoretical Criminology*, and *Law & Social Inquiry*.